"Just as it was in the days of Noah, so also will it be in the days of the Son of Man"

LUKE 17:26

THE
SUMMONING

PREPARING FOR THE COMING
DAYS OF NOAH

CARL GALLUPS

Critically Acclaimed Best-selling Author of
The Rabbi, the Secret Message, and the Identity of Messiah

DEFENDER

CRANE, MO

Dedicated to my great-grandson
Haddon Parker Gallups

You became an unspeakable blessing to us from the
moment we first knew of your existence.

CONTENTS

Acknowledgements. ix
Foreword xi
A Word from the Author xiii

PART ONE: THE SURREAL

1: The Gathering Tempest: March 2020 3
2: Relentless 9
3: The Shattering 15

PART TWO: THE JOURNEY

4: The Deluge 21
5: The Spectacle 23
6: The Day the Earth Cried. 27
7: Day by Day 31
8: Along the Way 35
9: When Will It Happen? 39
10: In the Same Manner 43
11: The Choice 49
12: The Temple Courts 53
13: One Last Nail 57
14: The Sound 61

PART THREE: THOSE WERE THE DAYS

15: Descending Darkness 69
16: Shades of the Prescient. 75
17: Rome Is Burning 83

18: Of Plagues and Pandemics 89
19: The Great Reset 93
20: We Know Where You Are 97
21: Convergence of Pieces 105
22: The First Time Ever 109
23: Final Warning 113

PART FOUR: DID IT REALLY HAPPEN?

24: Sticking to the Story 119
25: Global Graveyards 125
26: The Cryptograms 129
27: Rising Mountains 135
28: The Rocks Cry Out 139
29: Global or Not, Here It Comes 143
30: What We Know 147

PART FIVE: IT HAS ALWAYS BEEN

31: The Time of the End 155
32: A Certain Tree 161
33: Of Scholars and Figs 169
34: To the Exact Season 173
35: Two Resurrections 175
36: Because of the Gentiles 181
37: In the Day of Salvation 185
38: Heralds 191

PART SIX: A GENERATIONAL PHENOMENON

39: Summoning the Flood 199
40: A Flood of Border-Busting 205
41: The Shift That Triggered 211

PART SEVEN: THE DAYS OF NOAH

42: Just Like This 219
43: The Great Brainwashing 225
44: The Sons of God 229
45: Killer Angels .233
46: Pervasive Degradation 239
47: The Elephant in the Room 243
48: The Sins of the Angels 247
49: Genesis 6 and Sodom 251
50: Organic Manipulation 257

PART EIGHT: THE VISITORS

51: The Corrupting Visitation 263
52: In the Temple of God 267
53: The Day of Evil 271
54: Casting Down .275
55: The Shaking 279
56: Falling Stars 283
57: From the Heart of the Earth 289
58: Clothed in Power 295

PART NINE: PREPARING THE ARK

59: The Eternal Pattern 303
60: The Closed Door 311
61: The Value of a Name 315
62: Kingdom Builders 319

Epilogue 325
Addendum 327
About the Author .369
Notes 371

Acknowledgments

My deepest gratitude goes to the editing and production staff of Defender Publishing—especially to Angie Peters, my ever-patient, attentive, and gracious editor. You are such a pleasure to work with!

My thanks as well go to Jeffrey Mardis, the creator of this stunning cover. You always know exactly how to express the foundational content of my books through a brilliantly designed cover. You have a real gift from the Lord.

Also to Pamela McGrew: Your interior design and layout work is, as usual, uniquely suited to each book—pleasing to the eye and thoughtfully applied. Thank you for your hard work.

And certainly to my wife, Pam, my very first manuscript copy critic, editor, and source of daily and divine encouragement: I love you dearly.

You guys really make me look good! Undeservedly so. Thank you so much.

Foreword

THE LAST NAIL HAD JUST BEEN DRIVEN INTO THE FRAME OF THE MASSIVE DOOR.

As the spike found its stopping point, it let out an earsplitting clang. Its trilling ring echoed throughout the surrounding terrain, reverberations racing through a world that would soon be immersed in a watery grave. It was as if the sound carried with it a warning that screamed, "Judgment is coming soon!"

Listening to the haunting sound ricocheting from tree to tree and rock to rock, the old man shuddered. The tenor of the blow had unnerved him. He sensed that very same clank, that precise intonation, would be heard again, somewhere in the distant future.

Noah knew he had heard that sound before. It was as familiar to him as the sound of his own voice. And he knew exactly where he had heard it. That was why he was standing there…shaking.

Those are the opening words of one of the first chapters of this book. Are you interested yet? Just wait!

If you're looking for an in-your-face unveiling of what's really happening in our world today and you want to know how all this ties to our very near future, then you've got your hands on the right book.

I have known Carl Gallups, and have ministered with him, for years. I've appreciated the way he approaches his biblical studies with the mindset of an investigator, though this fact should come as no surprise to his regular readers. Carl spent a little more than a decade in the field of law enforcement in Florida, serving the greatest part of that time as a sworn patrol officer with two different sheriff's offices. So, as with the rest of Carl's amazing bestselling books, *The Summoning* will also take you on a journey of contextually accurate, well-researched, and thrilling theological discoveries.

I can assure you, today's whirlwind of global events buffeting our own generation are soon to become a collection of living, breathing spiritual harbingers appearing right before your eyes. The world in which we're living is going to make a lot more sense to you as Carl's biblical, historical, and scientific investigation unfolds.

You'll also find the information that Carl includes in the addendum section to be particularly useful. Those pages read like a fascinating handbook of practical and biblical preparation for these uncertain times, answering just about every major question you might have on the topic. Again, drawing on his many decades of combined law enforcement and direct ministry experience, Carl speaks with not only a pastor's heart but also from the vantage point of having dealt with many of these situations firsthand.

Keep your highlighter pen handy. This is a book that you'll not only want to read and reread, and keep in your personal library, but you'll also probably find yourself sharing these biblical treasures with many others for years to come.

Enjoy the ride!

Dr. Tom Horn

A Word from the Author

IS OUR WORLD ACTUALLY REELING TOWARD THE PRESCIENT DAYS OF NOAH—
that time of unparalleled global turmoil foretold by Jesus in the Gospels
of Matthew and Luke? Are we truly on the brink of a *universal shaking*,
as a number of today's prophecy watchers are warning?

How one might answer these questions depends on how he or she
understands the unfolding of prophetic convergences characterizing our
own unique generation. And there's the rub.

A number of people in today's largely anesthetized institutions of
the "visible church"[1] don't appear to be aware of anything prophetic
occurring at all—never mind the fact that Christianity is already "by far
the most persecuted religion on the planet."[2] And now, even the leading edges of government-sanctioned discrimination against the Body of
Christ have come to America, rushing upon us like a flood. Yet, for the
most part, the Church still sleeps.

Do you wish to know what the Word of God says about where we're
situated within the ultimate scheme of things? Do you want to find out
how to prepare yourself for the future, both logistically and spiritually?
Would you like to discover how to embrace your days on this earth as a
victorious ambassador for the coming Kingdom of Jesus Christ? You'll
find the answers to those questions and many others in the following
pages.

Along the way, you'll also glean a treasure trove of biblical, scientific,
and historical information that will prove invaluable to your personal

witnessing and teaching opportunities. And—as you reach the last pages—your life, and this increasingly bizarre world we're living in will finally make much more sense.

I promise, you'll not regret the time you invest to embark upon this journey. Thanks for taking it with me. I'm honored that you have.

The Summoning

*The Mighty One, God, the Lord, speaks and summons the earth
from the rising of the sun to the place where it sets.*

From Zion, perfect in beauty, God shines forth.

*Our God comes and will not be silent; a fire devours before him,
and around him a tempest rages.*

*He summons the heavens above, and the earth, that he may
judge his people: "Gather to me my consecrated ones,
who made a covenant with me by sacrifice."³*

*And the heavens proclaim his righteousness,
for God himself is judge.*

—PSALM 50:1–6

PART ONE

◁◆▷

The Surreal

For several years before writing this book, on numerous television and radio programs, I asserted that I couldn't help but believe something was getting ready to prophetically "snap."

I even preached about it from my own pulpit and in prophecy conferences, and I wrote about that overwhelming hunch in a couple of books prior to the one you're reading now. The more I expressed my impressions, the more correspondence I received from believers all over the world telling me that they were sensing the same thing.

At the time that I was trying to properly articulate this warning, I had no idea how close we were to the commencing of that *snapping* event. But now, I'm fairly certain I understand *what* it was that actually occurred.

And when.

And why.

1

The Gathering Tempest

March 2020

*A couple of days later, you wake up to find your home
surrounded by multiple government vehicles...*

"IT WAS A MOMENT IN HISTORY THAT CHANGED EVERYTHING."

How many times in the course of humanity's rather ignoble existence could a statement like that be accurately made, and without exaggeration? Probably in many hundreds of instances, at least.

However, as you'll soon discover, this period of time was truly unique, and in myriad prophetic ways. But let's be brutally honest: As the ordeal was initially unfolding, few understood it to be quite as dramatic as all that.

In reality, however, the *snapping* event would eventually grow to become something much more prophetically intense than what most first imagined. As a result, it really doesn't matter *when* you're reading this book. Even if it's decades from the time of its writing, the perspective you're about to gain will help you make biblical sense of the times you're living in—even then—*especially then*, I assure you.

Because, as it turns out, that relatively small dot on the overall timeline of history was tied to something unique and specific—something

Jesus Himself spoke about two thousand years earlier. And it was coming to fruition within the precise timeframe that He said it would.

Imagine

Think of it like this:

What if you were living in a world where, across the country, thousands of hardened criminals were "quietly released" from prison...for "their safety."[4] And what if this unthinkable absurdity were to occur at the time when pastors and churchgoers were accused of being "mega-dangerous,"[5] then were fined and/or arrested simply for meeting at their places of worship?

Or, what if the National Guard were dispatched to your church by your governor on the Lord's Day, because a group of about two dozen people tested positive for an upper-respiratory virus from your congregation? A group that *volunteered* to get tested. No hospitalizations. No one on respirators. No one died. They simply tested positive.[6]

Also, at the same time prisoners were being released around the nation, regular, law-abiding citizens were mandated to shelter in their homes and wait for the government to *tell them* when they could come out—or else, they would be subject to fines and/or jail. The day before, they were free citizens, having broken no laws; the next day they were effectively placed under house arrest...because the government "said so."

What if?

Church Under Fire

Now, envision that an openly gay mayor of one of the largest cities in the United States, after first having issued orders for churches to shut their doors, were to order police raids on several congregations within her jurisdiction. What if she were to instruct her police force to swoop down upon the churches because she was furious that they were still holding services in spite of her coronavirus lockdown orders?

And, what if one of the best known mega-church pastors in America were to be threatened with fines and arrest because he finally reopened his church without the government's permission?

This atrocity happened after many months of the pastor patiently complying with state-ordered lockdowns, until his city was informed by the mayor that there was no apparent end in sight—*especially* for venues like churches.

It happened to Pastor John MacArthur of the Grace Community Church in Los Angeles, California, in August 2020. When asked where he stood concerning those threats, Pastor MacArthur explained:

> We will obey God rather than men…. We will not bow to Caesar. The Lord Jesus Christ is our king. We will meet as the church of Jesus Christ because we're commanded to do that. We will sing, we will pray, we will fellowship, we will proclaim the Word of God far and wide and even around the world.[7]

Pastor MacArthur's attorney, Jenna Ellis, who at the time was a special counsel with the Thomas More Society, asserted:

> After Grace Community Church voluntarily complied with state orders for nearly six months, California's edicts demanding *an indefinite shut down* have gone now far past rational or reasonable and are firmly *in the territory of tyranny* and discrimination. This isn't about health. It's about *blatantly targeting churches.*[8] (Emphasis added)

While Pastor John McArthur was desperately fighting to get his church opened back up, the president of the world's largest conservative

evangelical denomination—the Southern Baptist Convention—shuttered the doors to his own megachurch until the end of 2020.[9]

This same man—Pastor J. D. Greear—publicly addressed his
immense denomination through an online video in which he spoke to
SBC churches concerning the Black Lives Matter riots that had just broken out around the nation and in other parts of the world. He issued
this admonition: "And, oh by the way, let's not respond by saying 'all
lives matter.'"[10]

Never mind that the pervasive biblical truth "all lives matter" is also
the very heart of the gospel message of salvation.

Let's get back to another "what if": What if the commissioner of
health in one of America's largest cities threatened to bulldoze your
church facilities to the ground if you continued to worship in spite of
the fact that the "government" had *ordered* you to stop meeting? That
sounds like something Communist China might do, doesn't it?[11]

> Chicago officials are **threatening to close or even bulldoze** a
> church that has continued meeting in defiance of a state order,
> saying **the governor's action has the "force of law."**[12] (Emphasis
> added)

Surely *this* couldn't happen.
Could it?

Then, to further emphasize the nature of the "normally" improbable
and surreal world we're describing, what if the United States Supreme
Court actually issued a ruling effectively declaring that a casino, restaurant, or bar had more of a constitutional right to congregate than
a church—regardless of how savagely the court had to violate the First
Amendment of the Bill of Rights in order to make that ruling?[13]

*"All we are seeking is the same consideration and trust that is being ten-
dered toward the liquor stores, abortion clinics, and Walmart,"* one pastor
said.[14]

Something like that would never happen in America....*right?*

Home Sweet Home

Now imagine this nightmare scenario:

You and your family voluntarily get screened for the virus. You believe this is simply your civic duty. You're found to be positive, but asymptomatic. Your spouse and infant child test negative.

After the test, you're ordered by a local health agency to "self-quarantine" in your own home for at least two weeks. The agency's rep pushes an "order" in front of you requiring your signature, thus legally obligating you to the government's oversight. *For your own safety.*[15]

Since you have no symptoms, you decline to sign the document, but you assure the agent, in your own handwriting, that you'll stay at home as much as possible—*voluntarily*—like any other free American citizen. You also say that you'll take every reasonable precaution to protect yourself, your family, and anyone in the public you might occasionally contact.

A couple of days later, you wake up to find your home surrounded by multiple government vehicles and personnel, as well as the county sheriff armed with a court order and ankle monitors. You've committed no crime, yet your constitutional rights have been summarily thrown in the garbage by government officials.

Imagine living in America in a state wherein the governor issues an order requiring criminal misdemeanor charges, fines, and potential jail time for public school teachers, *as well as for students in K–12*, who don't obey his mask "order"? That's right. Send your children to school in America, and you might get them arrested and saddled with a criminal record.[16]

Or what if the US government could literally force you to take the newest COVID-19 vaccine? What if it threatened to limit your access to jobs or schools—even fine you or put you in jail—if you or the dependent members of your family don't take it? Imagine if longstanding SCOTUS-ruled vaccination laws were touted by "experts" as the ultimate *police power-weapon* of the "state"?[17]

Yes—imagine *that* ridiculously insane world.

That couldn't *really* happen, *could it?*

———

One evening we went to bed and that make-believe world didn't exist— at least, not in America. It was only the stuff of dystopian science-fiction movies and novels. Nothing to worry about.

The next morning, everything changed. Every single bit of what was just described had actually happened, and more. And, not just in America.

But…could any of these events actually indicate biblically prophetic connections?

2

Relentless

The truth is that something prophetic
is always happening.

NOT TOO LONG AGO, ANY OF THE AFOREMENTIONED SCENARIOS WOULD HAVE been considered inconceivable, especially to those living in the largest "Christian" nation and the most powerful republic the planet has ever known. After all, we had a Constitution to protect us from such outrageous atrocities.

But during the first few months of 2020, each of those unthinkable events did in fact occur. Further, many other bizarre instances just like them, or even worse, not only continued to unfold in our own nation but practically all over the world—for the first time in history.[18]

The prophetic pummeling seemed to arrive in waves, almost like a "flood." Medical and scientific truth was thrown to the ground. Multitudes of doctors were silenced by the newly appointed "Masters of the Universe." Prominent schools of medicine from major universities and their scientifically based medical reports were ignored and/or castigated by the mainstream media.[19] Lawlessness at every level of society was unleashing its reign of tyranny. And it was happening globally...because of a new coronavirus strain.

But that wasn't all.

By mid-July 2020, the mainstream media was breathlessly warning that an even deadlier virus had already been loosed upon the planet. And we were only barely in the middle of this one. The media warned that we'd be "confronting these threats again," and in "wave after wave."[20]

Blood was in the water. The sharks were circling. Absolute panic became the order of the day. It was the "new normal."

Is It Prophetic?

During those days, I was often asked, "Do you think this global coronavirus pandemic and the resulting worldwide political and societal upheaval have any prophetic significance?"

Serving as the senior pastor of a Gulf Coast church since 1987, I've been through several scenarios that produced similar atmospheres of panic-driven fallout—especially with Saddam Hussein's launching of Scud missiles into Israel in 1990 and the resulting Gulf War in 1991… then the 9/11 terrorist attacks of 2001. The same with Arab Spring in 2011 and the hugely prophetic shifts that resulted from that globally impacting calamity. In each of those situations and several others like them, I was pelted with the same question.

Time to Choose

After decades of preaching the Word of God, I've discovered that relatively few people seem to give much thought to biblical prophecy. Nor do they, for the most part, understand the complexities of the prophetic times in which we've been living for the last century or so—that is, until "something" happens. Then, and almost *only* then, do people want to know if a revelatory event might be occurring. Otherwise, it's simply life as usual. Or, so they think.

The truth is that something prophetic is always happening. Throughout every generation, God is constantly at work weaving together the fabric of His preannounced revelations. And through those ancient pronouncements, Yahweh is forever proving Himself faithful to give humanity ample hints of what He's up to.

That's why Noah was building a ship in his backyard—for a dozen decades.[21] The door to that gigantic boat stood wide open all that time. It was God's provision, given for the singular chance of escape from the soon-coming judgment. But no one—and I mean *no one*—chose to go through that door except Noah and his family.

The Trigger

Here's something else to remember: Genuine prophetic events always run in a line, like a string of dominoes arranged to begin falling in a certain pattern. But the chain only comes to life after the first plank is toppled over. Then, the continuous toppling of the tiles ripples right through every generation, until the last domino finally falls.

However, the process always begins with *a single tile* in the chain, like when the floodwaters of Noah's day finally commenced. The whole episode started with just one drop of water spilling from above, followed by infinitely countless more raindrops, and then finally followed by the deluge—on a specific day, in a precise instant. After it was done, the world was forever changed.

It was the same way in that one split second when Moses raised his staff to the heavens as he stood at the edge of the Red Sea. Or at the moment the walls of Jericho toppled and the Israelites conquered the Promised Land for the first time. Or when Caesar Augustus issued a decree ordering all of the citizens to travel to their towns of origin, thus putting Mary and Joseph in Bethlehem. And as in that exhaled exclamation when a tiny baby boy lying in a manger let out His very first cry.

Each of these seemingly minuscule points in time later proved to have been ticks of the clock that altered the entire course of human events. Once those moments snapped into existence, there was no turning back. Nothing was ever the same.

It Is Finished

Or, what about that one, precise, preordained spark of an instant when Jesus cried out, "It is finished!"? The message of that divine cry effectively decreed: *God's plan of personal salvation is finally coming to fruition, and everything will now begin to lurch forward towards restoring that which was corrupted in Eden.*

Once that "Word" fell from Heaven's lips, the prophetic conglomeration that followed had been activated. With that cry also came an interdimensional call to battle. Regardless of the resulting ebbs and flows that are left lapping the shores in the aftermath of the 2020 *snapping*, the first prophetic domino of that unprecedented chain has been eternally toppled over. In that process, the demonic powers were freshly awakened. Satan knows his time is getting short. He's filled with rage (Revelation 12:12).

In the meantime, the people of each successive generation must choose where their allegiances will align. That's where we come into the picture. *This is our generation.* It's our time to choose. It's our time to step up and make a genuine difference in the overall Kingdom mission.

Two thousand years of humanity's reckoning of time have ticked off the clocks and calendars since Jesus cried out from the cross. A little more than twenty complete *one-hundred-year generations* of humanity have come and gone since then. But never forget, those same two thousand years were actually only two brief "days" within the cosmic framework of God's perspective:

A thousand years in your sight are like a day that has just gone by, or like a watch in the night. (Psalm 90:4)

But do not forget this one thing, dear friends: With the Lord a day is like a thousand years, and a thousand years are like a day. The Lord is not slow in keeping his promise, as some understand slowness. Instead he is patient with you, not wanting anyone to perish, but everyone to come to repentance.[22] (2 Peter 3:8–9)

And then, after those two short *days* had passed, came 2020.

The prophetically promised shaking had begun. As you'll soon discover, God had not kept this day a secret from us.

Summer was growing nigh.

The fig tree had been shaken.[23]

The fruit was starting to fall.

3

The Shattering

Things appeared to point to a
threshold-crossing moment in history.

THE SHOCK OF THE ALMOST INSTANTANEOUS EVENT UNNERVED PRACTICALLY THE entire planet.

Were we really this vulnerable? Could the whole world actually change so quickly? So viciously? So senselessly? And were we really this helpless to do anything about the systematic and often lawless dislodging of the elements of basic sanity from our everyday lives? What were the insufferable "new norms" going to turn out to be in the aftermath of this melee?

The COVID-19 virus quickly became more than simply a brand-new strain of an age-old virus. The newest "invisible" enemy to invade humanity also brought with it a mega dose of irrational panic and fear. And that global atmosphere became the catalyst that shifted the prophetic nature of our day into high gear.

Soon, the pervasive *spirit of fear* was politically weaponized by malevolent people the world over. And, it was manipulatively moved along by the ubiquitous *zeitgeist* of our day—a palpable *spirit of Antichrist*. Demonically driven agendas began to pour out of the halls of darkness. A prophetic squall was on the way.

Just Like This

Yet, we haven't been without biblical warning concerning such a day. Within just a few consecutive weeks of Jesus' earthly ministry, He twice hammered home what now appears to be an increasingly *relevant-to-our-time* prophetic truth: "Just as it was in the days of Noah, so also will it be in the days of the Son of Man."[24]

With those words, Jesus assured His followers there *would be* a future generation that would live in conditions that most certainly rival the circumstances in the days of Noah's generation. It would be a time of unequaled worldwide turmoil—with definitive biblical indicators of even more to come.

But, Jesus effectively warned, the pervasive attitude of the planet's collective population would be: *Oh well, don't worry. Soon, everything will go back to normal. It always happens that way. Eat! Drink! Buy and sell! Of course, we'll have to adapt to a few adjustments, perhaps make a few compromises. But, all will be just fine! There's nothing to see here...*

It Wasn't the Virus

Let me be very clear about this next point.

Even though the SARS-CoV-2 virus was labeled as "the biggest challenge to global health and prosperity since World War II,"[25] a number of us who carefully analyze what is *really* occurring in our generation didn't necessarily believe that the newest coronavirus strain *itself* was the presenting problem. After all, numerous variations of that upper-respiratory disease have been seasonally ripping through the human race for a long time. And, certainly, over the ages, the planet has endured a multitude of much worse plagues.

There was also a good chance that, similar to influenza, this latest strain of coronavirus would eventually become just another part of life on a relatively dangerous planet, something we'd simply have to learn to deal with maybe for a long time to come—perhaps forever.[26]

So, no; the virus itself wasn't the presenting problem.

The real issue was the resulting onslaught of continually unfurling prophetic events, coupled with the corresponding worldwide "attitudes" that were created in the midst of them, especially the mindset concerning the unprecedented assaults upon the church. These things appeared to point to a threshold-crossing moment in history. The virus—or, rather, the irrational and unmitigated terror of it—was just the trigger, *one of the first dominoes* causing everything else prophetic to begin to topple. Caesar's decree had been signed. The staff had been raised. The walls were tumbling down. The first splats of the ominous warnings from Heaven's throne had already hit the ground.

Yet, most of the world's population—even a large portion of *the visible church*—went on with the routine tasks of daily life as though *all was good*, waiting for everything to return to "normal." Even though the governments of the world effectively slammed the door shut on numerous aspects of their previous manner of daily life. Maybe forever.

Exactly what was it that Satan seemed to know about those days—a time that was unlike any time before it—and a thing that so many Christians appeared to be overlooking?

You're about to find out.

As we continue our journey, let's go back to the beginning. Back to the place and age where it all started.

Or, rather, where it all *started over again.*

✧

PART TWO

The Journey

Teach these things to your children, talking about them when you sit at home and when you walk along the road, when you lie down and when you get up.

—DEUTERONOMY 11:19

4

The Deluge

All of this would be gone within days.
—Circa 2350 BC

THE LAST NAIL HAD JUST BEEN DRIVEN INTO THE FRAME OF THE MASSIVE DOOR.

As the spike found its stopping point, it let out an earsplitting *clang!* Its trilling ring echoed throughout the surrounding terrain, the reverberations racing through a world that would soon be immersed in a watery grave. It was as if the sound carried with it a warning that screamed, *"Judgment is coming soon!"*

Listening to the haunting sound ricocheting from tree to tree and rock to rock, the old man shuddered. The tenor of the blow had unnerved him. He sensed that very same *clank*, that precise intonation, would be heard again, somewhere in the distant future.

Noah knew he had heard that sound before. It was as familiar to him as the sound of his own voice. And he knew exactly *where* he had heard it. That was why he was standing there…shaking.

He had heard the clanging echo in several prescient visions—deep in the silky dark hours of the night. This particular moment in which he now stood had subconsciously awakened within him those memories. *Pa-Pinggg. Pa-Pinggg. Pa-Pinggg!*

But there was something else. The ringing from his dreams had been accompanied by a haunting human cry. It had burst from the tortured

21

lungs of a shadowy figure, one who had been cruelly impaled through his hands and feet...on what appeared to be some sort of suspended wooden beam. The shouting figure had also been surrounded by a vile mob huddled together under his blood-soaked body. *Cursing. Mocking. Reviling.*[27]

Noah was certain that the nighttime revelations were in some way intertwined with what he was doing this very moment—*building a gigantic wooden vessel,* a ship of potential salvation that was offered for his entire world. If the world would only listen, and come...and be saved. So far, they had not come; they only mocked.

He had erected the multilevel boat in the field beside his house, visible for miles around, available for all who cared to inquire. They couldn't miss it! It was Noah's divine assignment. Driving the nails, *driving the nails, driving the nails*...day in and day out. For decades. *And decades...*

Noah now reached up to where he driven that final spike. He gently rubbed his hand over the crown, its cap barely protruding from the wood. He took his index finger and methodically encircled the nail's head, tracing its rugged iron edges...slowly...contemplating. Mesmerized by it.

Then the vision was gone, as quickly as it had come.

5

The Spectacle

*As he finished speaking, the earth began to
roll under their feet.*

FOR NOW, HOWEVER, THE ANIMALS WERE SECURELY ENSCONCED INSIDE. EACH pair was situated in its own specially constructed enclosure. Seven days ago, the dreamlike procession had finally started. The beasts came streaming in from around the countryside, headed straight toward the vessel. They came of their own accord, faithfully hearkening to a voice apparently heard only by them…the beckoning sound of their Creator.[28]

What a beautiful thing to behold! Here was a virtual parade of created beings coursing to his own front door. *It was as if the animals knew.* But this spectacle was exactly what Yahweh had told Noah would happen. He had never doubted it would be so, even though from the beginning it had still been a thing hard to imagine. But actually seeing it with his own eyes—right this moment—this was something else altogether!

Noah and his family stood in awe as the animals entered. From the smallest to the greatest, the creatures moved forward in pairs…each according to its own kind.

So many thoughts poured through Noah's mind as he watched the animal parade. *Is this really happening? Why didn't these hard-hearted people listen? Family, friends, fellow citizens…they have all been warned, and for such a long time! But they refused to heed the message. Instead, they mocked and cursed us!*

Then Noah turned to look at his wife, his sons, their wives. "Take a look around!" he said. "You'll never see anything like this again!"

Noah's sons and daughters-in-law, all with widened eyes, began to circumnavigate their surroundings. *Father was right. All of this world would be gone within days. It* would *happen.* His family didn't doubt him. Especially now.

The Snapping

It was at the end of the seven days of receiving the animals and securing them safely within the ark when it commenced.

Noah spoke up as he and his family were just finishing the final preparations. "Yahweh has again spoken to my soul…just now!" he said. "Everything is getting ready to burst asunder, my dear family. This is it! It's about to come to pass…"

"Don't be frightened!" he continued, surveying the faces of those around him. "God has not given us a spirit of fear. We are to be strong. We're wrapped in His divine protection. He Himself will carry us along, *above* the waters of His wrath, as if we are carried upon the wings of His messengers!"

As Noah finished speaking, the earth began to roil under their feet as though the fabric of the earth's foundation was beginning to rip apart at the seams. The door to the great vessel suddenly snapped loose from its thick mooring ropes. The giant wooden entryway came crashing down against the cradle of its frame. At the thundering impact, they were sealed inside.

At that same moment, an unearthly explosion filled the air, causing their ears to reverberate with a pummeling, thumping sensation. After that, yet another otherworldly sound—a metallic groaning—burst forth from the heavens. It sounded as if ten thousand resounding trumpets had unleashed their doleful notes throughout the earth.

As the terrain continued to churn, a lingering light illuminated the interior of the ark. The animals cowered when they saw it, and they hushed. The presence of something holy was among them. They knew they were safe—protected inside the ark Noah had built...at God's command.

The Wrath

Then, on that very day, in the six hundredth year of Noah's life, on the seventeenth day of the second month—the torrents came. They started with one single solitary *splat!* Then another *splat!* And then another.

Finally, after the first few spatters, vast oceans poured from the sky as if a canopy of previously unseen water had been violently released upon them. Within moments, the landscape was engulfed in cascading streams. The streams churned and frothed into roaring rivers, then the rivers melded into gigantic, bubbling lakes. Soon, the lakes merged their watery arms and finally became a never-ending sea, stretching to every horizon.

The earth was being covered over in water! The white-capped oceans steadily rose, creating violent, foam-covered, blackened depths...a foreboding chasm of watery death. At this rate, the rising waters would consume the mountains themselves!

Just then, another loud, cracking sound raced across the surface of the deep. With that last sound, portions of the earth opened up like giant, gaping mouths. Cavernous fissures burst forth from the deepest pits of the planet's crust. Geysers of water blasted miles into the air, intermingling their inundation with the torrential columns of water emptying from the heavens.

The ominous fissures popped up all around, as far as their eyes could see. Noah and his family stood slack-jawed, peering through the tiny portholes. The blackest clouds they had ever witnessed canopied the sky like a divine vestment of inky-black cloth draped over the tabletop of the entire universe. The middle of the day had become as dark as midnight. The stars were gone. The sun and moon were nowhere in sight, completely blanketed out of view. *Would those glorious heavenly lights ever be seen again?*

Their eyes had never beheld, their ears had never heard, their minds had never before contemplated such raw, unmitigated, majestic power. The gigantic boat that once had looked so enormous to them now felt so very small.

The family gathered in the center of the ship as it started to groan under the strain of its weighty living cargo. The vessel was moving! They could feel it beginning to float! They fell to their knees in prayer.

What was left of Elohim's first creation finally let forth a long, *heaving* sound, like that of a grief-stricken mother groaning over her dying child's last breath of life.

The end had come.

So far...they had survived.

But what happened next covered them in unspeakable grief.

6

The Day the Earth Cried

*They vanished into the darkness
as if they had never existed.*

HUSH!

What was that noise? Noah and his family scrambled to peer through the tiny portals. But it was too dark to see anything, so they pressed their ears against the ship's walls.

They finally deciphered the sounds.

Could it really be?

This is unthinkable! Must we now be forced to endure this additional sorrow?

All around, they heard the cries. Close by. Even right beneath them.

They realized that masses of people on the outside of the vessel were clinging to the hull, as if searching, frantically scratching and clawing, looking for a life-saving crevice they could take hold of. The desperate people screamed and pleaded, their pitiful cries occasionally muffled by the moaning of the wind and the slapping of the angry waves against the ark—and the *pounding, beating, drumming, wretched,* never-ending *rain...*

As if this wasn't enough, the ark's occupants heard the agonizing pleas coming from far off as well. They could make out mingled wailing and cursing, even above the tumult of the geological upheaval. Surely there were tens of thousands! Great roars would suddenly emerge, sounding like a massive throng that had gathered for a sporting event. The planet itself seemed to be weeping, grieving from its own heartbreaking depths of anguish.

The wrenching pleas for mercy were shouted over and over again, as if the mere repetition would somehow cause the doors of the vessel they had previously ignored to fling open and relent...ultimately inviting them all inside. But the portal would not concede. It had been sealed by the divine hand of Yahweh.

No one was coming to their rescue.

Those inside the undulating, wave-tossed ship grieved over the screams that cruelly violated the depths of their hearts. They agonized over those they used to live among, only hours earlier. Many of them they knew by name. But Noah and his family were now helpless to save a single person, or to even offer comfort. All of them...*perishing*...just outside the walls of the ark.

At times, it was hard to distinguish between the bellows of the humans and those of the beasts. And every now and then, they thought they actually recognized an individual voice. A friend? A family member? A personal acquaintance? The horrors were ceaseless. The ark's inhabitants covered their ears as they wept, praying for the cries to come to an end.

Eating and Drinking

It had only been a few days ago that some of those on the outside had been planning huge wedding celebrations. Others had been feasting at their wild and raucous parties, reveling in their debauchery and insolence. Mocking God and reviling God's servants. Counting their piles of money. Planning their next business ventures. Parading about in their fancy clothes and fine jewelry. But now it was too late. None of it mattered anymore. As they were gasping for their last breaths of life, none of them thought of any of those things anymore.

For 120 years, the mocking ones had been reasoned with. At times, they had even been begged. And now, by their own choosing, they were all being wiped out as if they were a mere anthill, destined for annihilation. What a difference just one day could make in the scheme of all things. It didn't *have* to be this way. It didn't. They could have been saved, too.

None of their previously presumed legacies would ever again mean a thing *to anyone*. Their best-laid plans had come to naught. They had lustfully clung to the demonically corrupted world to which they had become so attached, and they had lost their souls…forever.

Multitudes were finally giving up, too exhausted to struggle any longer. They reluctantly released what little strength they still had as that one last gasp filled their lungs with a burning gulp of putrid, muck-laden water. The oceans of black swallowed them whole, like a gigantic ravenous beast. They vanished into the darkness as if they had never existed. Some were still shaking their fists toward the heavens and screaming vile words of rebuke at their Creator while they slipped out of sight…never to be seen again.

And slowly, but surely, through the last few hours that ensued…the screams of agony, the shrieks of unmitigated pride stopped. All the evil that had lived in their hearts went down to the depths with them.

Mercifully so.

7

Day by Day

The divine "reset" button had been pushed
by the finger of Yahweh Himself.

SOON, THE ONLY SOUND THAT ENVELOPED THE EARTH'S NEW FAMILY WAS the storm. The relentless, crashing waves. And animals. Multitudes of animals.

The rocking, creaking, groaning of the boat now set the predominate ambiance of their new home—their fortress of safety. The persistent mooing, moaning, crying, yelping, bellowing, and bleating of the beasts undulated throughout the craft. The animals had survived something unspeakable, and they seemed to sense it. A new beginning was on the way.

But, there was still work to be done. *Always* work to be done....

There were mouths to feed. Baby animals to be birthed. Putrid refuse to be jettisoned overboard. Rancid, reeking stalls to be cleaned. Life-sustaining vats of gruel to be prepared. Relentless leaks to be plugged. And occasionally, the sweet release of sleep.

Then it started over. Get up, get a little something to eat, and do it all again. And again...and yet again.

Time was now largely irrelevant. For the longest, there was no sun or moon by which the ark-dwellers could measure their lives. There was just work. And precious moments of blissful slumber. Then more work. More pounding rain. More rocking back and forth. More irritated protestations from the animal-passengers. More wretched seasickness. More filth to clean up.

Each and every day, for forty days and forty nights, the heavens and the earth emptied out pent-up oceans of water. For a hundred and fifty days, the swirling waters covered the earth. Finally, as far as the eye could see, not even a mountaintop was visible. The divine "reset" button had been pushed by the finger of Yahweh Himself.

Everything New

Then…finally…Yahweh spoke.

He sent a mighty rushing wind over the earth. The waters bucked against the wind, but the mountain-like waves ultimately relented and began to recede. Yahweh spoke yet again, and the springs of the deep and the floodgates of the heavens sealed shut, and the rain stopped falling from the sky. Instantly.

The water began its withdrawal, swallowed up by the gaping fissures in the earth's crust. At the end of 150 days, the swirling torrents of the newly created oceans had gone down considerably. And on the seventeenth day of the seventh month, the ark finally came to rest on the mountains of Ararat. The waters continued to recede until the tenth month, and on the first day of that month, the tops of the mountains became visible.

By the first day of the first month of the next year, Noah's six hundred and first year, the flooding waters of death had significantly retreated from the surface of the earth. By the twenty-seventh day of the second month, the ground was completely dry.

On that day, Noah's oldest son, Shem, approached his father, his hair tangled and matted, his beard long and shaggy.

"Father," he asked, "Is this really *the end* of everything? What's to become of us now?"

Noah looked outside the portals, toward the heavens, as the clouds were parting and the first rays of sun the family had seen in months began to stream through. Brilliant, multicolored bands of shimmering light filled the crystal blue skies above them.

"On the contrary, my son," Noah answered. "This is only the beginning. This is where it starts over! Here. Now!"

Shem smiled at the comforting tone of his father's infectious enthusiasm. It was one of the things he had always loved most about his dad. Ham and Japheth moved closer to their brother and father. They understood.

Noah leaned in toward the three men, grabbing them together in a gripping bear hug as if they were still his little boys. "*Come, my sons*! Help me open this door! I'm ready to put some solid ground under my feet! How 'bout you?"

All four men beamed, wide-eyed, at their wives. Finally, they would step on firm soil as earth's *new family*. With the eight of them and Yahweh's hand of mercy, everything would begin again.

"Hurry up!" Noah shouted, as he scrambled toward the door. "There's work to be done! *A lot of work*.... We have a new world to build!"

The family snickered among themselves as they piled out of the ark.

It seemed that Noah, the carpenter, was always looking to build *something*.

8

Along the Way

Near the Jordan River highway
Around AD 33

HE HAD ONLY A FEW MORE WEEKS TO LIVE.

Even though it was the beginning of spring, the Mediterranean sun was already unseasonably warm. There wasn't a comforting cloud of shade to be seen. It would be a hot day, to be sure. But there was work to be done.

Almost 2,400 years had passed since the Flood. Yahweh, the Creator of every living thing, was now standing in the midst of His own creation. Surreptitiously clothed in the flesh of humanity, He was currently on the last leg of His journey, headed to a cross. The grueling sacrificial process of setting everything right was quickly closing in on Him. At times, the thought of the ordeal awaiting Him at the end of the road was suffocating. Yet, He knew it was coming soon. So, He pressed on....

It had been almost three years since Jesus began His earthly ministry. Presently, He and His burgeoning entourage—the twelve disciples of His inner circle as well as the crowds that constantly followed after them—were moving among the villages of the Jordan River Valley. They had come from the north of Judea, down through Galilee, along the region of Samaria.[29]

Following the main road between the various hamlets of civilization, they would eventually arrive at Jericho, several weeks from now. From there they would finally ascend to Jerusalem one last time. The entire trip would take weeks and would culminate with a brutal disfigurement of Yeshua's body, wrought under a Roman soldier's thoroughly humiliating scourge. Then He would be finished off with the slamming of three thick spikes through His hands and feet. *Pa-Pinggg! Pa-Pinggg! Pa-Pinggg!*

Jesus often heard the sound…ringing in His head, especially at night. But, for the moment at hand, He steeled Himself *and pressed on.* This is why He had come.

The Inquisition

Jesus' group stood on the outskirts of yet another village. The blazing sun now beat down from directly overhead, forcing rivulets of sweat to pour down His face. As He wiped them away with the back of His sleeve, Peter ambled up to Him with a waterskin.

"Master, drink this…it's already been a long day." Jesus smiled, slipped the container from Peter's hands, and swigged down a couple of refreshing gulps.

"I have a feeling it's about to be even longer," Peter said, jerking his head in the direction of the village's main entrance and rolling his eyes.

A gaggle of Pharisees—*the Jewish keepers of religion*—were making their way toward them. They didn't look happy. They never did, especially when Jesus showed up among the throngs over which they normally held the sway.

Jesus winked, gripping Peter's shoulder. "We've seen that sight many times before, my good friend. These are always such fun *conversations,* wouldn't you agree?"

Peter snorted. "You mean *confrontations,* don't you?"

Before Jesus could acknowledge Peter's remark, the Pharisees were upon them. *"Teacher! Teacher!"* the leader of the ecclesiastical parade shouted, "Please. Give us a hearing! If you would be so gracious. *Please.* We only ask for a moment or two of your time."

Jesus nodded His permission and motioned with His hand for the approaching men to continue. A "moment or two" almost always meant an "hour or two" with this bunch. But Jesus would oblige them, yet again.

"My name is Baruch,"[30] the speaker declared as they arrived. He jutted his chin toward the others with him. "We're the ones who minister the Word of *Hashem*[31] among the people of the villages of this region."

"Yes. I remember you, Baruch," Jesus said. "I'm more than familiar with your work." He slightly chuckled.

He liked Baruch. He had spoken with him before, a couple of years back. The elder Pharisee had seemed, at that time, to have been sincerely searching out the truth of Jesus' Kingdom teachings.

Jesus stood waiting for the inquiries that were certain to come.

They didn't disappoint.

9

When Will It Happen?

*Their lack of response quickly grew to a
blossoming, inward embarrassment.*

BARUCH SPOKE ON BEHALF OF THE GROUP. "WE'VE HEARD OF YOUR TEACHINGS concerning the coming Kingdom of God," he said. "We are, as you might imagine, most interested to learn of your deepest thoughts on the matter—"

Jesus slightly nodded, indicating that Baruch should proceed. The Pharisee cleared his throat, attempting to compose himself.

"Well...I suppose what we would like to know is...exactly *when* is the Kingdom of God going to come? We've waited so long! We can almost feel its approach. It's thick in the air! It seems that we're living in undeniably prophetic times. We all agree, there's a uniqueness about our days, like at no other time in our remembered past. It's as though something is getting ready to *snap*. Do you feel it too?"

He searched Jesus' face for a reaction. The others indicated by their body language that they agreed with their leader. "Teacher, what do *you* say about this?" Baruch's voice held a sense of urgency.

Jesus answered, "The coming of the kingdom of God is not something that can always be observed with bubbling explosions of obvious revelations—not in the context of everyday life, anyway."

He stepped a bit closer to the Pharisee. "Because it's in the middle of each day's living and each generation's passing, the Word of God and the declarations of the ancient prophets are continually unfolding.

"Most of the time, it's in the little things, Baruch."

"Please!" Baruch appealed. "Explain more!"

Jesus accommodated. "The coming of Messiah was foretold in the Scriptures, of course. And those Scriptures promised that He would come first unto His own people."

Baruch slightly shook his head. So far, so good.

"Messiah's birthplace was foretold as well," Jesus continued. "The divine miracles that He would minister were also foreseen. They were to be wonders that could only be explained by the fact that Messiah had indeed arrived upon the earth, directly from the throne of God. Yet, at the same time, He would also come unto His own creation through very specific generations of humanity itself. This is why He would be known as the Messiah of Heaven, but also as the Son of David."

Jesus looked up at a circling vulture, shading His squinting eyes with a cupped hand. He spoke again, still looking at the bird. "Messiah's humble earthly beginnings were clearly revealed to you as well. Even the final work that He would come to accomplish was laid out through the prophets Zechariah and Isaiah, even by King David."[32]

He lowered His hand and smiled at the Pharisee, "It's all there in your Scriptures."

Baruch was speechless, as were those with him. Some of those revelations were also matters of heated debate among their various orthodox factions. Their lack of response quickly grew to a blossoming discomfort. *Who was this one, to think that he could teach us, especially in such matters of well-known controversy?*

But Jesus knew their thoughts. Turning to Baruch's entourage, He quizzed them further. "Do you have a hard time pondering these things, gentlemen?"

He paused a few seconds, then continued before they could answer. "People will not be able to accurately say, 'Here it is!' or 'There it is!'

because of any one specific instance. When God's Kingdom first appears in your midst, you'll simply have to have the discernment to identify that presence. Many things will be happening at once—some little, some bigger. It is a keen spiritual discernment that you'll need in order to see it and correctly tie it together. It's a sensitivity that comes from touching the throne of God through your uninhibited love for your Creator."

Jesus glanced around at His disciples, then back to the Pharisees. "God's work is to be accomplished this way for now, in order to remain veiled from the sight of the evil one. Only those with eyes to see will be able to truly recognize it when it happens."

"Can you show it to us, Teacher?" Baruch pleaded. "We have those eyes *to see*! We'd love to see it now! Is that even possible?"

Jesus leaned into Baruch and murmured, for his ears only, "The Kingdom of God is in *your midst* right now my friend. It is right before you."[33]

With that, Jesus stepped back from Baruch and simply stood there for a moment, begging the man's soul *to see*. But there was no indication that the elder Pharisee understood the revelation. *Not yet.*

Jesus continued speaking to them as a group. "After this age has rejected what it has seen," He said, "the Kingdom of God will return again, but not to *this* generation. It will come in a future one."

Baruch's mouth fell open. His eyes widened. Before the Pharisee could express his thoughts, Jesus turned to survey the crowd gathered behind Him. Multitudes had been following Him before He even arrived outside this little village. He gazed down the path ahead, deep in thought.

Jesus knew an exceedingly dark day awaited Him...just down that ancient roadway.

But not quite yet. That dreadful day would come soon enough.

Right now, there was still work to be done.

Always...work to be done.

10

In the Same Manner

Whoever tries to keep their life will lose it,
and whoever loses their life will preserve it.

Jesus motioned for His own inner circle to draw closer.

He spoke to the Twelve in such a manner that Baruch and his entourage could also hear. "The time is coming when you, too, will long to see one of the days of the Son of Man, but you will not see it. People will tell you, 'There He is!' or 'Here He is!' But do not believe them."

He continued, "I'm serious when I tell you this. Do not go running off after them. For the Son of Man in His day will be like the lightning, which flashes and then lights up the sky from one end to the other. No one will miss Him! But first He must suffer many things and be rejected by this generation."

Baruch spoke up. "Are you saying we have already missed the Messiah? Are you telling us that our generation has forfeited His blessings and somehow overlooked His appearance?" Those with him began to mutter among themselves, whispering words of growing resentment.

Jesus replied, "I tell you the truth, Baruch. This generation is in fact largely missing the entire event, *yes*. Again, it's all right there, open before you. It really couldn't be any plainer. The Word of God is *living*, right before your eyes."

"But…*but*…" Baruch struggled for his next words, his frustration growing more obvious.

When he had finally gathered his thoughts, the elder Pharisee continued, his eyes narrowing, "Are you then asserting that the people of our own day have actually *seen* the Messiah, but failed to recognize Him? *How is this even possible?*"

Baruch moved closer to Jesus, a hint of indignation in his voice. "Surely our high priest would have recognized Him? Certainly our elders would know the Messiah? How could it be that Messiah would not have gone straight to our elders and reported to them? After all, it is we who are Messiah's forerunners, His divine messengers, and heralds. Why wouldn't He have come to us *first?*"

"It is the same in every generation my friend," Jesus responded. "Yahweh is always moving, He's always working. He's always confirming the ancient prophecies by pushing them right along through every epoch of time. But one has to properly put together the full picture of His Word in order to *see* it happening and to correctly *understand* it. Messiah doesn't 'report' to any man, Baruch. He does not move in the direction or the manner in which man's 'teachers' have determined."

This further elucidation appeared to grip Baruch's heart. Jesus could sense wheels of meditation grinding away deep within his soul.

"You see," Jesus continued, "the world is moving toward a great and terrible day of judgment. It's still in the distance, but it *is* coming. God *will have* His Paradise restored. The evil one will not prevail in the end. In the meantime, Yahweh is patient, holding out His offer of salvation to all. Each generation is held responsible for what it does with God's movement among them—"

"These are hard sayings, Teacher!" Baruch interrupted. He looked at his feet, shaking his head. "I don't understand how an entire generation could miss the warnings of God's Word, especially the prophetic promises."

"Oh…but they do!" Jesus rejoined. "And it's happened before, even in the most unlikely of times!"

"It's like this," Jesus said, as He turned toward the crowd.

"*Just as it was* in the days of Noah, *so also will it be* at the final coming, in the days of the return of the Son of Man." The crowd snapped to attention at these words.

"Think about those days of old!" Jesus went on. "People were eating, drinking, marrying and being given in marriage right up to the very day Noah entered the ark. But they were also immersed in all manner of wickedness, thinking that God was not watching their vile affairs! They spurned their love for their Creator, and even intimately consorted with the fallen ones! Then, right in the midst of everyday life, like a thief in the night, the Flood came and destroyed them all!"

Jesus paused as the crowds gasped at these difficult reminders of the folly of past generations, then He spoke up again. "In Noah's day, the people didn't seem to expect what was coming upon them…until it was entirely too late."

Jesus looked away, searching for another platform from which to speak. He saw a large boulder with a flattened top and climbed upon it. From there, He continued; now the crowd would be sure to hear His next words:

"But that generation was without excuse! They had been warned! Yahweh never brings judgment without first issuing a merciful warning. Yet, they refused to see the utter vileness and corruption in which they dwelt, and to which they had yoked themselves. They declined to even acknowledge the enormous ship standing in the field at Noah's house. It was there for all the world to see! And, *see it* they did! But rather than rejoice at the sight of the ark of their potential salvation, they mocked it! They loathed its presence. It was an object of embarrassment and shame to them!"

Jesus paused to scan the faces in the crowd. "That vessel was God's vehicle of deliverance, erected and lifted up high, for all to behold. It had been built by a master carpenter. A man of God. And it was available for *any* who would come. In it, men and women would have found safety. But no one came, except Noah and his own family, and the animals that God brought to Noah."

The crowd stood amazed by these words. Only the whispering sounds of the breeze and the occasional screech of a gliding hawk looking for his next meal wafted against their eardrums. Other than that, all ears and eyes were directed toward Jesus.

The Pharisees took note of the compelling sway Jesus had over the people. He *always* held that power, wherever and whenever He spoke. By and large, the Jewish elite hated Him for it.

See how the people love Him!

Who is this man?

"And it was the same in the days of Lot," Jesus said. Once again, He wiped the sweat from His eyes and cheeks before continuing:

"In the wicked cities of Sodom and Gomorrah, the people were also eating and drinking, buying and selling, planting and building—just like they had done during the days of Noah before them. But the very day Lot left Sodom, spirited away by angels, fire and sulfur rained down from heaven and destroyed them all. So it will be again, in the last days. It will be just like that."

The listeners understood these marvelous scriptural accounts. They had studied them in their synagogues. They had shared the sacred stories with their children and discussed them over meals and in family prayer times. But what in the world did those pieces of ancient history have to do with *them* and *their* current generation—a time filled with all the technological wonders of the ages? Would these same kinds of horrible things really come to pass upon them as well?

Then, Jesus startled His listeners with yet another sudden exclamation, "*It will be just like this* on the day the Son of Man is revealed! On that day no one who is on the housetop, with their possessions inside, should go down to get them! Likewise, no one in the field should go back for anything. *Remember Lot's wife!* Whoever tries to keep their life will lose it, and whoever loses their life will preserve it. I tell you, on that night, two people will be in one bed; one will be taken and the other left. Two women will be grinding grain together; one will be taken and the other will be left!"

"Where will these things take place, Lord?" someone shouted from the crowd.

Jesus bellowed back, "They will happen *wherever* it is necessary for them to happen! And *whenever* Yahweh chooses!"

Jesus stepped down from his boulder-perch, the last words of His public message having concluded for the day.

Once on the road again, Jesus walked toward the village with His disciples close on His heels. He made no grand announcement, nor did He give any particular instructions. He simply started walking. The crowds moved along the road behind Him as one huge mass of humanity. They wanted—*they needed*—to hear more.

Jesus kept to His private teaching, however. "It's just like the birds of the air," He explained to the dozen closest to him. "You understand, don't you? Where there is a dead body, there the vultures will also gather. Therefore, wherever the wicked are, those who have marked themselves for eternal ruin because of their rebellious hearts—they, too, shall be found out by the judgments of God. The stench of their vileness reaches the nostrils of Heaven."

The vulture was circling them again, just overhead. It was as if the revolting thing were following them. Jesus looked up at the bird and said to His disciples, "In the same way that a carcass cannot hide from a vulture, neither can a world of evil hide from its righteous Creator. That thoroughly evil generation is on its way, my brothers. Just as surely as it appeared in Noah's day, it is coming once again. *But, it is not yet the time.*"

He suddenly stopped in the middle of the road. Seeming to peer into the distant future, He spoke again:

"And when *that day* arrives, it shall indeed come...like a roaring flood."

11

The Choice

*A handful of days before the
commencing of Passover week*

JESUS AND HIS DISCIPLES SPENT SEVERAL MORE WEEKS IN THE JORDAN VALLEY, moving among the hamlets, then eventually ministering for another few days in the region of Jericho, just down the mountain from Jerusalem.

As always, the crowds followed them. Watching. Waiting. Hoping to witness another miracle. Hoping to *receive* a miracle! Desiring to hear more about the coming Kingdom. Most were sincere seekers, hearts full of earnest expectation. Others were spies. *Always, there were the spies.* And traitors.

Passover was approaching. The throngs, including Baruch and his crew, would soon be on the road to Jerusalem in order to celebrate. Jesus gathered up His disciples and started out again. Leaving Jericho, they went up through the narrow valley that led to Jerusalem.

As they started along the way, the disciples inquired, "Lord, why did you tell Baruch that the kingdom of God was among them now?"

"You've been uniquely blessed, my friends," Jesus replied. "You don't need to look for the coming of the Kingdom in marvelous signs, because its King is presently right before you, living in your midst. But the display of power they vainly seek will one day become visible to all. The whole earth will see it...and will mourn when it happens. But God's people will not need to stumble around in the dark to find the signs of the coming Kingdom. When the signs begin to appear, they will be vividly apparent to my sheep, those who hear my voice and who have the eyes to see. Of this I can assure you."

As they walked, Jesus reminded them, "As I have told you before, we're going up to Jerusalem. There the Son of Man will be delivered over to the chief priests and the teachers of the law. They will condemn Him to death and hand Him over to the Gentiles to be mocked and flogged…and crucified."

The disciples gaped at Him. Why did He always insist on speaking this way?

"But, on the third day," Jesus said, "He will be raised to life."

Knowing their thoughts, He quickly offered comfort: "I know you don't fully understand what I'm saying right now. You're wondering why I'm telling you such hard things. But remember. I've told you this ahead of time so that when they come to pass, you'll remember, and then you'll know that *I am He*."

Just like in the Jordan River Valley, Jesus was once again shadowed by the crowds of pilgrims who were drawn to the Holy City either by the coming Passover or by their curiosity about this Jesus who was also headed that way. Most in the procession desired to discover exactly what part the prophet from Nazareth would play in the festivities. Throughout the multitude, there was an atmosphere of feverish expectation. They expected that Yeshua might at last announce Himself as the Christ and claim His Kingdom. Even the Twelve still didn't understand the full measure of who Jesus really was and what He had come to do.[34]

The travelers finally arrived at the diminutive village of Bethany on the summit of the Mount of Olives, a short walk from Jerusalem. It was early Friday, now just six days before the Passover.[35] They remained at Bethany for the Sabbath and spent most of that day together. As Saturday evening fell, the disciples sat with Jesus on the hillside overlooking Jerusalem and the Temple Mount, admiring the aureate sun as it slipped below the horizon.

The Arriving King

The next day, at dawn of the first day of the week, the group made their way to the city. They crossed the Kidron Valley and entered Jerusalem through the East Gate, with Jesus riding on the back of the foal of a donkey that belonged to a friend. The crowds overwhelmed the entrance pathways as the news washed over the city: "*Yeshua is entering Jerusalem!*" At the gate, the mass of humanity grew so enormous that it attracted the agitated attention of the religious elite, as well as of the Roman soldiers and Temple guards.

Jesus' entry became a spectacle of pageantry, thoroughly unnerving those who were already plotting His death. Palm branches and articles of clothing were strewn into the street in front of the donkey's path so that He might pass over them.

It was an entrance fit for a conquering king. But the Jewish elite labeled the event as outright blasphemy. And, as far as the Romans were concerned, the spectacle could be the makings of a coming insurrection. Scrutinizing eyes followed His every move.

On that day, the crowd at the gate represented all of humanity. Of course, there were beggars, as always. Insanely rich people were present as well, attracted by the attendance of the Prophet and Miracle Worker. People from every race, culture, and walk of life mingled...children, young adults, middle-aged folks, elderly—all were there in massive numbers, a sea of integrated humanity.

Those of royalty and from the households of royalty were also there. Businessmen, prostitutes, merchants, traders, thieves, soldiers, and law enforcement officials were crammed together in the belly of the great crowd. Freedmen, citizens of Rome, slaves, indentured servants, and homeless people were packed into the throng, too.

Certainly, the religious were present. From every denomination of Judaism they came, as well the Roman and Greek pagans—not to mention those who believed in no god at all.

And on that same day, at that precise moment—without even

making a conscious decision to do so—the various representatives of humanity began to choose sides. Every reaction one might imagine was on display, aimed squarely at the One riding the donkey.

The scene morphed into a logistical nightmare as the crowds rolled as one, trying to get a closer look, to touch Him, or to have Him acknowledge their presence with just a glance. Cries of "Hallelujah!" sporadically arose to the heavens and bounced off the great walls of the city, echoing down the Kidron Valley and throughout the surrounding terrain. Plots of murder were murmured through scrunched-up and twisted-sideways mouths. Their diabolically influenced words were accompanied by seditious winks and self-congratulating slaps on backs.

It had begun.

But, this is why He had come. Not for the accolades and adoration of the crowds. *No*...He had come so the people could *choose*. He had come here on this day, and in this manner, *on purpose*.

He was here to fulfill the sound of the repeated crack of a whip. He had arrived so that thick, long spikes would slam through His flesh, muscle, tendon, and bones. He had come to lay down His life—lay it down even for those who hated Him. He had come to hold open the door of the "ark" for as long as possible...because there was yet another certain day to come.

Another ear-splitting wave of "Hallelujah!" hurtled through the Passover crowd. More weeping. More shouting.

More promises of allegiance, sworn with solemn oaths...vows that most never intended to keep.

More whispered threats. More plotting.

This opportunity must not go to waste! Perhaps now we can finally catch Him in a trap.

We can shut down this whole operation—this "church" of which He continually speaks.

We will slay their shepherd!

And the sheep will scatter.

12

The Temple Courts

About that day or hour no one knows,
not even the angels in heaven.

FOR THOSE FIRST FEW DAYS, THE CITY WAS ABUZZ BECAUSE OF JESUS' PRESENCE.

They were intense days, filled with intrigue. Conspiracies were still developing. And an unknown betrayer had been diabolically manipulated to be living right in the midst of the disciples.

Deals had to be made. Important secret meetings must be held. Payoffs still needed to exchange hands.

There were crowds to be instructed. Disciples to be prepared. False teaching to be set straight. Friends to be made. Enemies to arise, from deep within the bowels of the dark shadows of the unseen realm. A few more miracles were still to be wrought. Money changers' tables still needed to be overturned.

And, most importantly, there were souls to be collected into the Kingdom's harvest.

Evening on the Mount

He had only a few more days to live. It was now late in the afternoon on Monday. The Temple courts had been sweltering. The people flowed into the city in great droves. It was an exhausting day, one of unrelenting confrontation.

At the end of it, Jesus retired once again to the Mount of Olives. It was there where He and His disciples would spend every single night of His last week on earth. If the disciples could have only fathomed what they would eventually be forced to endure in just a few short days, perhaps, by now, they would have already absconded.

Olivet Discourse

As Jesus sat upon a tabletop ledge of rock jutting out of the mountainside, the disciples quietly, reverently, slipped to His side and sat down. Another day was coming to an end. The men commented upon the serenity of the moment, and especially noted the magnificent beauty of the Temple below them. Jesus had interrupted their wonderment by assuring them that soon the structure they were admiring would no longer exist at all.

"Tell us Lord," a forlorn Peter inquired, "when will all these things actually happen…and what will be the sign of your coming, and of the end of the age?"

Jesus paused, then, without directly addressing His pronouncement about the Temple's destruction, He instead spoke of the signs of His final return.

"Watch out that no one deceives you, my brothers," He said. "Many will come in my name, claiming, 'I am the Messiah,' and will deceive many. You'll hear of wars and rumors of wars, but see to it that you are not alarmed. Such things must happen, but the end is still to come. Nation will rise against nation, and kingdom against kingdom. There will be famines and earthquakes in various places. All these are the beginning of birth pains."

Jesus continued laying out the litany of last-days' signs. They were ominous words, even frightening at times. But the disciples were captivated by each one He uttered.

"Then," He said, "after all these things have come to pass, the sign of the Son of Man will appear in heaven. And then all the peoples of the earth will mourn when they see the Son of Man coming on the clouds of heaven, with power and great glory. And he will send his angels with a loud trumpet call, and they will gather his elect from the four winds, from one end of the heavens to the other."

When He had finished, the disciples remarked among themselves: "Just like Lot! The angels of Yahweh rescued Lot and his family just before God poured out His wrath on those great and perverse cities!"

A Certain Tree

"Now learn this lesson from the fig tree—" Jesus continued.

These words commanded the disciples' attention. They remembered that Jesus, that same morning, had actually condemned a fig tree on their way into the city. He had merely spoken to it, as if it were a person. Then they watched the tree wither and die, right before their eyes.[36]

Jesus kept on with His lesson. "As soon as its twigs get tender and its leaves burst forth again," He said, "you know that summer is near. Even so, when a person sees all these things, they know it's near, right at the door. Truly I tell you, the generation of that day will certainly not pass away until all these things will have come to pass—every single one of them. Heaven and earth will pass away, but my words will never pass away."

The disciples looked around at each other. Did Jesus just say what they thought He said? Was this mysterious utterance yet another vital clue concerning the arrival of His Kingdom?[37]

"But about that day or hour no one knows," Jesus said, "not even the angels in heaven, only the Father." Once again, Jesus surveyed His friends' attentive faces, pausing as He glanced at Judas.

Then, before the disciples could settle that thought in their minds... He did it again. He invoked the name of Noah, just as He had done weeks before, down in the Jordan River Valley.

"As it was in the days of Noah," He said, "so it will be at the coming of the Son of Man. For in the days before the Flood, people were eating and drinking, marrying and giving in marriage, right up to the day Noah entered the ark; and they knew nothing about what would happen until the Flood came and took them all away. That is how it will be at the coming of the Son of Man."

Darkness Descends

As evening fell on the Mount of Olives and Jesus had slipped away to retire for the night, the disciples discussed the evening's teachings.

"The clue about the 'days of Noah' must be extremely important!"

"Twice in a matter of weeks Jesus emphasized this point. Could the world really grow that vile again?"

"How could it be worse than it is right now?"

If they had only known…

For tonight, however, they would rest well. They prepared for their evening slumber by promising each other that they would stay by Jesus' side through thick or thin. They would never leave Him. They would never deny Him.

Most of them would not keep that promise.

Within moments, they drifted off into blissful slumber.

In so doing, they became a living metaphor of a prophetic generation yet to come.

13

One Last Nail

Passover Eve

PA-PINGGG! PA-PINGGG! PA-PINGGG!

Hours ago, the last nail had been driven.

But the executioners didn't need the nails to hold the One in the middle to His cross. This was exactly why He had come. The night before, He had purposely delivered Himself into the hands of His eventual executioners.[38]

Just now a cry rang out. It shot from the tortured lungs of the brutally mangled figure, the One who had been cruelly impaled through His hands and feet…hanging on a suspended wooden beam, between two common criminals.

The crowd moved closer.

"What is He trying to say now?"

"And…by the way…where are His disciples?"

"Only one of them is here. Just a youngster. We think his name is John. But the others…they aren't anywhere to be seen!"

"We heard, just a few moments ago, that they had run for their lives!"

"Cowards!"

The pathetic visage of the flesh-mangled man was encircled by the mob. They stood there, gathered near His blood-soaked body, just in front of the soldiers who were holding them back from the cross. He had been beaten beyond recognition before the Romans had nailed Him there…with three thick, long spikes.

Just days before, as He had made His way into Jerusalem on the back of a donkey, many in this same crowd had welcomed Jesus as the possible Messiah. They had scattered palm branches and even articles of their own clothing in His path…welcoming Him, worshiping Him.

But today…they hated Him. The fickleness of humanity's flesh had overwhelmed them.

"He had to die. Doesn't everybody understand that?"

The Sanhedrin, together with the Roman governor, had seen to the affair. After all, the event was orchestrated through a perfectly legal decree. It simply had to be done. Life with Jesus in their midst had become…well…*too dangerous.* So the government must be obeyed. *It was the right thing to do—perhaps even the godly thing to do. Right?*

Somebody had to pay. *Better Him than us…*

Clenched fists were lifted up in anger and raised toward His face in defiance.

"He claimed He could save others!"

"But look at Him now!"

"He can't even save Himself!"

"Let the Lord deliver Him, since He trusts in Him!"

"Liar!" "Fraud!" "Trickster!"

A pack of black-robed elites stood at a distance, at the back edges of the crowd that had gathered in front of the Crucified One. Their slight smirks betrayed their inner arrogance and deluded visions of self-importance.

They were also relieved. Soon this insufferable, insolent, agitating "teacher" would be gone, and then they could finally get on with their normal, so very important lives. They would now go back to the way it used to be. With *them, not Him,* commanding the crowds.

The voice coming from the roughly hewed cross shouted again. He looked up into the blackening sky and cried out—

"*Father!*"

"He speaks again!" "Listen!"

A hush fell over the crowd.

"*Forgive them! They don't understand what they are doing!*"

"What is this? In His dying moments this Crucified One is praying for *our* forgiveness?"

Deep contemplation. Then growing realization. Then a panicked doubt.

"Who is this Man? Have we perhaps made a mistake? Is this thing turning out to be a terrible blunder, something we can never undo?"

Sounds of sniffling began to ripple through the crowd. It was as if this spirit of self-doubt had come down upon them all at the very same moment.

Jesus looked down from the cross. He looked at the faces through blood-streaked eyes, stinging with salty sweat…and tears.

Baruch was there. His cohorts had accompanied him.

But now, he stood ashamed. Ashamed that he had not spoken up in defense of Jesus when he had the chance to do so. Embarrassed as he felt the depths of his own guilt, now more apparent to him than ever. Mortified that this event was even under way, and infuriated that he had been forced to witness the horrifying spectacle.

It didn't have to come to this…

It didn't have to be so.

14

The Sound

*That last spike may as well have been driven
through Baruch's heart.*

BARUCH HAD ARRIVED ON THE SCENE EARLIER, EVEN BEFORE THE FIRST NAIL HAD
been driven.

He had been there when the two thieves were first spiked to their
beams of death and then lifted up to be placed on each side of Jesus.
Their animal-like shrieking had been pitiful. Horrific to hear. Excruciating to watch. A sound and sight he would never forget.

But Baruch stayed. And because he remained there, he was present
when the nails were slammed into Jesus' hands. In fact, he was just a few
yards away when it happened. He kept watching until the last one was
driven into Jesus' feet, one foot placed on top of the other to accommodate that one final spike.

As that last blow rang out, it unnerved him.

That sound!

That clash of metal had been different! It was an intonation clearly
distinct from the other two. That last spike may as well have been driven
through Baruch's heart. He heard it echoing off the towering stone walls
of Jerusalem and reverberating through the valleys.

That had been hours ago. Six long, merciless hours ago.

But right now, Jesus' eyes caught those of Baruch.

What's this? Is Jesus looking directly at me?

Did He just smile at me? Is my mind playing tricks on me?

Baruch saw the men. Roman soldiers, casting lots for Jesus' clothing. Under the cross…. *Revolting! Despicable! Heathens!*

He now had only a few more minutes to live. Jesus cried out again— "My God! My God! Why have you forsaken me?"

Waa…wait! Why did Jesus say this? What could He mean?

Then something bizarre happened.

In that moment, the centurion removed his helmet and dropped to the ground, onto his knees under the feet of Jesus. The two looked at each other briefly. As Jesus' head fell to His chest, their eyes met. Although many missed the intimacy of the exchange, Baruch had seen it. He stood dumbfounded as he watched.

Jesus said something to the centurion, only slightly moving His lips, barely able to speak. No one in the belly of the crowd could possibly hear what Jesus said to the man. But the huge soldier began to weep, lowering his head in apparent remorse, grieving in his soul—his wide, armor-covered shoulders heaving. Something primordially deep had unnerved him.

The next words the centurion uttered stunned those who were close enough to hear. They were painfully articulated through streaming tears and quivering lips: "Surely, this man was the Son of God!"

Baruch felt his pain, too. He was certain that others were experiencing a similar emotion. *Such guilt. Such remorse. Such a crime!*

Suddenly, an ancient Psalm came to the old Pharisee's mind. *That's it!*

It was David's song Jesus had started to speak! Number twenty-two. Its opening words resounded through Baruch's head: "My God. My God. Why have you forsaken me?" *That's it!*

Baruch's mind now raced through the stanzas of that Psalm. Was there a key he was missing? Had Jesus just given another mystical clue? Baruch had known that thousand-year-old song by heart since he was a boy, but now it was living and breathing, right in front of him! He began to murmur the verses as he stood, stupefied, in front of Jesus:

All who see me mock me; they hurl insults, shaking their heads. "He trusts in the Lord," they say, "let the Lord rescue him. Let the Lord deliver him, since he delights in him."

My mouth is dried up like a potsherd, and my tongue sticks to the roof of my mouth; you lay me in the dust of death.

Dogs surround me, a pack of villains encircles me; they pierce my hands and my feet.

All my bones are on display; people stare and gloat over me.

They divide my clothes among them and cast lots for my garment.[39]

Oh. My. God!
This can't be happening!

As the knot in his throat almost strangled him, Baruch suddenly remembered what the "teacher" had revealed to him that day in the village, several weeks back, when Jesus and His disciples had stopped to address the group's questions about the coming Kingdom of God.

He had asked Jesus if it were really possible for an entire generation to miss the Messiah when He finally came. Jesus had responded, "The Kingdom of God is in your midst right now, my friend."

Then Jesus had said something else that day: "I tell you the truth, Baruch. This generation is in fact largely missing the entire event, *yes*. Again, it's all right there, open before you, in your Scriptures. It really couldn't be any plainer. The Word of God is *living*, right before your eyes."

Baruch's memories were interrupted, because, that's when it happened...

Jesus now had only seconds left. He grunted as He pushed Himself up. The sound came from deep within His heaving chest.

Cavernous. Guttural. Excruciating.

Jesus gathered what appeared to be the last of His remaining reserves of strength. With wild eyes, He strained against the tormenting final spike that had been driven into the top of His feet. He pushed up on it and winced in the agony caused by His action.

He quickly gasped for one final breath. His lungs filled with the pungent air that enclosed Him. He heaved out the last inhalation His lungs would ever hold…and shouted at the top of His weakening voice.

"It!"

"Is!"

"Finished!"

Instantly, His head dropped to His chest.

He never took another breath.

But how can this be? How can someone "will into existence" the exact second at which they will die? This is impossible!

Unless…

Upon hearing those last three words issued from the cross, Baruch now, finally, understood the message of that echoing last nail: Three dying men. Three unnecessary nails buried in the flesh of the One in the middle. Three painfully uttered last words.

The world would never be the same again.

Divine judgment is on its way. Humanity will not stand guiltless for what has happened here this day!

It's their fault! Baruch pointed to the Romans, as he spun around facing them.

It is our fault! He turned again and motioned to the Jews with an outstretched index finger.

This is my fault! He punched himself in his chest with a balled-up fist and wept bitterly.

When he had finally composed himself enough to speak, Baruch looked up at Jesus hanging on the cross. He called out to the lifeless form, "Lord! Please remember me also, when you come into your Kingdom! I understand it now! *I do!*"

Baruch smiled through bitter tears. A liquid warmth washed over him. Calming him. Soothing him. Assuring him. He was unashamed. *Strengthened.*

At last…he was finally beginning to understand.

But three days from now, the planet would be knocked off kilter.

Absolutely nothing would ever be the same again.

And Baruch's world would be eternally transformed along with the resultant shaking.[40]

PART THREE

Those Were the Days

Yesterday, I was speaking with my sister in Florida about what everyone is talking about COVID-19, and how it has spread around the world…. She asked me if I had considered that God was trying to get the world's attention….

Suddenly I started thinking how God in the past had managed to get people to listen to Him and what effect it had on the population.

My first thought was Noah and the Ark. Even though God's patience is vast there comes a time when He says enough is enough and so it was in Noah's day. God gave the world's population **the chance to repent while Noah was building the ark,** but sadly, God's invitation was rejected and **our world changed forever.**[41] (Emphasis added)

—TERRY COPELAND, WRITER FOR THE
CUMBERLAND TIMES-NEWS

This wasn't just happenstance that this pandemic happened. **And it wasn't just happenstance that it happened in this day and age.…** Some people **think this is the end of the world.** Some people don't know which way to go; they've lost their jobs and they've lost their hope.[42] (Emphasis added)

—REV. JOHNNY HARRIS, UNION BAPTIST CHURCH,
EATONTON, GEORGIA

15

Descending Darkness

Religion is supposed to be a source of comfort in times of confusion and suffering. And yet everywhere you look, services are being suspended.[43]

—Mattia Ferraresi, Italian journalist,
New York Times, March 10, 2020

The unfurling events in the early days of 2020 proved to be so profoundly surreal that even the largest part of the world's "visible church" panicked when it happened. The whole planet had careened around a sharp corner. And it left skidding tire marks when it did.

That one thing—*the panicking church*—seemed to scream the loudest about the prophetic reality of the days the world had just entered. Never since the birth of the church had this kind of globally pervasive fear factor occurred among the people of God. *Never.*

It was as though the church collective had been forced before the crucifix of decision once again. *Which will it be: The government or the Word?* And instead of standing as one, most of the sheep scattered into the night of fear and doubt. The church was losing its "saltiness" and was now being trampled underfoot.

But that haunting, omnipresent spirit wasn't relegated to the church alone. Governments worldwide began to react to the deliciously tempting openings that had finally presented themselves. Here was an opportune "crisis." *It must not be allowed to go to waste.*

Within weeks, edicts, orders, and quickly passed laws were put into place. Law-abiding citizens were herded into their homes. Various brands of governmental authorities began determining which businesses and organizations were "essential" and which were not. Multitudes of businesses were ordered shut.

Sports arenas, movie theaters, civic centers, conference centers, churches, and myriad other venues where large crowds normally gathered were shuttered through the power of quickly cobbled-together government decrees. Even various robust economies, the dynamic engines of international sustenance, were allowed to grind to a halt.

The world was effectively closing down. The *spirit of dread* had been unleashed. The new *caesars* had spoken. The loyal legions of the nascent empire were on the prowl, and they had been given authority to *handle* the disobedient ones.

Drunk on their newfound power, the insatiable appetite of the world's propaganda-driven media machine made certain to keep the embers of the newly formed global-terror narrative stoked. They had finally discovered what could make practically the entire global population—even the church—cower in dark corners.

Failing Hearts

Universal anxiety levels went through the roof. The sale and use of antidepressants reached all-time records.[44] The numbers of suicides and overdoses skyrocketed.[45] Social isolation syndrome became a serious international health crisis.[46] The combined effect was like gasoline being power-sprayed into a pit of glowing coals.

The ordeal of those days brought to mind the foreboding words of Jesus, spoken two thousand years earlier, as He warned of the prevailing nature of earth's final days under human rule:

Men's hearts [will be] failing them from fear and the expectation of those things which are coming on the earth, for the powers of the heavens will be shaken. (Luke 21:26, NKJV)

The *Jamieson-Fausset-Brown Bible Commentary* notes:

Nearly every expression [using this verb in the Scriptures] will be found used of the Lord's coming in *terrible national judgments.* Though its **ultimate reference** beyond doubt is to *Christ's final coming.*[47] (Emphasis added)

The 2020 COVID-19 "fear-demic" was relentless in its buildup, valiantly riding atop an incoming wave of irrational dread. It came barreling towards the borders of the global community like a Viking marauder with an insatiable bloodlust for the conquest of new territories finally within view.

Early breathless predictions estimated that well over a million people in the United States alone could perish in the pandemic. By March 2020, the *Washington Post* reported:

In the worst-case scenario, America is on a trajectory toward 1.1 million deaths. That model envisions the sick pouring into hospitals, overwhelming even makeshift beds in parking lot tents. Doctors would have to make agonizing decisions about who gets scarce resources.... Scientists bluntly stated the coronavirus is **the most serious respiratory virus threat since the 1918 flu pandemic.** If no action to limit the viral spread were taken, **as many as 2.2 million people in the United States could die over the course of the pandemic,** according to epidemiologist Neil Ferguson and others at the Imperial College Covid-19 Response Team.[48] (Emphasis added)

Even in April 2020, NBC News was still pushing the terror-invoking narrative, announcing: "As many as 240,000 people in the U.S.

could die from Covid-19—and that's only with strict social distancing measures in place."[49]

And four months later, in August, Texas Tech University's Department of Mechanical Engineering was still pushing the same panic narrative: "New epidemic model indicates **COVID-19 here to stay**, *likely to cause 235,000 U.S. deaths* by October"[50] (emphasis added).

Not to be outdone, in early September 2020, the Institute for Health Metrics and Evaluation (IHME) at the University of Washington offered up its own dire predictions, claiming that there might be more than 410,000 total coronavirus-related fatalities in the United States by the start of 2021 and warned that the "worst is yet to come."[51]

So, it was no surprise that in the earliest parts of 2020—by the time the rogue wave finally crashed ashore and the global death count appeared to be dutifully accelerating—just as experts had warned—international economies fell into various arrays of chaos.

Roiling in the frothy turmoil were the devastations of the fortunes and futures of family legacies, entire industries, and lifelong dreams of financial independence. Businesses scrambled to reformulate their operational models. Unemployment levels rose to historic heights. For millions around the world, the perceived *uncertainty index* began to bounce off the chart.

Step by Step

In the midst of the incoming flood of anxiety, a huge swath of the world's panicked population jumped aboard the bandwagon of political correctness. All of a sudden, they gobbled up every piece of "expert" information and advice that the previously tagged "fake-news machine" spewed. No one wanted to appear insensitive; even worse, they didn't want to be labeled as a "science denier" or "insensitive."

Again, for many students of biblical prophecy, it was staggering to observe how many people who had, just days before, professed deep faith in Jesus Christ but who were now suddenly willing to give up their daily activities of living—because they had become overwhelmed with the dread of dying.

Then, once the media elite felt it was in a comfortable position to further stoke the flames of the newly found pandemic power, God's people were subjected to further shocking headlines.

Slowly, the proverbial frog was being boiled alive.

16

Shades of the Prescient

The outlandish, hate-filled attacks on Christians were not just relegated to America's churches.

IN THE MIDDLE OF THE PANDEMIC, THE NEW YORK TIMES ALLOWED ITS publication to be employed as a shameless propaganda vehicle. In an incendiary opinion piece, evangelical Christians were labeled as the driving force that would eventually allow the "killer virus" to rampage across the world. Collectively, "religious ultraconservatives" were summarily labeled as "science deniers" and lacking in the abilities of "critical thinking."

The article's headline asserted: "The Religious Right's Hostility to Science Is Crippling Our Coronavirus Response."

This denial of science and critical thinking among religious ultra-conservatives now haunts the American response to the coronavirus crisis.

Donald Trump rose to power with the determined assistance of a movement that denies science, bashes government and prioritized loyalty over professional expertise. In the current crisis, we are all reaping what that movement has sown.[52] (Emphasis added)

That overtly bigoted piece was only the first of many that would follow. America's enormous Christian community was placed squarely within the crosshairs. The scope of the targeting was unparalleled.

By early April 2020, the British publication, *The Guardian*, jumped on the bandwagon with this headliner: "The Rightwing Christian Preachers in Deep Denial over Covid-19's Danger." The article stated:

> A number of American religious leaders have endangered their flock by holding services—and by claiming the virus can be defeated by faith in God.
>
> [Pastors of] the Christian right...are endangering their flocks and the rest of America by claiming the virus is a hoax, or that it can only be defeated by supernatural means, rather than solid healthcare policy.[53] (Emphasis added)

Later that month, *The Atlantic*, another mainstream leftist publication, dutifully did its part in perpetrating the anti-Christian talking points as well. Its headlines screamed, "Some of the Most Visible Christians in America Are Failing the Coronavirus Test."

If the coronavirus is a test of our collective character, some American Christians are flat-out flunking.

Consider the popular pastor John Piper, who was asked what he would say to pastors who claim that the pandemic is God's judgment on sinful cities and arrogant nations. **"God sometimes uses disease to bring particular judgments upon those who reject him and give themselves over to sin,"** Piper responded.

Or perhaps look to R. R. Reno, the editor of the conservative Christian journal *First Things*, who argued that **it's not worth a "mass shutdown of society" just to fight the virus.**

"There is a demonic side to the sentimentalism of saving lives at any cost."[54] (Emphasis added)

The outlandish, hate-filled attacks on Christians were not uniquely relegated to America's churches. The leftist media and other legitimized hate groups continued to pile on Christians living all over the planet, as evidenced through the following samples of international reports:

England | Northern Ireland | Scotland | Wales Evangelical Alliance—"Covid-19 Conspiracy Theories Putting Christian Minorities at Risk":

Persecuted Christian minorities around the world are at heightened risk due to a wave of conspiracy theories **blaming them for the spread of Covid-19.**[55] (Emphasis added)

Christian Today—"More Suffering for Persecuted Christians as They're Blamed for Coronavirus":

Ron Boyd-MacMillan, Open Doors' Head of Strategic Research, said, **"Ever since a plague that ravaged the Roman Empire in 180 AD, Christians have been unfairly blamed for natural disasters like these with a rise in persecution."**[56] (Emphasis added)

Vision.org—"Coronavirus Sparks New Persecution Threat for Christians":

Christians in countries where persecution is prevalent are coming under a new threat. Conspiracy theories are **blaming them for the spread of Covid-19.** Some **radicalized Muslims in Africa are blaming Christians for the pandemic,** claiming that Allah is punishing mankind because Christians in China supposedly burned the Koran.[57] (Emphasis added)

Criminalizing Church Attendance

Meanwhile, back in America, the vitriolic attacks against the few Christians still gathering in their churches continued. In late March of 2020, the Democrat governor of Virginia, Ralph Northam, issued an executive order making it a *criminal offense* for more than ten people to gather for a church service. His order allowed for up to a year in jail for violators.

Yet, the same governor had already declared liquor stores and pet stores "essential services," with no threat of jail if they opened. A pet store was essential. A church was not. A liquor store was "safe." A church was "dangerous."[58]

This type of anti-church lunacy continued even after America, by mid-June 2020, was beginning to return to a relative degree of normalcy. An example of the media's relentless attempts to spread its spirit of dread among churchgoers is illustrated in a June 16 headline from a West Virginia CBS News affiliate channel: "Covid-19 Hits Five W. Virginia Churches."

Following are a few quotes from that news outlet:

> **Five** churches across West Virginia are experiencing **outbreaks**.... The **National Guard was called out to the Graystone Baptist Church** which has 28 positive cases....
>   "With this COVID-19 stuff, it **absolutely is a mega-killer and mega-dangerous**," said Gov. Jim Justice, West Virginia.[59] (Emphasis added)

Of course, the implication of the governor's remarks appeared to be that since COVID-19 is a mega-killer, then these churches that were still meeting were being complicit in the *mega-killing* nature of the disease. Had the National Guard been called to the scene of a casino, restaurant, bar, big-box store, grocery outlet, or even most of the riots that were ensuing around the nation? Nope. Only to a church, where people had gathered to worship Jesus and voluntarily take a COVID-19 test.

Duplicity

Then, on July 8, 2020, the agenda-driven *New York Times* doubled down on its anti-Christian rhetoric. And this time, it wasn't an "opinion" piece they printed. The Internet search engines read: "Churches Emerge as Major Source of Coronavirus Cases."[60]

Even though the article's displayed headline was a bit tamer, that Google headline was specifically coded in its underling HTML language to display that particularly sensational and incendiary caption.[61]

The message had been sent—loud and clear. It wasn't the nation-wide riots that were the problem; those were fine. It wasn't the thousands of protesters gathered at those unruly events. It wasn't casinos, big-box stores, or restaurants. Nor was it the day-to-day mingling of families, friends, and community in gatherings that had now been occurring across the country for more than a month as state-by-state restrictions were loosened. Nope. According the *New York Times*, it was the "churches" that were the problem in the world. They, and they alone, were the "major source" of coronavirus cases.

However, during much of the time the world's major media was declaring that going to church could be a "mega-killer" and a "major source of coronavirus cases," several of America's top "health experts" were claiming that protesting in massive crowds in the heart of America's largest cities was actually a "healthy" activity for our nation.[62] *Yes.* You read that correctly—protesting is *healthy*.

That surreal juxtaposition became a media refrain sung to various tunes of madness. For example, just a couple of days after the National Guard had been called out to the West Virginia Graystone Baptist Church, the following headlines adorned the top spots on Internet's search engines:

The *Wall Street Journal*—"Early Data Show No Uptick in Covid-19 Transmission from Protests: Public Health Experts Say Preliminary Test Results Are Encouraging":

Early coronavirus testing data from a handful of U.S. cities and states suggest that recent protests against racial injustices haven't yet led to a marked uptick in new cases.[63]

MedPage Today—"So Far, So Good: No Covid-19 Spread from Protests":

Despite large protests, Washington, D.C., continues to see a decline in cases, with fewer than 100 a day since June 4.

"It's been reassuring that there hasn't been a large spike over the past couple of weeks," Monroe [Anne Monroe, MD, MSPH, an epidemiologist with George Washington University] told MedPage Today. "So far, thankfully, it does not appear that the protests have impacted current case counts."[64]

Twin Cities (Minneapolis-St. Paul)—"Early Test Results Show Few Protesters Caught Covid-19":

Early data from coronavirus tests of Minnesotans who participated in demonstrations after the death of George Floyd suggest the mass gatherings may not result in a spike in Covid-19 infections.[65]

Violence Is "Good"

Then, as if to take the madness up yet another notch, in late June 2020, a study conducted by economics professor Dhaval M. Dave of Bentley University and four other economists suggested that the riots probably helped to lower the COVID rates.

They actually claimed that the more violent the riots became, the greater the likelihood that people would stay at home, even if it was out of fear. By doing so, they said, the panicked populace would finally practice the government-mandated "social distancing" edicts on a more consistent basis.[66]

Apparently, the ever-present fake-news message was something along these lines: Going to church is "mega dangerous and mega deadly." But going to violent riots and mass protests appears to be perfectly healthy and might even be a "lifesaving factor," helping to lower our nation's overall infection rate.

The demonically twisted information flow grew more absurd—and disturbing—every day. For the first time in history, the church as a whole was globally mocked. Anti-Christian sentiment was whipped into a roiling froth of disdain.

But they weren't finished yet.

17

Rome Is Burning

And it happened just before Resurrection Sunday.

As those floods of national and international attacks were regularly unleashed in all of their vitriolic, nuanced language, it caused the biblically literate to shudder. Previous history lessons came to mind, especially those concerning Roman Emperor Lucius Domitius Ahenobarbus—more infamously known as Nero. He was the one who ordered the beheading of the apostle Paul in AD 67.

Nero, of course, is also infamous for having blamed *the Christians* for the Great Fire of Rome. That disastrous event was a mammoth, city-wide fire many historians believe the emperor most likely orchestrated himself. The blazing inferno burned ten of Rome's fourteen districts to the ground. Here's what an article on the PBS website had to say about the event:

> Nero himself blamed the fire on an obscure new Jewish religious sect called *the Christians, whom he indiscriminately and mercilessly crucified.* During gladiator matches he would feed Christians to lions, and he often lit his garden parties with the burning carcasses of Christian human torches.[67] (Emphasis added)

Could the world's peddlers of mass information have forgotten what this incendiary language could ignite? Worse yet, perhaps they knew fully well what they were doing. With the advent of 2020, it appeared that "Rome" was on fire—again—and once more, the Christians were blamed.

The quickly spreading philosophy that said "churches are evil spreaders of this disease, but mass shopping at big box stores or mass rioting in the streets of major US cities is not" was egged on by the left-wing media, as represented by an article from *The Hill*, titled, "Why the Government Can Shut Down Church Gatherings During a Pandemic."

> *Jesus might also be viewed as the first coronavirus offender,* because the Last Supper hosted three disciples too many under the social gathering limits in most states during this crisis. At the time, of course, Roman Governor Pontius Pilate was trying to contain Christianity itself, which now some church leaders accuse American governors of doing. *Some churches plan to defy state public health directives by carrying out large Easter services.*[68] (Emphasis added)

Stop the Singing!

As these bizarre societal twists on attending Christian church services were daily taking shape, a number of leftist local governments continued to push the limits to beyond the absurd. And it happened just before Resurrection Sunday, April 12, 2020.

Mendocino County, California, officials decided that small groups that were "governmentally allowed" to attend "limited" worship services were, at the same time, disallowed from singing and playing instruments. Remember, these Nero-like edicts were issued during the same time that chanting, screaming, crying, biting, and spitting on people at massive riots—attended by thousands standing only inches away from each other—were considered by the leftist media as "good for the country."

Fox News reported the governmental overreach:

Mendocino County, a coastal county with a population of 86,000, *banned churches from singing* while recording online worship services, unless the individuals sang from home. Four individuals only were allowed to record from one place and "*no singing* or *use of wind instruments*, harmonicas or other instruments that could spread Covid-19 through projected droplets *shall be permitted* unless the recording of the event is done at one's residence," according to the county order.

"It is an entirely different matter, however, to tell Christians that they cannot sing in praise and honor of God" [said Albert Mohler, president of the Southern Baptist Theological Seminary].

"Indeed, these orders came out just days before Resurrection Sunday—orders saying that Christians, on the day where they celebrate the resurrection of the Lord Jesus Christ, are prohibited from singing."[69] (Emphasis added)

Even by July, just days before America ironically prepared to celebrate its "independence," the state of California joined the *no-singing-in-church* bandwagon. With Nazi-like language, the bizarre order read:

Even with adherence to physical distancing, convening in a congregational setting of multiple different households to practice a personal faith carries a relatively higher risk for widespread transmission of the Covid-19 virus, and may result in increased rates of infection, hospitalization, and death, especially among more vulnerable populations. In particular, activities such as singing and chanting negate the risk-reduction achieved through six feet of physical distancing.

Places of worship must therefore discontinue singing and chanting activities and limit indoor attendance to 25% of building capacity or *a maximum of 100 attendees,* whichever is lower.[70] (Emphasis added)

The article also emphasized that "in March, *a choir practice*—without masks—was blamed for an acute outbreak of coronavirus in Washington State"[71] (emphasis added).

Yet, just one day before California banned singing in church, the *Los Angeles Times* gave a wink and a nod to mass protesting with this headline, "Experts See Little Evidence That Protests Spread the Coronavirus in U.S."[72]

But these *spirit of Antichrist* atrocities weren't just happening throughout America. They were occurring in many other areas of the world as well. It was as if most of the international governments were reading from the same, pre-planned script. For example:

> *Churches across Germany* [were told that]… Worshippers will have to wear masks, respect social distancing, **and *no singing* will *be allowed*** amid *fears* that **it spreads the virus more easily.**[73] (Emphasis added)

Tyranny

Then, on July 24, 2020, the Supreme Court of the United States weighed in concerning the constitutional rights of churches in America.

To America's Christians, the ongoing attacks against the church took a monumentally surreal—and highly prophetic—turn for the worse. The court effectively ruled that casinos, restaurants, and bars had more of a constitutional right to meet than did churches. The mainstream media gleefully reported the ruling. Conservative media went apoplectic.

Following is an excerpt from *The Conservative Review*:

SCOTUS rules **Nevada churches can be restricted more than casinos**.... In Calvary Chapel Dayton Valley v. Sisolak, a large church in Dayton, Nevada, sued the governor for limiting church capacity to just 50 people.

Meanwhile, in an obvious catering to special interests, **casinos, gyms, restaurants, and bars can entertain *up to 50 percent capacity*,** even if that includes *several hundred people.* Nobody thought this could pass constitutional muster, but **once again *Chief Justice John Roberts* sided with the four liberals and denied an appeal from the church.**

What has become clear is that ordinary Americans seeking to exercise their fundamental rights in the face of unprecedented tyranny *have no pathway to protection* through the courts.... At this point, our *only appeal must be to the heavenly court.*[74]

In August 2020, Dr. John MacArthur, pastor of Grace Community Church in Los Angeles, summed up the unprecedented government assault on America's churches like this:

Never before has the government invaded the territory that belongs only to the Lord Jesus Christ and told us we can't meet, we can't worship, we can't sing. There's no power given to the government to make those kinds of calls against us.[75] (Emphasis added)

However, our ancient brothers and sisters in Christ had been through plagues, pandemics, and outlandish persecution before. And, it had suffered much worse than what we were presently enduring. When, during those days of old, the church had faithfully persevered, they didn't close their churches. Nor did they stop singing. Nor did they practice "social distancing" from each other, much less from the world around them.

In fact, they increased their worship, they enlarged their fellowships, they amplified their missions outreach, and they sang louder. And they ran headlong into the killing fields of mortal danger, often coupled with ever-increasing persecution. They did it in order to minister to the dying world around them.

By faith, they didn't hide from the rigors of life in a fallen world, as did the frightened pagans of their times. Neither did they shirk from touching, feeding, clothing, and ministering to those who were on the brink of death, suffering from the most hideous of the latest killer diseases.

History is replete with these accounts and the amazing miracles that came to life in their midst.

18

Of Plagues and Pandemics

Of course, no one listened in Noah's day either.
Literally—no one.

DR. RODNEY STARK[76] IS AN AMERICAN SOCIOLOGIST OF RELIGION. HE
served as a long-time professor of sociology and of comparative religion
at the University of Washington. He is now Distinguished Professor of
the social sciences department at Baylor University.

In his book, *The Triumph of Christianity: How the Jesus Movement
Became the World's Largest Religion*, we read:

> In the year 165, during the reign of Marcus Aurelius, a devastat-
> ing epidemic swept through the Roman Empire. Some medical
> historians suspect this was the first appearance of smallpox in
> the West…. During the fifteen-year duration of the epidemic, a
> quarter to a third of the population probably died of it.
>
> At the height of the epidemic, mortality was so great in many
> cities that the emperor Marcus Aurelius (who subsequently died
> of the disease) wrote of caravans of carts and wagons hauling out
> the dead. Then, a century later came another great plague….
> No one knew how to treat the stricken. Nor did most people
> try…. Hence, when their first symptom appeared, victims often

were thrown into the streets, where the dead and dying lay in piles.

As for action, Christians met the obligation to care for the sick rather than desert them, and thereby saved enormous numbers of lives…. It is entirely plausible that Christian nursing would have reduced mortality by as much as two-thirds!

The fact that most stricken Christians survived did not go unnoticed, lending immense credibility to Christian "miracle working." Indeed, the miracles often included pagan neighbors and relatives. This surely must have produced some conversions, especially by those who were nursed back to health….

What went on during the epidemics was only an intensification of what went on every day among Christians…. Indeed, the impact of Christian mercy was so evident that in the fourth century when the emperor Julian attempted to restore paganism, he exhorted the pagan priesthood to compete with the Christian charities.

But there was little or no response to Julian's proposals because there were no doctrines and no traditional practices for the pagan priest to build upon…. Christians believed in life everlasting.

Thus, for Galen to have remained in Rome to treat the afflicted during the first great plague would have required far greater bravery than was needed by Christian deacons and presbyters to do so. **Faith mattered.**[77] (Emphasis added)

Yes. Faith mattered.

And faith—simply taking God at His Word—has always mattered for the genuine Church of Jesus Christ. The world has never understood it, and probably never will. Thus, we shouldn't be shocked by the world's response to our faithfulness while ministering in the middle of yet another pandemic. The "real" Church of truly born-again believers has been called to move in that same faith today—*especially* in today's world.

We are not to cower in fear while the world comes unglued. We are supposed to be the *Noahs* of our own generation. The *ark* of our day is our walk of faith and our message of the Good News of Jesus Christ. That message is largely the same as Noah's: *Repent and turn to the Lord God for your salvation, for His judgment is soon to fall upon the entire planet.*

Of course, no one listened in Noah's day either. Literally—*no one.* And the scoffers perished. Every single one.

> [Jesus said,] And **they knew nothing about what would happen** until the flood came and **took them all away. That is how it will be** at the coming of the Son of Man. (Matthew 24:39; emphasis added)

The global pandemic of 2020 brought a wave of panic and fear that rolled across the planet like a tsunami. Biblically knowledgeable Christians believed that the universal and vitriolic anti-Christian narrative that came with that wave was being choreographed in the deepest halls of the unseen realm of darkness. The Scriptures had warned us of just such truths:

> For our struggle is not against flesh and blood, but against the rulers, against the authorities, against the powers of this dark world and against the spiritual forces of evil in the heavenly realms. (Ephesians 6:12)

As time moved forward, that scriptural truth and others like it began to take on an increasing relevance to the world's truest believers.

The demonic assault was shameless, and smothering.

And it grew even more so.

19

The Great Reset

The purpose of the Great Reset...is to completely overhaul the world's existing structures and institutions.[78]

THE THING THAT MADE THE VICIOUSLY ANTI-CHRISTIAN *NEW YORK TIMES* HIT piece all the more ominous was the fact that, just one day before the story was written, the world's elites had already introduced the planet to yet another provocative scheme. The revelation came from Great Britain's *The Guardian* with a headline that proclaimed: "Gordon Brown Calls for Global Government to Tackle Coronavirus."

So, at the beginning of a pandemic touted as one of the worst the planet had ever experienced, we were also issued a clarion call preparing us to bow to a "global government." Ostensibly, this worldwide government would be absolutely necessary for our own *safety*—for the *good of the planet.* And, that eminent body of governance planned on being placed in firm control of the world's health concerns, as well as of its various economic priorities.

Gee. What could go wrong with that plan?

Following are the first two paragraphs of the *Guardian* article:

Gordon Brown has urged world leaders to create a temporary form[79] of **global government to tackle the twin medical and economic crises** caused by the Covid-19 pandemic.

The former Labour prime minister, who was at the centre of the international efforts to tackle the impact of the near-meltdown of the banks in 2008, said there was a need for a task-force involving world leaders, health experts and the heads of the international organizations that would **have executive powers to coordinate the response.**[80] (Emphasis added)

Almost one month to the day after Gordon Brown called for a universal government, Yahoo News got in on the action as well. It assured the world: "Coronavirus Marks the **Real Beginning of the End of Cash.**"

The coronavirus pandemic has placed front and center before us the question of whether societies need to use physical money. In fact, it reignites the rolling debate of whether hanging onto the use of physical cash is a wasted endeavor.

Necessity is the mother of invention. In today's climate, where the global health crisis of Covid-19 means we are now in lockdowns and varying levels of social distancing, **the need to improve and use digital payments is more important than ever.**[81] (Emphasis added)

Pushing the Button

By the last few days of June 2020, the idea of a global government took yet another dangerous turn. Fox News reported the Orwellian dream with these words: "Al Gore, UN Secretary-General, Others Now Demanding 'Great Reset' of Global Capitalism: These are truly dangerous times for those who support individual liberty and free markets."

Following are a few quotes from that article:

While most **Americans have been preoccupied** with protests and pandemics, a potentially bigger story has managed to slip beneath the radar: **a growing movement** among the world's most powerful leaders to **call for a "reset" of the entire global economy.**

It's a proposal they acknowledged has **only been made possible** because of **the "opportunity" provided by the economic destruction** caused by the novel coronavirus.

"**Every country,** from the United States to China, **must participate,** and every industry, from oil and gas to tech, *must be transformed.* In short, we need a 'Great Reset' of capitalism."

The purpose **of the Great Reset** isn't merely to enact policies that would lead to additional wealth redistribution, but rather *to completely overhaul* **the world's existing structures and institutions.**[82] (Emphasis added)

And from the Great Reset Initiative official website, we find these declarations:

The Covid-19 crisis, and the political, economic and social disruptions it has caused, is *fundamentally changing* the traditional context for decision-making...

As *we enter a unique window of opportunity* to shape the recovery, this initiative will offer insights to help inform all those determining the future state of global relations, the direction of *national economies, the priorities of societies, the nature of business models and the management of a global commons.*[83] (Emphasis added)

The Language of Antichrist

Then, so as not to give up the incessant demand emanating from the self-appointed "Masters of the Universe," the United Nations once again doubled down in the opening days of July 2020, as reported in an article headlined "U.N. Chief Guterres Renews Call for More Global Governance, Bureaucratic Regulation":

> **U.N. Secretary-General Antonio Guterres renewed his call for "more robust global governance"** Wednesday, adding the World Bank and the International Monetary Fund (IMF), regional authorities such as the African Union and the European Union (E.U.) to a list of organizations **he says *can bring "order" to a future world* disrupted by the coronavirus pandemic.**
>
> In an essay titled "Global Wake-up Call," the unelected head of the globalist body said "from Covid-19 to climate disruption, from racial injustice to rising inequalities, **we are a world in turmoil.**"[84] (Emphasis added)

Does this sound like the "spirit of Antichrist" to you?

20

We Know Where You Are

*Plans for micromanaging the daily coming and going of the
planet's entire population were finally underway.*

THEN CAME THE NEWLY IGNITED FEARS OF FORCED VACCINATIONS AND THE
digital tracking of the world's population. These seemingly nefarious
agendas further ramped up the speculations of a last-days global marking system spoken of in Scripture (see Revelation chapters 13 and14).

However, the truth is that most Americans are acutely aware that,
over the past several centuries, vaccines have been developed that have
eliminated or nearly eradicated a long list of diseases.[85] A number of us
are grateful for those wondrous medical breakthroughs. Some of us are
even alive today because of them.

But, at the same time, we also realize that we're living within a
brand-new paradigm of never-before-imagined technological *signs and
wonders.* And we know that malicious people and the organizations they
manage would most assuredly attempt to use the technologies of our
day to bring about a long-dreamed-of global system of governance and
control. How could we miss it? This was no longer relegated to the mere
stuff of conspiracy theories. Now we were seeing "movers and shakers"
openly boasting about these same goals in mainstream media sources.[86]

It's also a sad fact of history that the US government—as well as
other administrations of the world—have flatly lied to their populations

in the past about vaccines and healthcare. Some, including the US, have actually run grotesque "experiments" on unsuspecting, select groups of people under the guise of providing "free healthcare."[87]

We also discovered, in the middle of the newest pandemic of panic, that the reporting of infection rates and deaths supposedly related to the virus has most likely been nefariously manipulated. Many suspected this to be the case, but now, apparent proof of it began to surface. *Business Insider* and a Fox News affiliate out of Florida were among several who were exposing the apparent ruse:

> The White House's coronavirus task force response coordinator, Dr. Deborah Birx, said in a recent meeting that "there is nothing from the CDC that I can trust." ...Birx and others reportedly feared that the Centers for Disease Control and Prevention's data-tracking system was *inflating coronavirus statistics like death rates and case numbers.*[88] (*Business Insider*, May 2020; emphasis added)

> Since a FOX 35 investigation, last week revealing some laboratories weren't reporting negative COVID-19 results, the state has updated some numbers. However, many others, are still the same, with hundreds of labs showing a positivity rate of 100%.
> **Now, another FOX 35 investigation** is underway, looking into claims that **people were *receiving* [positive] *test results* even though *they were never tested.*** Florida Gov. Ron DeSantis said he has heard this enough to believe its happening and the state has already investigated its test sites.[89] (Fox 35-Orlando, July 2020; emphasis added)

Massive Distrust

It has only been a few decades since the unprecedented era of almost unmitigated technological advancements exploded upon the world like a long-simmering volcano that suddenly blew its lid. So it didn't help, in the time of this new and blossoming COVID-19 pandemic, that the mainstream media was continually running articles like the following:

Digital Certificates of Vaccination

- GatesNotes.com (Bill Gates' personal website)—"31 Questions and Answers about Covid-19":

  Eventually we will have some digital certificates to show who has recovered or been tested recently or when we have a vaccine who has received it.[90] (Emphasis added)

- CNN—"Fauci: There Might Be "Merit" to the Idea of Coronavirus Immunity Certificates":

  It's one of those things that we talk about when we want to **make sure that we know who the vulnerable people are and not.**[91] (Emphasis added)

- Institute of Electrical and Electronics Engineers [IEEE]— "Quantum Dots Encode Vaccine History in the Skin: Invisible to the Eye, the Dots Glow under Infrared Light from Modified Smartphones":

  "We started thinking about **using a dye that's not visible by the naked eye,**" but that would be persistent and inexpensive to detect, says senior paper author Ana Jaklenec, a research scientist at MIT's Koch Institute for Integrative Cancer Research. Together with MIT's Robert Langer, **she came up with a solution—quantum dots.**[92] (Emphasis added)

Global Vaccination—Every Person on the Planet

- GatesNotes.com—"What You Need to Know about the Covid-19 Vaccine":

  In order to stop the pandemic, we need to make the vaccine available to almost every person on the planet. We've never delivered something to every corner of the world before…. We need to manufacture and distribute at least 7 billion doses of the vaccine.[93] (Emphasis added)

- CNBC—"Bill Gates Denies Conspiracy Theories That Say He Wants to Use Coronavirus Vaccines to Implant Tracking Devices":

  "We have never, never as a globe made a vaccine of this type before nor of this scale before *ever*."—Melinda Gates.[94] **(Emphasis added)**

- *Scientific American*—"Genetic Engineering Could Make a COVID-19 *Vaccine in Months* Rather Than Years: Candidates Are Speeding toward Human Trials":

  Within days his laboratory and dozens of others around the world started designing vaccines that they hoped could protect billions of people against the SARS-CoV-2 virus, **the biggest challenge to global health and prosperity since World War II.**

  Three different *techniques based on DNA and RNA molecules are speeding to human trials*, but whether they will work, or can be scaled up to millions of doses, is unclear.[95] (Emphasis added)

- *Science* magazine and the *Journal of the American Association for the Advancement of Science*—"Abortion Opponents Protest COVID-19 Vaccines' Use of Fetal Cells":

Several promising COVID-19 vaccine candidates are **manufactured using cells derived from human fetuses** electively **aborted decades ago**.[96] (Emphasis added)

Force Them to Take It!

- Famed constitutional attorney Alan Dershowitz:

You have no right to refuse to be vaccinated.

Let me put it very clearly, you have no constitutional right to endanger the public and spread the disease even if you disagree, you have no right not to be vaccinated, you have no right not to wear a mask, you have no right to open up your business.

And if you refuse to be vaccinated the state has the power to literally take you to a doctor's office and plunge a needle into your arm.

If there's a disease that will kill you, you have the right to refuse that, but **you have no right** to refuse to be vaccinated against a contagious disease for public health. **The police have the power of the Constitution that gives the state the power to compel that.**[97] (Emphasis added)

By mid-July 2020, those closely watching the unfolding of these seemingly prophetic events had even more reason to be concerned as the following headline appeared: "Africa to Become Testing Ground for 'Trust Stamp' Vaccine Record and Payment System."

Portions of that article follow:

A new biometric identity platform partnered with the Gates-funded GAVI vaccine alliance and MasterCard will launch in West Africa and combine Covid-19 vaccinations, cashless payments, and potential law enforcement applications.

In early June, GAVI reported that Mastercard's Wellness Pass program would be adapted in response to the coronavirus (Covid-19) pandemic.

Around a month later, Mastercard announced that Trust Stamp's biometric identity platform would be integrated into Wellness Pass as Trust Stamp's system is capable of providing biometric identity in areas of the world lacking internet access or cellular connectivity and also does not require knowledge of an individual's legal name or identity to function.

The Wellness Program involving GAVI, MasterCard, and Trust Stamp will soon be launched in West Africa and will be coupled with a Covid-19 vaccination program once a vaccine becomes available.[98] (Emphasis added)

As if all of that wasn't enough, *USA Today* got in on the action with yet another mainstream piece aimed squarely at people of faith. The provocative article—written by three physicians—flatly calls for "mandatory vaccinations," with severe penalties for those who refuse. The words sounded like something ripped straight from the pages of the book of Revelation:

The only answer is compulsory vaccination—for all of us.... Simply put, getting vaccinated is going to be our patriotic duty.

So here's what **America must do** when a vaccine is ready....
- Do not honor religious objections.
- Do not allow objections for personal preference, which violate the social contract.

- How can government and society assure compliance with protective vaccines? Vaccine refusers could lose tax credits or be denied non-essential government benefits. Health insurers could levy higher premiums.
- Private businesses could refuse to employ *or serve unvaccinated individuals*, schools could refuse to allow unimmunized children to attend classes, public and commercial transit companies—airlines, trains and buses—could exclude refusers. Public and private auditoriums could require evidence of immunization for entry.
- A registry of immunization will be needed with names entered after immunization is completed.[99] (*USA Today*, August 2020; emphasis added)

It seemed that the long-hoped-for goals of every serious globalist began to revolve around the world's newest and most convenient "crisis"—SARS-CoV-2. The elite denizens of the "new world order" had discovered the elusive starter mechanism for which they had been frantically searching. Their plans for micromanaging the daily coming and going of the planet's entire population were finally underway.

To a number of those who had long been cataloging these kinds of prophetic events, it appeared as though the perfect storm of an ominous biblical convergence might be lurking just right around the corner. And it was all hidden behind the demonic mask of "Come now. You understand, don't you? It's all being done for your own good."

Just trust us.

21

Convergence of Pieces

The societal atmosphere was genuinely beginning to boil over with irrational, anxiety-ridden fears.

ADMITTEDLY, WHEN WE EXAMINE MORE CLOSELY THE ARTICLES REFERENCED IN the previous chapter, a few—but certainly not all—appear to be fairly sincere attempts to employ the wonders of the most recent technologies in order to provide a safer and healthier planet.[100]

Additionally, constitutional attorney Alan Dershowitz's stunning claims of governmentally "forced vaccinations" actually have valid standing through long-held Supreme Court precedent, regardless of how shocking that might sound to a number of US citizens.[101]

But here's the problem....

The societal atmosphere was genuinely beginning to boil over with irrational, anxiety-ridden fears. The citizenry of the planet was dealt a daily barrage of forced church closings, government-imposed stay-at-home orders, and Orwellian mask mandates, as well as draconian and newly minted legal ramifications for violators of the latest imaginative government directives.

So, naturally, the words about universal vaccination programs, coupled with "certificates of immunity" and "quantum dot" tracing and the digital cataloging of personal information and immunity identification, were still rather unsettling proposals for a large portion of America's populace—especially when these proposals were coming from the world's elitists, those already well known to be admitted globalists.

And that's not to mention, as illustrated in the previous chapter, that we were discovering that case and death numbers were actually being manipulated. That shocking revelation was then attached to the exposure of yet another highly suspicious pattern. In April 2020, *USA Today* reported, "Fact Check: Hospitals Get Paid More if Patients Listed as COVID-19, on Ventilators":

> Sen. Scott Jensen, R-Minn., a physician in Minnesota, was interviewed by "The Ingraham Angle" host Laura Ingraham on April 8 on Fox News and claimed hospitals get paid more if Medicare patients are listed as having COVID-19 and get three times as much money if they need a ventilator.
>
> [Sen. Scott Jensen posted:] "How can anyone not believe that increasing the number of COVID-19 deaths may create an avenue for states to receive a larger portion of federal dollars?"
>
> "Hospital administrators might well want to see COVID-19 attached to a discharge summary or a death certificate. Why? **Because if it's a straightforward, garden-variety pneumonia** that a person is admitted to the hospital for—if they're [on] Medicare—typically, the diagnosis-related group **lump sum payment would be $5,000.** But *if it's COVID-19 pneumonia, then it's $13,000,* and if that *COVID-19 pneumonia patient ends up on a ventilator, it goes up to $39,000.*"[102] (Emphasis added)

USA Today concluded that its in-depth fact check was: *True.*

> We rate the claim that hospitals get paid more if patients are listed as COVID-19 and on ventilators as TRUE.
>
> Hospitals and doctors *do get paid more* for Medicare patients diagnosed with COVID-19 or if it's *considered presumed* they

have COVID-19 *absent a laboratory-confirmed test*, and *three times more* if the patients are placed *on a ventilator* to cover the cost of care and loss of business resulting from a shift in focus to treat COVID-19 cases.[103] (Emphasis added)

Did you catch that? Patients didn't have to actually test positive for COVID-19. They only had to be *presumed* to have it. Then, in would flow the bucket loads of federal funding the medical industry so desperately needed. Next, a hospital could put patients on a potentially deadly respirator and the medical facility would receive three times the amount of federal compensation!

To top all this off, Americans were heavy-handedly reminded that *forced vaccinations* were indeed supported by several longstanding legal precedents, lawfully solidifying that *this* convenient legal tool was the *one thing* that could be used to force people to "take a mark" against their will—or else.

How could this collision of surreal events not be considered a runaway train ride of epically prophetic proportions?

22

The First Time Ever

*An explosion of unrestrained chaos might
be just around the corner.*

To put the preceding information into clearer focus, let's quickly recount this collision of unparalleled convergences.

1. **In 2020**, a viral pandemic sweeps the planet.

2. **For the first time since the Flood of Noah**, fear, panic, and pandemonium clutch the hearts of almost everyone in the global population—practically overnight.[104] Depression, anxiety, and the use of antidepressant drugs reach historic levels.

3. **For the first time in history**, governments the world over (aided by the newest technologies), began to capitalize upon that fear and—almost in choreographed fashion—seized as much control as possible over their respective jurisdictions, often leveling draconian and liberty-restricting decrees upon their citizenry.

4. **In 2020, for the first time in history**, one of the most obvious groups specifically targeted for "closure" and routinely appearing in the latest vitriol-filled headlines of news reports around the world was—*the church.*[105]

5. Then, **2020 became the first year since the birth of Christianity** in which barely a church on the planet was open for services on Resurrection Sunday…the one day in all of history that represents *Satan's defeat.*

6. Seven weeks later, **2020 also became the first year since the birth of the church** in which barely a live congregation on the planet was open for Pentecost services. That, of course, is the Feast of the Lord that represents both the birth of Israel[106] and of the church (Acts 2). The supernatural birth of the church was yet another monumental sign of Satan's defeat. And this was the year that the "spirit" of Satan wouldn't "allow" that global celebration to take place.

7. **The year 2020 became the first ever** when a multitude of churches around the world were told that *when* they *were* "permitted" by their government officials to finally return to their services, they were not allowed to sing.

8. **In 2020, for the first time,** it became globally *unacceptable*—with some even losing their jobs, ministries, and friends over the issue—to utter the phrase, "All lives matter."[107] Without doubt, those three words also embody the heart of God's Word and express the indisputable theme of the message of the gospel itself. Yet they were suddenly deemed to be hateful, racist words the world over.

9. **In 2020, for the first time in America's history,** the Supreme Court of the United States effectively ruled that casinos, restaurants, and bars had more of a "right" to meet than did churches. America's sacrosanct 1st Amendment rights were summarily thrown to the ground.

10. **In the midst of these *unprecedented events*—**clearly smacking of the prophetic—the world was consistently pummeled with amplified and serious cries for forced vaccines, gene-altering vaccines, vaccines created from aborted fetuses, digital tracking systems, global governance, and biometric identification of the citizenry of the entire globe. This doesn't even include the incessant demand for a complete "resetting" of global capitalism and individual liberties, along with the international elimination of paper currency.

Prophetic Stew

It seemed to a great number of people that the recipe for an explosion of unrestrained chaos might be just around the corner. The prophetic ground roiled under the feet of the world's population. The heavenly trumpets were resounding, for those with ears to hear. But few were listening, just as it was in the days of Noah.

The planet, almost overnight, had become a vitally different place. In the midst of the seismic shift, most of the world's churches were still in the process of shuttering their buildings, sometimes spurred on by a pervasive spirit of unreasonable alarm. They could be presented with hard facts and reports like what you've just read, and it still didn't matter. Their doors were shut, their masks dutifully covered their faces, and they huddled in fear until the "government" told them what to do next.

The much-ballyhooed "faith of God's people" appeared to take wings and fly out of the stained-glass windows all over the world.

And the "Masters of the Universe" took note.

They rubbed their hands together and thought, "We had no idea this would be so easy."

23

Final Warning

Was this the beginning of a divinely prophesied cosmic wake-up call?

THINK ABOUT THIS SOBERING TRUTH.

If, within a single generation, one or two unprecedented prophetic fulfillments come to light, that generation better sit up and pay attention.

And if a dozen or more of those events or circumstances have occurred, as they have in our own generation, then there should be no denying the obvious. Think of how many times in this book alone we've listed events and circumstances that happened "for the first time in history," or "only in our historical generation," or that were "unprecedented."

Further, if a fistful of even more right-off-the-pages-of-the-Bible prophecies came to life in a matter of months—as happened when 2019 turned the corner into 2020—then the *shaking* has already started.

These truths caused many serious prophecy researchers to ask: What is it that Satan seems to know that most of today's church apparently doesn't even wish to acknowledge?

The Word of God has the answer.

Therefore rejoice, you heavens and you who dwell in them! **But woe to the earth** and the sea, because **the devil has gone down** to you! **He is filled with fury, because he knows that his time is short.** (Revelation 12:12; emphasis added)

Once those days began to break upon us, some began to wonder: Could it be that God was *allowing* Satan to manipulate the governmental powers as a part of the final "weeding-out" process? Maybe it's a kind of final warning to the planet, even to our nation specifically?

Fulfilling Prophecy Unawares

Sadly, as the spirit of fear and deception continued to mushroom, an alarming number of people who professed to be Christians turned to their favorite outlets of "social" expression. A number used those forums to attack other Christians. Believers began to viciously critique other believers online, in front of the rest of the world.

Others openly ridiculed faithful pastors and their congregations, ministers who were simply trying to retain the normalcy of meeting as a congregation as the Word of God commands us to do. Some church leaders were even arrested, fined, or jailed for doing so. Others who had online ministries or television and radio ministries were attacked by godless mainstream media. Then, they were further reviled by yet a number of other online "Pharisees" claiming to be believers.

All of this took place with barely a whimper coming from the nation's larger Christian community. Many of the "Christian" aggressors reasoned in online rants: "We must obey the government! After all, that's what Paul told us to do in Romans 13. *Right?* Those churches and pastors should have known better. They were acting so dangerously! They should have obeyed the law."[108]

In the meantime, business owners turned against other business owners. Family members became enraged with each other. Good friends found themselves at seemingly irreconcilable odds. Some even reported friends and family members to the "authorities."

It was like watching a badly produced, B-quality, end-of-days movie—except these things were actually happening. Indeed, a portentous wind was howling, and it was warning of a coming storm. But few seemed to be listening.

It was uncanny how many people—those caught in the whirlwind of the COVID-confusion—didn't seem to notice that they themselves were sometimes fulfilling ancient prophecies that directly tied to the days just before the Lord's return. They didn't appear to have the slightest idea that the world might actually be racing toward the foretold days of Noah.

Let us hold unswervingly to the hope we profess, for he who promised is faithful. And let us consider how we may spur one another on toward love and good deeds, **not giving up meeting together, as some are in the habit of doing, but encouraging one another—and all the more as you see the Day approaching**. (Hebrews 10:23–25; emphasis added)

You will be betrayed even by parents, brothers and sisters, relatives and friends. (Luke 21:16; emphasis added)

At that time **many will turn away from the faith** and will **betray and hate** each other. (Matthew 24:10; emphasis added)

But if you suffer as a Christian, do not be ashamed, but glorify God that you bear that name. **For it is time for judgment to begin with the family of God;** and if it begins with us, what will the outcome be for those who disobey the gospel of God? (1 Peter 4:16–17, Berean Study Bible; emphasis added)

The kingdom of heaven is like a man who sowed good seed in his field. But *while everyone was sleeping*, his enemy came and sowed weeds among the wheat, and went away. When the wheat sprouted and formed heads, then the weeds also appeared. (Matthew 13:24–26; emphasis added)

Jesus had warned the church from the beginning of His earthly ministry:

You are the salt of the earth. But if the salt loses its saltiness, how can it be made salty again? It is no longer good for anything, except to be thrown out and trampled underfoot. (Matthew 5:13)

Unbeknownst to many, the *sifting* was beginning to take place.[109]

PART FOUR

Did It Really Happen?

But at your rebuke the waters fled, at the sound of your thunder they took to flight; they flowed over the mountains, they went down into the valleys, to the place you assigned for them.

—PSALM 104:7–8

24

Sticking to the Story

As it turns out, tales of a catastrophic flood
of one magnitude or another extend back to
the Bronze Age and Neolithic history.

THE ACCOUNT OF NOAH'S FLOOD IS THE MOST DETAILED OF ANY SINGLE EVENT in the Bible.[110]

Most biblical scholars agree that the first eleven chapters of Genesis supply the bulk of the doctrinal foundation for the rest of the Word of God. A large portion of those eleven chapters includes the account of Noah's Flood. Even so, the Flood narrative is not without its share of worldwide controversy, as well as outright ridicule.

I'm aware that a number of readers might be willing to declare something like, "The Bible says Noah's Flood is true, and I believe it is! That's good enough for me. I've already got this issue settled!"

Don't worry, I'm right there with you.

However, a shockingly large number of America's professing flock of Christians might not hold that same passion—especially as our ranks reach new lows concerning belief in the fundamentals of biblical creationism, as well as the authenticity of the account of Noah's day.[111]

Certainly, the world of *unbelievers* isn't even in the same universe with us in this matter. By holding to a thoroughly secular worldview, they've been duped. So, let's not fall into that same category of being deceived, misinformed, or even intimidated into merely uttering trite platitudes and pseudoscientific dribble when addressing the truths that surround the Flood of Noah's day.

Stories, Myths, and Truth

As it turns out, tales of a catastrophic flood of one magnitude or another extend back to the Bronze Age and Neolithic Period. And, they make their way into the midst of a diverse range of cultures. These accounts span virtually every part of the globe that has been regularly inhabited by humans—from Europe through Asia, Africa, the Americas, and into Oceania.

A flood is usually said to have been directed by a "god" or "gods" for the purpose of extinguishing an utterly depraved human race. In other words, there is an ancient global recognition—intended or not—of a pervasive sin nature that winds itself throughout the entire human species. Imagine that.

Myth or Fact?

Within secular academic circles, the various versions of a great flood are often called "flood myths" or "flood legends." Some historical sources claim there are well over 270 such independent international accounts.[112]

Admittedly, not all the legends of the flood are analogous, and not all speak of a *global* flood. Each legend possesses certain variations—some slight, others extreme. However, dozens of explanations are strikingly similar in many details, and many even eerily relate to the biblical Flood of Noah.

In early 2020, a PBS article summed up the matter like this:

While not all flood stories are the same, the description of **the destruction of the world by water is a common theme in many religions and cultures.** Most flood stories include an angry God or deity, and a catastrophic water event that destroys the world but is only survived by a chosen few.

These flood stories also seem to have significant roots in science. Flood stories may explain geological phenomena such as volcanoes, earthquakes, floods, *fossils*, and other *natural features of the landscape.*

Flood stories pervade hundreds of cultures and there are striking similarities to many of the accounts. It seems that at least some of these stories *could be based upon actual events.*

After the flood [as related in Genesis], the *ark came to rest* on a mountain top, *a detail that is repeated in many stories* across different cultures. This was an attempt to show the immense depth of the water, that it was *higher than the mountains.*[113] (Emphasis added)

Think about it. If a catastrophic flood like the one spoken of in the Word of God never happened—as many naysayers want us to believe—then why are there so many different intercultural accounts of just such an event? And why do these flood stories emanate from practically every continent? Furthermore, how could it be that so many of these stories, told through the filters of extremely diverse cultures, are still so very similar to each other?

Even in accounts with details that vary greatly, the foundation is nevertheless true: *In antediluvian times, somewhere in the deep past of human existence, the planet—or at least huge, sweeping portions of it—was subjected to a great flood.*

Even the left-leaning publication *Time* weighed in on the topic in an online article titled, "Before Noah: Myths of the Flood Are Far Older Than the Bible."

The legend of the Great Flood almost certainly has prebiblical origins,[114] rooted in the ancient civilizations of Mesopotamia. The Sumerian Epic of Gilgamesh dates back nearly 5,000 years and is thought to be perhaps the oldest written tale on the planet. In it, there is an account of the great sage Utnapishtim, who is warned of an imminent flood to be unleashed by wrathful gods. He builds a vast circular-shaped boat, reinforced with tar and pitch that carries his relatives, grains and animals. After enduring days of storms, Utnapishtim, like Noah in Genesis, releases a bird in search of dry land.[115] (Emphasis added)

ABC News reports:

"The earlier Mesopotamian stories are very similar where the gods are sending a flood to wipe out humans," said [renowned] biblical archaeologist Eric Cline.[116] "There's one man they choose to survive. He builds a boat and brings on animals and lands on a mountain and lives happily ever after? I would argue that it's the same story" [as Noah's Flood].[117] (Emphasis added)

While we're at it, let's take a quick look at just two examples of the uncanny resemblances that some of these flood legends share with the biblical account. And keep in mind that there are many others similar to these.

Nu'-u

According to Hawaiian folklore, just before the great flood erupted, a man named *Nu'u* built an ark—a great canoe with a "house" on top of it. He loaded his handcrafted ship with various animals and his family. Those people and animals were the only living creatures to survive the global deluge.[118]

The legend describes how Nu'u mistakenly credited his survival to the moon, and subsequently offered up sacrifices to it. Kane, the merciful creator "God," then descended to earth on a rainbow. From the rainbow Kane explained Nu'u's mistake.[119]

Did you notice?

Nu'u sounds suspiciously like Noah, doesn't he? Also, this Hawaiian legend comes complete with an "ark," animals, a single surviving family, and a Creator that mercifully speaks words of comfort to the castaways. He speaks those words from a rainbow. And, oh yeah, the Hawaiian legend also has Nu'u's vessel eventually coming to rest on top of a great mountain—a Hawaiian one, of course.

Fuhi

Then there's the Chinese flood legend. Coming from one of the most ancient areas of civilization, it records that *Fuhi* and his wife, along with their three sons and three daughters, escaped a great flood and, afterwards, were the only people alive on the earth. After the flood subsided, they were responsible for repopulating the world. That legend is over four thousand years old.[120]

A Collective Dream

A number of renowned archaeologists suggest there was indeed a historical deluge between five thousand and seven thousand years ago—the approximate timeline the Bible supports for Noah's Flood. They theorize that it actually descended upon the territory ranging from the Black Sea to what many call the "cradle of civilization," the flood plain between the Tigris and Euphrates rivers. This is the region where Noah and the people of his early world were living.[121]

However, those who simply can't stand the thought of a calamitous flood that mirrors the biblical narrative are still left with a major problem. How do they account for the anomaly of the hundreds of flood stories? Well, they do indeed have an answer. Here's an example of their response, from the *Time* article we looked at earlier:

> **Flood myths are so universal** that the Hungarian psychoanalyst Geza Roheim thought **their origins were physiological**, not historical—hypothesizing that **dreams of the Flood** came when **humans were asleep** with *full bladders.*[122] (Emphasis added)

Yes, that's got to be it: The worldwide stories of a gigantic flood are really just the result of humans having dreams about having to "go" in the middle of the night. That makes perfect sense...*to no one.*

The lengths to which some "experts" will reach in order to explain away the obvious often borders on the ridiculous. I am reminded of another passage of Scripture that seems applicable to our study at hand:

> **If you point these things out** to the brothers and sisters, you will be a good minister of Christ Jesus, **nourished on the truths of the faith** and of the good teaching that you have followed. **Have nothing to do with** *godless myths and old wives' tales.* (1 Timothy 4:6–7; emphasis added)

25

Global Graveyards

It seems quite apparent that, in ages past,
something unspeakable happened that
traumatized the collective human psyche.

As we move along in our quest for truth, please don't forget this next significant scientific fact.

In the production of a genuine fossil, a geological disturbance happens suddenly. It occurs with such rapid elemental power that entire communities of creatures and vegetation are trapped and buried—often alive—under unimaginable pressure and heat. Volcanic eruptions, earthquakes, and rapid catastrophic flooding can bring about such fossilization. *Normal burial processes simply do not produce fossils.*[123]

This science has been confirmed many times over. For example, paleontologist Dr. John R. Horner, in his book, *Digging Dinosaurs*, tells us:

> There were 30 million fossil fragments in that area. At a conservative estimate, we had discovered the tomb of 10,000 dinosaurs...**there was a flood.** This was **no ordinary spring flood** from one of the streams in the area **but a catastrophic inundation.**... That's our best explanation. **It seems to make the most sense,** and on the basis of it we believe that this was a living, breathing group of dinosaurs **destroyed in one catastrophic moment.**[124] (Emphasis added)

The Reality of Noah's Flood

In 2012, Dr. Robert Ballard,[125] acclaimed underwater archaeologist, was quoted in an ABC News online article titled, "Evidence Noah's Biblical Flood Happened, Says Robert Ballard."

Dr. Ballard, while not yet certain of an actual *worldwide* flood, appears convinced that the biblical account of Noah's Flood is truly meaningful for our own age.

Following are some excerpts from the article, as well as comments made by Dr. Ballard.

> The story of Noah's Ark and the Great Flood is one of the most famous from the Bible, and **now an acclaimed underwater archaeologist thinks he has found proof that the biblical flood was actually based on real events.** In an interview with Christiane Amanpour for ABC News, Robert Ballard, **one of the world's best-known underwater archaeologists,** talked about his findings.... **He is on a marine archeological mission that might support the story of Noah.**
>
> "We went in there [the area of the Black Sea] to look for the flood," he said. "Not just a slow moving, advancing rise of sea level, **but a really big flood** that then stayed.... The **land that went under stayed under.**"
>
> Four hundred feet below the surface, they unearthed an ancient shoreline, **proof to Ballard that a catastrophic event did happen in the Black Sea.** By carbon dating shells found along the shoreline, Ballard said he believes they have **established a timeline for that catastrophic event...around the time when Noah's flood could have occurred.**
>
> Ballard **does not think he will ever find Noah's Ark,** but he does think he may find evidence of a people **whose entire world was washed away** about 7,000 years ago. He and his team said they plan to return to Turkey next summer.

"It's foolish to think you will ever find a ship," Ballard said, referring to the Ark. "But can you find people who were living? **Can you find their villages that are underwater now? And the answer is yes.**"[126] (Emphasis added)

In an article in the June 1981 edition of *New Scientist*, Dr. David M. Raup, Chicago Field Museum professor of geology at the University of Chicago, attests:

> **A large number of well-trained scientists** outside of evolutionary biology and paleontology have **unfortunately gotten the idea that the fossil record is far more Darwinian than it is.** This probably comes from the **oversimplification inevitable in secondary sources:** low level textbooks, semi popular articles, and so on. Also, there is probably **some wishful thinking** involved.
>
> **In the years after Darwin, his advocates** *hoped to find predictable progressions.* In general, *these have not been found.* Yet the optimism has died hard, and *some pure fantasy* **has crept into textbooks…. One of the ironies of the creation-evolution debate** is that the **creationists have accepted the mistaken notion that the fossil record shows a detailed and orderly progression and they have gone to great lengths to accommodate this "fact" in their Flood Geology.**[127] (Emphasis added)

Renowned geologist Dr. Andrew Snelling holds a PhD in geology from the University of Sydney in Australia.[128] Arguing for the scientific evidence of a literal global flood, he explains:

> [If there had actually been a flood of the magnitude of Noah's], wouldn't we expect to find rock layers all over the earth filled with billions of dead animals and plants that were buried rapidly and fossilized in sand, mud, and lime? Of course, and that's exactly what we find. Furthermore, even though the catastrophic

geologic activity of the Flood would have waned in the immediate post-Flood period, ongoing mini-catastrophes would still
have produced localized fossil deposits.

Countless billions of plant and animal fossils are found in
extensive "graveyards" where they had to be buried rapidly on
a massive scale. Often the fine details of the creatures are exqui-
sitely preserved....

Notice in many of these examples how marine and land-
dwelling creatures are found buried together. **How could this
have happened unless the ocean waters rose and swept over the
continents in a global, catastrophic Flood?**[129] (Emphasis added)

It seems quite apparent that, in ages past, something unspeakable
happened that traumatized the collective human psyche. In a collection
of hundreds of ancient stories, the cause of that trauma is specifically
described as a "great flood."

The born-again believer most likely has no problem understanding
that such a catastrophic flood, as described in Genesis, is scientifically
plausible. However, for those who are still a bit wary of buying into the
totality of that account, there's still more.

26

The Cryptograms

The evidence is all around us, staring us in the face.

By the turn of the twenty-first century, even the Smithsonian Institute decided to weigh in on the most recent evidence pointing toward Noah's Flood.

In fact, that article begins with a Scripture quote:

The fountains of the great deep [were] broken up, and the windows of the heavens were opened. And the rain was upon the earth forty days and forty nights.

This quote from the **Book of Genesis** is part of a familiar tale—the story of Noah's flood. Scholars have known for a long time that the Bible isn't the only place this story is found.[130] (Emphasis added)

All Hell Broke Loose

Preferring to relegate Noah's Flood to a more regional area—yet, still, an extremely large region encompassing great swaths of the biblical lands—the Smithsonian article admits several astonishing geological truths:

Recently scientists have started to uncover evidence that Noah's flood may have a basis in some rather astonishing events that took place around the Black Sea some 7,500 years ago....

The idea that ocean basins can flood catastrophically during periods of rising sea levels is nothing new in geology....

We know such things because sediments reveal history....

The cores [containing the various evidentiary sediments] **seemed to be telling a strange story indeed....** At the very bottom of the cores, dozens of feet below the present seafloor, **they found layered mud, typical of river deltas....**

It is the interpretation of **these layers that tells us what happened on that inevitable day** when **rising sea levels** in the Mediterranean reached the base of the sediments at the bottom of the Bosporus—**and all hell broke loose.**[131] (Emphasis added)

Seashells Everywhere!

In the United States alone, we find seashells in the oddest of places— piles and piles of them. They are found in the middle of the continent and in the deserts, as well as in the floors of dried-out gullies and valleys.

They are embedded high up the towering sides of canyon walls. They are found in California, South Dakota, Kansas, and on the mountaintops in western Texas. Fossilized oyster and mollusk shells are among the oddly amassed seashells. So are the remains of coral reefs. In fact, some of the coral is of a variety found only in the Atlantic, three thousand miles away from the reef's remains.[132]

Ancient shale exposures also exist in numerous states, including South Dakota, Colorado, Nebraska, Minnesota, New Mexico, and Wyoming, as well as in Canada. Those shale deposits contain tons more fossilized shells, including ammonites, which are ancestors of the spiral-shaped nautilus seashell.[133]

In another deposit called Smoky Hill Chalk in western Kansas, an additional anomaly can be found: giant *clamshells*. Some of these shells are four feet or more in diameter. Other fossils contain up to a hundred fish fossils.[134]

Between New Mexico and Texas is a four hundred-mile-long fossilized reef called the Captain Reef, one of the largest of this type of incongruity in the world. Parts of this reef, found in the Guadalupe Mountains National Park, reach to the mountaintops—eight thousand feet in altitude. Thousands of years of weather erosion have exposed to the world what is at the top, sticking out of the giant cliffs like an enormous biblical billboard. At the same time, other sections of this same reef are still underground, in the desert, miles from any ocean.[135]

In a reference to his exploration of the California desert in 1776, Father Pedro Font[136] wrote:

> **I have come to surmise** that in olden times **the sea spread over all the land,** and in some of the great recessions which histories tell us about, it left these salty and sandy wastes uncovered. Indeed one finds on the way many piles of oyster shells, mixed with earth and half buried, and **other shells and maritime signs. It is not possible** that people should have made such mountains of shells by carrying them from the sea so far a distance **merely to bury them in piles.**[137] (Emphasis added)

Do you want more evidence? An article published in *Live Science* in 2009 attempted to "explain" the existence of the massive number of fossils and animal remnants that shouldn't normally be where they were found. Of course, their explanation comes from a strictly evolution-based standpoint. Following are some telling quotes from that article:

> The famed Sharktooth Hill Bone Bed in California **is loaded with shark teeth as big as a hand** and each weighing a pound, **from giant prehistoric killers** called megalodon.
> Intermixed with copious bones from extinct seals, whales

and fish, as well as turtle shells three times the size of today's leatherbacks, all these relics seem to tell of a *15-million-year-old disaster.*[138] (Emphasis added)

Seeing what certainly appears to be evidence of a catastrophic and potentially global flood, it seems the "scientists" simply couldn't abide that possibility. So, in order to discount what would normally appear rather obvious, they arrived at the following explanation:

But scientists *now suggest* this vast graveyard *might not* have resulted from **a sudden catastrophe**. Instead, they *suggest* it formed *slowly over a long span* of time, *potentially* serving as a window *into thousands of years* of ancient history.[139] (Emphasis added)

Fluffy Words

Note the frequent use of the nonscientific, "fluffy," words: "suggest," "might," and "potentially." Sound familiar? Of course. That's the evolutionist's way of trying to make something sound scientific while leaving room for plausible deniability, in case the fluffy science is proven incorrect in the future. And, as you saw, their highly questionable theory also contains another useful answer for everything: "It formed slowly over a long span of time." Yet, we've already discovered that fossils simply do not "slowly" form over "long periods of time."

Also notice that their "long periods of time" is listed as "thousands of years," not millions or even billions of years. The phrase "thousands of years" actually fits nicely with exactly what the Bible says.

Here's a useful, revealing exercise. Cross out every word in that paragraph that's part of the fluffy language. Without those words, the sentences are scientifically useless. They merely telegraph the idea that "we sure *hope* this is the case." The remaining words actually admit: "We don't know what happened, or how long ago."

When we perform this quick exercise, look at what's left: "This vast graveyard [of fossils] [serves] as a window into ancient history."

That's it! When all the guessing is taken out, we are left with a truly scientific declaration of undeniable fact. *Fossils serve as windows into ancient history.* But wait. There's still more to that Live Science piece:

The Sharktooth Hill Bone Bed is the richest and most extensive marine deposit of bones in the world, averaging roughly 200 bones per square yard. All in all, the bed is a six-to-20-inch-thick layer of fossil bones, 10 miles of it exposed, which covers nearly 50 square miles just outside and northeast of Bakersfield....

The absence of volcanic ash makes a volcanic catastrophe unlikely as the origin of the bones, while **the puzzling presence of land mammal fossils, such as tapirs** [a pig-like animal that inhabits South America, Central America, and Southeast Asia] **and horses** that **must have washed out to sea** and into the bed, makes it improbable that some toxic sea phenomenon such as red tide was the cause....

Many bones had manganese nodules and growths, which form on bones that sit for long periods in seawater before being covered by sediment.

In the layer above the bone bed, *most skeletons were found with the bones encased* in sediment and articulated together *as they were in life.*[140] (Emphasis added)

Here's the problem. If this amazing fossil site was the only one in the world, or if there was only a single pile of fossilized seashells in the middle of a desert somewhere, or if there was only one mountaintop that contained a variety of marine fossils, all of this might be a bit easier to explain. But that "if" scenario simply isn't the case. These ecological anomalies are *global.* Seashells and other marine-life fossils are found on mountaintops and cliff outcroppings all over the world, including the Matterhorn and the Himalayas.

But, how can this be?

The plain fact is that there was a cataclysmic Flood, just like the Word of God asserts. The evidence is all around us. It's staring us in the face.

It's written in stone, emblazoned upon the face of cliffs.

And it's buried at the tips of the world's mountaintops.

27

Rising Mountains

Actually, it's really not that hard to imagine at all.

YOU MIGHT ASK: WHAT ARE THE BEST ANSWERS THAT EVOLUTIONISTS HAVE FOR the mountaintop fossil mounds, evidence that points directly to what the text of Genesis states?

Have a look at a couple of representative samples of the answer. The first one comes from a NASA article:

> Centuries ago, scholars puzzled over how seashells could wind up on the tops of mountains. Fossil seashells are now recognized as the **remains of ancient sea floors** *raised* **to high altitudes by** *mountain building.*[141]

Gee. I wonder where they could have gotten that idea. We know the One who categorically declared this fact many thousands of years before it was possible for NASA to speculate upon the possibility:

> **The mountains rose, the valleys sank down** to the place that you appointed for them. (Psalm 104:8, ESV; emphasis added)

Consider the commentary on this verse by several classical scholars *before* NASA even existed:

Jamieson-Fausset-Brown Bible Commentary:

These verses describe the *wonders of the flood* [rather than of] **the creation** (Ge 7:19, 20; 2Pe 3:5, 6). God's method of **arresting the flood** and **making its waters subside** is poetically called a "rebuke" (Ps 76:6; Isa 50:2), and the **process of the flood's subsiding** by undulations among the hills and valleys is vividly described.[142] (Emphasis added)

Adam Clarke Commentary:

Some have thought there is a reference to the breaking up on the fountains of the great deep, *at the time of the flood;* while the protrusion of the waters would raise the circumambient crust, so as to form mountains, the other parts, falling in to fill up the vacuum occasioned by the waters which were thrown up from the central abyss, would constitute valleys.[143] (Emphasis added)

Cambridge Bible for Schools and Colleges:

The rendering of the A.V. and R.V., which is also grammatically possible, **appears to describe the commotion of the waters as the great deep**[144] **breaks up** [*Cambridge* is using language from Genesis 7:11—Noah's Flood] and they seek their appointed place.[145] (Emphasis added)

Again, acclaimed geologist Dr. Andrew Snelling agrees with the biblical account.

We must remember that the rock layers in the Himalayas and other mountain ranges around the globe were deposited during the Flood, well before these mountains were formed. In fact, many of these mountain ranges were pushed up by earth movements to their present high elevations at the end of the Flood.

There is only one possible explanation for this phenomenon—the ocean waters at some time in the past flooded over the continents.

Could the continents have then sunk below today's sea level, so that the ocean waters flooded over them?

No! The continents are made up of lighter rocks that are less dense than the rocks on the ocean floor and rocks in the mantle beneath the continents. **The continents, in fact, have an automatic tendency to rise, and thus "float" on the mantle rocks beneath, well above the ocean floor rocks.** This explains why the continents today have such high elevations compared to the deep ocean floor, and why the ocean basins can hold so much water.[146] (Emphasis added)

A second example of today's "newly discovered" secular postulations, according to the evolutionary models, comes from *Weather.com*:

> The mighty **Himalayas, also known as "The Roof of the World,"** rise up to an incredible height, disappearing into the clouds on some days. **Some of the world's highest peaks** are in the Himalayas, including Mount Everest, which at 29,029 feet is **the highest mountain in the world.** ... These mighty mountains are **hundreds of miles away** from the closest sea. **So how is it possible that marine fossils have been found in multiple locations in the Himalayas?**
>
> *It's hard to imagine* that this vast expanse of weather-bleached land *was once a thriving ocean bed*, with fish and marine creatures populating the water.[147]

Actually, it's really not that hard to imagine at all—especially once one comes to the scientific, and rather obvious, understanding that the earth's surface, or at least a huge portion of it, was once covered over in water. Isn't this also what most of the more than 270 "flood myths" have been telling us for thousands of years? More importantly, it's what the Word of God has been telling us for thousands of years as well, except in much more striking detail.

And, it's what *the Word that Became Flesh*—Jesus Christ—also declared, as He resoundingly affirmed the reality of Noah's Flood.

> Just **as it was** in *the days of Noah*, **so also will it be** in the days of the Son of Man. (Luke 17:26; emphasis added)

So, just what is it that the fossils of the world have been trying to tell us?

Their message is clear.

Something earth-shattering happened in earth's primordial past.

28

The Rocks Cry Out

*Every time you pick up a fossil, you're holding a
gospel tract in your hands—written in stone—
by the finger of God Himself.*

By Jesus' day, thousands of years after the biblical account of Noah's Flood, that ominous event was still a central theme of eschatological teaching among the Jews, especially in the early church.

This fact shouldn't be surprising in the least. Those people were over two thousand years closer to the cataclysmic occurrence than we are now. Knowledge of it was still burning deep within their generational memories, as we see in the New Testament itself.

Jesus wasn't the only one to speak of Noah's Flood. The writer of Hebrews mentions Noah, the ark, and the Flood. Peter, the early church's first preacher and senior pastor, spoke of the days of Noah in both of his letters to the first-century church. In each of those letters, Peter also ties Noah's day to the last days, that generation just before the return of the Lord Jesus Christ.[148]

Rocks That Talk

Think about it! Every time you pick up a fossil, you're holding a gospel tract in your hands—written in stone—by the finger of God Himself.[149] What is its message? Perhaps it is meant to read something like this:

> About five thousand years ago there was a catastrophic Flood. It was initiated by the hand of God as His holy judgment upon a world steeped in unimaginable wickedness. You are holding the evidence in your hand. It is evidence that His Word is true.
>
> That evidence is also tangible testimony that God's judgment *will come* once more, one final time. And it is testimony that the very same Word of God assures us His Kingdom *will be* restored.
>
> It also tells of how *you* can be a part of His glorious Kingdom that's on its way. You can escape the coming judgment, like Noah did in the ark. God has made a way for you, through the blood-sacrifice of His Only Son, Jesus Christ. (See Romans 10:9–13)

This idea should give a fresh nuance of meaning to a familiar passage of Scripture:

> "I tell you," [Jesus] replied, "If [my followers] keep quiet, **the stones will cry out.**" (Luke 19:40; emphasis added)

Romans and the Flood

Even the first chapter of Paul's letter to the Romans appears to give a nod toward the Great Flood of Noah as well:

> **The wrath of God is being revealed from heaven against all the godlessness and wickedness of people,** who suppress the truth

by their wickedness, since what may be known about God is plain to them, because **God has made it plain to them.**

For since the creation of the world God's invisible qualities—**his eternal power** and divine nature—**have been clearly seen**, being understood from what has been made, **so that people are without excuse.** (Romans 1:18–20; emphasis added)

Gill's Exposition of the Scriptures (Romans 1:18):

[There are] many instances and **examples of divine wrath** and displeasure; as in **the total destruction of the old world** *by a worldwide flood....* This wrath is said to be **God's wrath "from heaven."** (Emphasis added)[150]

Dr. Stephen J. Cole (On Romans 1):

A glance through **past history**, both in the Bible and outside of it, **shows the ongoing wrath** of God. **He destroyed the whole world** *through the flood.*[151] (Emphasis added)

We really are without excuse before our Creator—every single generation of us.

Once again, the entire planet is staring down the barrel of God's impending wrath. With each passing year, people all over the world can sense the coming of it, deep within their souls.

Perhaps the prophet Daniel saw our day, or a time close to it. He declared that those last days of mankind's wicked rule would come sweeping down upon the earth just like—*of all things*—"a flood."[152]

But this time when it comes, it will be God's final word.

29

Global or Not, Here It Comes

*The problem most of us have in this regard is that the Bible,
itself, appears to insist that the Flood in question
truly was a universal one.*

HOW DO WE RECONCILE WHAT THE BIBLE APPEARS TO DECLARE IN THE MATTER
of a *global* flood with what most of the world's scientists believe? Those
scientists and geologists insist that the geographical evidence is indisputable—*there were catastrophic regional floods, but there was never a literal,
worldwide flood.*

It is often quite shocking for most to learn that even renowned
Christian scholars do not find it essential to insist that Noah's Flood was
a global event. The problem most of us have in this regard is that the
Bible itself *appears* to insist that the Flood was universal.

From the Face of the Earth

Let's have a closer look at the passages in Genesis often interpreted to
mean that the deluge was planet-wide.

> So the Lord said, "I will wipe *from the face of the earth* the
> human race I have created—and with them the animals, the

birds and the creatures that move along the ground—for I regret that I have made them." (Genesis 6:7; emphasis added)

Seems pretty clear, right? Not so fast....

Actually, that text, written in Hebrew, does not contain the word "earth." The original language simply says "I will wipe from *the face*." The problem is that in the same book of Genesis, in several other chapters, we discover a similar phrase. And in those verses, the phrase "I will wipe from the face" is either accompanied by the Hebrew word *adamah* or the Hebrew word *erets*. So, let's have a quick look at the interesting meanings and usages of these words.

Adamah

Adamah (from where the word *Adam* derives) means "the soil, ground, or the land"—thus that part of the "earth" that is visible from its "face."[153]

This word is most frequently translated as local or regional. However, it can also be correctly translated into the English word "earth"— but even then, it usually means "the soil" upon which one is standing at the moment. We use our English word "earth" in much the same way:

"When that baseball hit me in the head, I fell to the earth like a rock!"

"When that train came by, I was standing so close to the tracks that I felt the earth move!"

Here is how the first chapter of Genesis uses the word:

God made the wild animals according to their kinds, the livestock according to their kinds, and all the creatures that move **along *the ground*** [*adamah*] according to their kinds. And God saw that it was good. (Genesis 1:25; emphasis added)

However, in the same verse, the word *adamah* could also be translated into English as "the earth," as in fact it has been done by several other translations[154] in which we see the word *adamah* rendered, in the same verse, as either "ground" or "earth." And there's where we find room for differences in understanding concerning the scope of Noah's Flood.

Erets

The Hebrew word *erets* is similar to *adamah*. It is most frequently translated as "earth." Sometimes the context requires that *erets* must mean the entire globe. But *erets*, like *adamah*, can also mean the "land," "soil," or a "regional area of the globe" as well, and is often used in that context.[155] Here is an example of how *erets* is translated into our English versions as meaning "the entire globe" of the earth:

In the beginning God created the heavens and **the earth** [*erets*]. Now **the earth** [*erets*] was formless and empty, darkness was over the surface of the deep, and the Spirit of God was hovering over the waters. (Genesis 1:1–2; emphasis added)

In that same chapter of Genesis, just a few verses later, the word *erets* is used again. But this time, numerous translations render it as "the ground" upon which one is standing—not the entire globe.

"And to all the beasts of the earth and all the birds in the sky and all the creatures that move along **the ground**—[*erets*] everything that has the breath of life in it—I give every green plant for food." And it was so. (Genesis 1:30; emphasis added)

So which is it? Was the flood regional or global?
Hang on, we're almost there.
And our final analysis is an important one.

30

What We Know

Even the most modern secular science acknowledges
three striking truths that cannot be discounted.

Are you confused?

Don't be.

If it helps, just remember that we use our English words for "earth," "ground," "soil," and "land" in the same interchangeable ways as does the Hebrew language. So, proper context of the word's usage in a particular passage becomes the all-important key to accurate interpretation.

Now, back to Genesis 6:7 and the other verses in Genesis that are similar to it.[156] The way most *English* translations state it, we're told that through Noah's Flood, God would wipe humans and beasts from the "face of the earth." It is also said that He would destroy everything "under the heavens" that had breath.

Knowing what you do now about the words *adamah* and *erets*, here is how several oft-quoted biblical scholars understand the verses in question.

Barnes' Notes on the Bible (on Genesis 6:7):

I will wipe away man from **the face of the soil.**—The resolve is made to sweep away **the existing race of man.**[157] (Emphasis added)

Ellicott's Commentary for English Readers (on Genesis 6:7):

I will destroy.—Heb., delete, rub out.
    From the face of the earth.—Heb., the *adamah*, the tilled ground which man had subdued and cultivated.[158] (Emphasis added)

The *Cambridge* commentary, like numerous others, takes the position that *to believe anything other than the Flood of Noah's day as a literal and global event* is nothing short of blasphemy.[159]
Cambridge Bible for Schools and Colleges (on Genesis 7:19):

It is this hyperbolical description which has naturally seized upon the imagination of readers. It is not necessary to enlarge upon the physical impossibility of such an event. If the literal interpretation were adopted, the waters would have submerged not only the mountains of Western Asia and of Europe, but also the Andes and the Himalayas. Water at that height would have been ice: organic life would have been impossible. Geology has shown that no such universal Deluge has ever occurred. **The accumulation of the vast amount of water represented in such a scene and encompassing the whole globe is beyond the range of physical possibility.**[160] (Emphasis added)

Even during the often romanticized classical days, biblical scholars were quite infamous for taking swipes at each other—sometimes, pretty vicious ones.
    Benson Commentary is another example of this dogmatism regarding Noah's Flood:

Therefore, there were hills and mountains before the flood. *Deists, and other infidels,* **would persuade us that this was**

impossible, because of the vast height of [the multitude of] hills and mountains.

It will be sufficient to observe here, that this cannot be thought impossible by anyone who believes in the existence of such a being as Jehovah, a God of infinite power, to whom it surely was as easy to bring forth a sufficiency of water for this purpose, as it was to create all things by the word of his power, or to say, Let there be light, and there was light.[161] (Emphasis added)

Universal or Regional?

Carol A. Hill has been a consulting geologist for more than forty years at several major universities. She has been featured in various PBS television specials, in the series *NOVA*, and on National Geographic TV. She also wrote the highly acclaimed book, *A Worldview Approach to Science and Scripture.*[162]

In 2002, while serving as the consulting geologist for California State University at Long Beach, Professor Hill wrote a lengthy paper titled, "The Noachian Flood: Universal or Local?"

In that paper, she lays out a salient argument for the literal "fact" of Noah's Flood, as recorded in Genesis, while at the same time asserting that the biblical language used in those texts simply does not *have to mean* a worldwide deluge.

Following are a few paragraphs from her article that summarize Hill's case:

Earth. The Hebrew for "earth" used in Gen. 6–8 (and in Gen. 2:5–6) is eretz ('erets) or adamah, both of which terms literally mean "earth, ground, land, dirt, soil, or country." **In no way can "earth" be taken to mean the planet Earth, as in Noah's time**

and place, people (including the Genesis writer) had no concept of Earth as a planet and thus had no word for it.

Their "world" mainly (but not entirely) encompassed the land of Mesopotamia—a flat alluvial plain enclosed by the mountains and high ground of Iran, Turkey, Syria, and Saudi Arabia...i.e., the lands drained by the four rivers of Eden (Gen. 2:10–14). The biblical account must be interpreted within the narrow limit of what was known about the world in that time not what is known about the world today....

Biblical context also makes it clear that **"earth" does not necessarily mean the whole Earth.** For example, the face of the ground, as used in Gen. 7:23 and Gen. 8:8 in place of "earth," does not imply the planet Earth. **"Land" is a better translation than "earth" for the Hebrew** *eretz* **because it extends to the "face of the ground"** we can see around us; that is, what is **within our horizon....**

All, Every, Under Heaven. While these terms also seem to impart a universality to the Flood event, all three are used elsewhere in the Bible for local events, and so—like the term "earth"—do not necessarily have an all-inclusive or universal meaning. For example, Acts 2:5 states: "And there were dwelling at Jerusalem Jews, devout men out of every nation under heaven."[163] (Emphasis added)

The Bottom Line

The point of this detailed study is to demonstrate that it's simply not necessary for our English translation of Genesis 6:7 to mean that the Flood was universal. It doesn't take away from the biblical account of Noah's day whatsoever, even if we *100 percent* discovered that it wasn't a global event that Noah's world experienced.

Please keep in mind that a number of biblical scholars, and even scientific scholars who happen to be of a sincere biblical faith, both modern and classical, don't agree on the resolution of the subject. And the language used in the original Hebrew of the biblical text apparently doesn't unequivocally resolve the question, either.

One can find plenty of scholarly papers, articles, or books that will support either position a student might wish to take. And each of those resources will be fairly dogmatic in its stance. But they can't both be right. And it could be that neither of them have every nuance of what happened more than five thousand years ago exactly correct.

If it makes you feel any better (or not), I teach a literal worldwide view of what happened in the Genesis Flood. However, neither the Word of God nor my faith is shaken by the other view. And I will not break fellowship with true born-again believers who disagree with me, unless they say the catastrophic Flood of Genesis never happened at all. Not only would that assertion deny God's clearly understood account, but it also refutes all reasonably collected scientific knowledge.

What's more important, however, is this: God is asserting through the Genesis narrative that He summarily wiped humanity off the face of the ground—wherever they lived. His Flood in Noah's day *reached them all.* It was calamitous. It was final. It was decreed from Heaven's throne. And, it was confirmed by Jesus in the New Testament.

When we assemble all these facts, we have no problem believing the Bible. The Flood happened. And most importantly, the same elements and attitudes of human life that led up to this devastating form of God's judgment way back in the times recorded in Genesis 6 will happen again.

Jesus said we can count on it.

PART FIVE

It Has Always Been

They will say, "Where is this 'coming' he promised? Ever since our ancestors died, everything goes on as it has since the beginning of creation."

—2 PETER 3:4

31

The Time of the End

*The message of the last days is one of gloom and doom only
for those who fit within the category of "scoffers."*

WE'RE LIVING IN THE LAST DAYS! THE END IS NEAR!

What do you think when you hear those words? Even a number of born-again believers are prone to become a little uneasy when an "overly sensational" preacher uses these phrases.

But the expressions "last days," "end of the age," "last times," "time of the end," and "day of the Lord" are all biblical terms. They're not merely religious slogans that histrionic evangelists concocted in order to scare people into heaven. They are, in fact, declared in the Word of God as absolute truth.

Following is an example of each of these phrases as used in the biblical message.

- **Last days:** "Knowing this first, that there shall come in the **last days** scoffers, walking after their own lusts, and saying, where is the promise of his coming? For since the fathers fell asleep, all things continue as they were from the beginning of the creation," (2 Peter 3:3–4, KJV; emphasis added).
- **Time of the end:** "And he said, Go thy way, Daniel: for the words are closed up and sealed till the **time of the end**" (Daniel 12:9, KJV; emphasis added).

- **The end:** "And this gospel of the kingdom shall be preached in all the world for a witness unto all nations; and then shall **the end** come" (Matthew 24:14, KJV; emphasis added).
- **The last times:** "But, beloved, remember ye the words which were spoken before of the apostles of our Lord Jesus Christ; how that they told you there should be mockers in **the last time**, who should walk after their own ungodly lusts. These be they who separate themselves, sensual, having not the Spirit" (Jude 17–19, KJV; emphasis added).
- **The day of the Lord:** "But of the times and the seasons, brethren, ye have no need that I write unto you. For yourselves know perfectly that the **day of the Lord** so cometh as a thief in the night" (1 Thessalonians 5:1–2, KJV; emphasis added).
- **The end of the world (age):** "And as he sat upon the Mount of Olives, the disciples came unto him privately, saying, tell us, when shall these things be? And what shall be the sign of thy coming, and of **the end of the world?**" (Matthew 24:3, KJV; emphasis added).
- **The coming judgment:** "**For when they shall say, Peace and safety; then sudden destruction cometh upon them,** as travail upon a woman with child; and they shall not escape" (1 Thessalonians 5:3, KJV; emphasis added).

In reality, when understood in proper context, the message of these phrases should ultimately comfort and encourage the Christian. Further, we are urged to pray to *speed the coming* of the last days:

For the Lord himself shall descend from heaven with a shout, with the voice of the archangel, and with the trump of God: and the dead in Christ shall rise first:

Then we which are alive and remain shall be caught up together with them in the clouds, to meet the Lord in the air: and so shall we ever be with the Lord.

Wherefore comfort one another with these words. (1 Thessalonians 4:16–18, KJV; emphasis added)

Seeing then that all these things shall be dissolved, what manner of persons ought ye to be in all holy conversation and godliness, **looking for and hasting unto the coming of the day of God**, wherein the heavens being on fire shall be dissolved, and the elements shall melt with fervent heat? (2 Peter 3:11–12, KJV; emphasis added)

Without a doubt, these biblical warnings are ominous to those who don't fully understand God's prophetic message. That's why we must remain ever diligent in taking the gospel to the ends of the earth. Time is growing shorter with each passing day.

However, to the born-again Christian who has been given glimpses of the magnificence that is to come, the promise of the end of this age in the fallen and depraved world should be considered a glorious thing. The "end of time" refers to the end of humanity's wicked rule over the planet and the beginning of God's new day of total restoration.

In a Snap!

Think of it. If you were given the power to snap your fingers right now—and by so doing, you could instantly end all death, pain, suffering, crime, corruption, pollution, and wars, along with murders, rapes, thieving, lying, disease, pestilence, famine, hunger, and terrorism—would you do so? Absolutely, you would! Who *wouldn't* wish for such a world?

God's Word declares that the "end" of all these things is indeed on its way. If you belong to the Lord, why wouldn't you long for that day to come soon—perhaps even today?

Do not love the world or anything in the world. If anyone loves the world, love for the Father is not in them.

For everything in the world—the lust of the flesh, the lust of the eyes, and the pride of life—comes not from the Father but from the world.

The world and its desires pass away, but whoever does the will of God lives forever. (1 John 2:15–17)

Then I saw "a new heaven and a new earth," for the first heaven and the first earth had passed away, and there was no longer any sea.

I saw the Holy City, the New Jerusalem, coming down out of heaven from God, prepared as a bride beautifully dressed for her husband.

And I heard a loud voice from the throne saying, "Look! God's dwelling place is now among the people, and he will dwell with them.

They will be his people, and God himself will be with them and be their God. 'He will wipe every tear from their eyes. There will be no more death' or mourning or crying or pain, for the old order of things has passed away."

He who was seated on the throne said, "I am making everything new!"

Then he said, "Write this down, for these words are trustworthy and true." (Revelation 21:1–5)

Gloom and Doom?

The message of the last days is one of dread only for those who fit within the category of "scoffers."

Knowing this first, that there shall come in the last days scoffers, walking after their own lusts, and saying, where is the promise of his coming? (2 Peter 3:3)

That time in humanity's story of which Peter is speaking points to the despair and disdain among those who are lost in the age of the last days. They cannot bear the thought of their "world"—the system in which they have invested their life's desires—not existing anymore. But this same attitude was the prevailing philosophy of Noah's time. And it cost the people of that day their eternal souls.

I Don't See It

Are you still having trouble with the concept?

Think of it like this. A community of fish and other sea creatures living at the bottom of a several-miles-deep cavern on the ocean floor cannot imagine the universe of life and creation that exists only a few miles above their heads.

Everything above the surface of their watery environment is most assuredly real. It's physically there. *We* are there!

That world is filled with more than seven billion human beings and well over twenty million other species of life. All of this exists in that "unseen dimension" just above. Regardless, every bit of it, and everything beyond it, out into the farthest reaches of space, is totally unimaginable to the ocean-floor aquatic life forms. Therefore, they do not *believe in* any of it. They can't even fathom it.

However, it really doesn't matter what those fish "believe," does it? We are real. They are real. They are in their dimension of reality, and we are in ours. They are below us. We are above them. We can enter into their environment and even manipulate and adjust it. There's nothing they can do about it. They have absolutely no say in the matter. But, they cannot enter our world, nor could they dream of manipulating it or having an impact on it.

That scenario is similar to the matters of the unseen spiritual realms and their interaction with our own earthly, physical dimension. The Word of God assures us that "they are there." From the opening paragraphs to some of the last words of the Bible, we are told that these things are true.

Of course, the unbeliever will laugh at our insistence that the prophesied "day of the Lord" is coming. They mock the notion of multiple dimensions of physical reality that contain intelligent life interacting with our own world, even though the Word of God has assured us of the certainty of these things for millennia.[164] They scoff only because they are swimming around in an ocean of unbelief and are thoroughly happy within their tiny world of reality at the bottom of the ocean. All the while, they are duly impressed with their self-proclaimed brilliance.

Nevertheless, no amount of denying the Word of God will stop His plan and purpose. It didn't stop the Flood about which Noah so desperately warned his own generation, and about which our own world is still debating.

Our Creator *will have* a new creation. He will bring heaven and earth together under one head, Jesus Christ. This new world will be populated with those who have passed the test of faith, *and believed.* They will inherit all that He has reserved for them, simply because they freely chose to follow the way of the Lord of Glory rather than the evil one and his rebellious legions.[165]

This is the promise of His Word. In the end, it's what life is really all about. It's a cosmic weeding-out process. And it will happen, on a grand scale. You can take it to the bank.

—

Now, let's go back to the Mount of Olives, a few days before Jesus delivered Himself to the cross. That evening, Jesus was sitting with His disciples, looking down upon the area of the Temple Mount.

It was then that Jesus gave them an eye-opening clue, one directed at the most important period of human history yet to come:

The age in which we are currently living.

Your day.

32

A Certain Tree

It is a well-known biblical fact that the fig tree is frequently
used, in both the Old and New Testaments,
to describe the nation of Israel itself.

ON THAT EVENING AT THE MOUNT OF OLIVES, JUST BEFORE JESUS REMINDED
the disciples of the prominence of the "days of Noah," He first revealed
to them an important key. It was a clue pointing them to when those
prophetic days of Noah would visit the world. And, it was one that His
disciples would have thoroughly understood.

> Now learn this lesson from the fig tree: As soon as its twigs get
> tender and its leaves come out, you know that summer is near.
> Even so, when *you see all these things*, you know that it is
> near, *right at the door*.
> Truly I tell you, **this generation** will *certainly not pass* away
> **until all these things have happened.**
> Heaven and earth will pass away, but my words will never
> pass away. (Matthew 24:32–35; emphasis added)

The Interpretive Principle

As with almost all the prophetic utterances concerning the time of the last days, there are often multiple veins of intended meaning. One understanding is usually aimed at the immediate audience. And often, at least one more thread of the prophecy is meant for that specific time of the end. Astute theologians understand this as a "compound prophecy."[166]

Several prominent scholars acknowledge the compound-prophecy pattern as being affiliated with the fig tree parable of the Olivet Discourse. Since a multiple fulfillment is often involved in these kinds of prophecies, there is frequently a real struggle among scholars as to how to properly interpret them.

A Speedometer

At first reading, it would seem that the most understandable meaning of the fig tree illustration would revolve around Jesus' words, "As soon as its twigs get tender and its leaves come out, you know that summer is near. *Even so, when you see all these things*, you know that *it is near*, right at the door."

Therefore, the most logical conclusion, and thus the first vein of interpretation, is that Jesus simply used the natural process of a blooming fig tree to describe the speed with which end-time prophecy would unfold. A fig tree blooms in early spring, in April–May. But within just a few weeks, summer arrives, and so does the ripest fruit.

Expository Notes of Dr. Thomas Constable:[167]

The lesson of the fig tree is quite simple. As the appearance of tender twigs and leaves on a fig tree indicate the nearness of summer, so *the appearance of the signs Jesus explained would indicate that His coming is near*.[168] (Emphasis added)

A Revenant Nation

However, other scholars have seen something much deeper in the message of this fig-tree teaching. The reason is because Jesus didn't choose just any tree as the example; He chose the fig tree. That particular tree is a metaphor His immediate audience was familiar with; it was an object lesson Jesus had used earlier that day.

> Early in the morning, as Jesus was on his way back to the city, he was hungry. Seeing a fig tree by the road, he went up to it but found nothing on it except leaves.
>
> Then he said to it, "May you never bear fruit again!" Immediately the tree withered.
>
> When the disciples saw this, they were amazed. "How did the fig tree wither so quickly?" they asked. (Matthew 21:18–20)

Arno Gaebelein's Annotated Bible:

> In Matthew 21:1–46, we see in *the withered fig tree* a *type of Israel's* spiritual and *national death*. That withered tree *is to be vitalized*. The fig tree *will bud again*.[169] (Emphasis added)

The lesson of that morning regarding the withered fig tree was still fresh in the minds of the disciples. For this reason alone, there is little doubt: They would not have missed the implications of Jesus' newest fig tree message, given on the evening of that same day.

The two fig trees represent one and the same thing. The disciples were intended to see a withered and dying Israel that was happening right before their own eyes within their own generation. It would be marked by the AD 70 destruction of the Temple and the ultimate expulsion of the Jews from the entire region by the Roman Empire. But they were also intended to see a resurrected, fully "bloomed," nationally revived Israel that would appear in the last days to *an entirely different* generation.

The fig tree is frequently used in both the Old and New Testaments to describe the nation of Israel itself, either in a physical/geographical sense or in a spiritual one.

A study of Judges 9:10–11; Jeremiah 8:13, 24:10, and 29:17; Hosea 9:10; Habakkuk 3:17; and Haggai 2:19; as well as the books of Matthew 21:19; Mark 11:13, 20–21; and Luke 13:6–7 bear out this biblical truth.

Here's an example from that group of Scriptures:

> **When I found *Israel*,** it was like finding grapes in the desert; when I saw your ancestors, *it was like seeing the early fruit on the fig tree.* (Hosea 9:10; emphasis added)

All the Trees

Interestingly, when Luke records this parable in his Gospel, he adds the words "and all the trees" to Jesus' teaching.

> Look at **the fig tree *and all the trees*.** When they sprout leaves, you can see for yourselves and know that summer is near.
>
> Even so, when you see these things happening, you know that the kingdom of God is near. (Luke 21:30–31; emphasis added)

On that night, Jesus' Jewish audience would have known that not only was the fig tree a symbol for Israel, but also that the phrase "all the trees" would indicate "the other nations" of the world that would be surrounding and/or affecting Israel.[170]

Arno Gaebelein's Annotated Bible:

The fig tree is the picture of Israel. The parable of the fig tree in Luke 13:1–35 is well known, and *its application is Israel,* to whom the Lord came, looking for fruit, and did not find it. Luke 21:1–38, the record there of this discourse, mentions likewise the fig tree and *all the trees*; these *are the Gentiles, the nations.*[171] (Emphasis added)

That Generation

Given these facts, it then becomes apparent that the second vein of Jesus' foretelling had something to do with the return of Israel in the very last days. In effect, He would have been telling the generation of the last days to "watch the nations" closely, especially as the fig tree—Israel—blooms again. Many scholars agree with this assessment. Following are a few examples:

Lange's Commentary on the Holy Scriptures: Critical, Doctrinal, and Homiletical:

This generation means the generation of those who know and discern these signs…. The continued use of (elapse or pass away) in Matthew 24:34–35, *should have saved the commentators from the blunder of imagining that the then living generation was meant,* seeing that the prophecy is by the next verse carried on to the end of all things; and that, as a matter of fact, the Apostles and ancient Christians did continue to expect the Lord's coming, *after that generation* had passed away.[172] (Emphasis added)

Expository Notes of Dr. Thomas Constable:

The demonstrative pronoun "this" (Gr. aute)…could refer *to the end times rather than to that generation….* Jesus meant that

the generation of disciples that saw the future signs would also witness His return…. The earliest signs then would correspond to
the branches of the fig tree becoming tender. This would be the
first evidence of fulfillment shaping up. "This generation" then
represents an evil class of people who will oppose Jesus, disciples
until the day He returns.[173] (Emphasis added)

John Trapp Complete Commentary:

That generation that *immediately precedes the end of the world*.
That ***this is the sense***, appears by the antithesis, Matthew 24:36;
"But of that day and hour knoweth no man"…the generation
and age wherein Christ shall come ye may know by the signs
that foreshow it.[174] (Emphasis added)

International Standard Bible Encyclopedia:

To be sure, the solution should not be sought by understanding "this generation" of the Jewish race or of the human race. **It
must mean, according to ordinary usage, *then living generation*….** all this **belongs to "the end"** itself, in the absolute sense,
and is **therefore comprehended in the Parousia** and excepted
from the prediction that **it will happen in that generation**,
while included in the declaration that only God knows the time
of its coming.[175]

The blooming of Israel would serve as an unmistakable sign to those
nations. The prophet Ezekiel spoke of the same thing Jesus did in this
parable, especially the involvement of "other nations" in the process.[176]

This is what the Sovereign Lord says: "When I gather the people
of Israel from the nations where they have been scattered, I will

be proved holy through them in the sight of the nations. Then they will live in their own land, which I gave to my servant Jacob.

They will live there in safety and will build houses and plant vineyards; they will live in safety *when I inflict punishment on all their neighbors who maligned them.* Then *they will know* that I am the Lord their God." (Ezekiel 38:25–26; emphasis added)

Since this interpretation appears to be the fullest meaning of Jesus' parable, then He was indeed telling us that the return of Israel would just precede the coming days of Noah.

So what does biblical scholarship, history, and even science have to say about these matters?

Turn the page to find out.

33

Of Scholars and Figs

The fig tree bloomed in 1948.
Jesus said the days of Noah would soon follow.

THE CLASSICAL SCHOLARS WROTE THEIR COMMENTARIES LONG BEFORE THE historically unprecedented return of Israel took place in 1948. Yet a number of them saw the *compound-prophecy* element of the fig tree parable as applying to an unrevived Israel, a nation that would spring to life in the end times as a divine signal.

Following are examples from that genre of well-known biblical commentators.

Pulpit Commentary (Spence-Jones, H. D. M. 1836–1917. Published 1883): The fruit of the fig tree appears before the leaves, as we learned in the story of the withered fig tree (Matthew 21:19), which the Lord may have had in mind when he gave this illustration. Did he intend to symbolize *the revival of the life of the withered Jewish race* in the *time of the end?*[177] (Emphasis added)

F. W. Grant's The Numerical Bible (1834–1902):

And the Lord now impresses upon His disciples **the suddenness** with which all this will be accomplished. **The fig tree is once** more *chosen as a figure of Israel*: and the fruit is there as soon as the leaves: **thus the development is sudden indeed;** summer in this way seems at once to set in: *Israel's hopes come thus to sudden fruitage.* **The very generation that sees the beginning of these things** *will see the end.*[178] (Emphasis added)

Israel's "hope" of which F. W. Grant speaks has always been, even during the days of Jesus' earthly ministry, the restoration of the nation of Israel back to its land and the eventual coming of their Messiah. Even the national anthem of Israel—the *Hatikvah*—speaks directly to this hope.[179]
Arno Gaebelein's Annotated Bible (1861–1945):

In Matthew 21:1–46, we see in the withered fig tree a type of Israel's spiritual and national death. But that withered tree is to be vitalized. The fig tree will bud again.

As soon as the branch becomes tender the fruit is found. It is a rapid development. This is the lesson here. *Israel's blessing, new life, fruit and glory will quickly be realized in those end days....*

The other application, that now we behold Israel like a budding fig tree, signs of new national life and in this a sign of the times, *is certainly not wrong.*

It tells us of the nearness of the end.[180] (Emphasis added)

Modern Commentators

There are also a number of scholars of our own day who understand that this parable was meant to point to the biblically prophesied return of a "last-days" Israel. Following are prominent examples.
Expository Notes of Dr. Thomas Constable:

A *popular interpretation* of this parable equates modern Israel's presence in the Promised Land with the budding of the fig tree…. This view…could be *at least part of what Jesus intended.*[181] (Emphasis added)

David Guzik[182]—*Enduring Word Commentary* (long-time Blue Letter Bible commentator and scholar):

The fulfillment of this prophecy was highly unlikely until *Israel was gathered again as a nation in 1948.* The restoration of a nation that the world had not seen for some 2,000 years is *a remarkable event in the fulfillment and future fulfillment* of prophecy.[183] (Emphasis added)

In the third example, note that Dr. Stan Rickard[184] additionally acknowledges the fact that a number of scholars "throughout church history" understood the fig tree to represent the revived nation of Israel in the last days.

Stanley Edgar Rickard, Jr. Ph.D.—*The Moorings Commentary on The Fig Tree of Matthew 24*:

Many commentators throughout church history have agreed that [the fig tree teaching] represents the nation of Israel. In this symbolism Jesus is alluding to a vision of Jeremiah (Jeremiah 24:1–10)…. The same imagery occurs more than once during Jesus' ministry (Luke 13:6).[185] (Emphasis added)

Dr. Rickard then goes on to lay out the reasons why the disciples, to whom this important clue was originally given, would have undoubtedly understood Jesus' meaning.

Why did Jesus curse the fig tree—a mere tree whose only fault was that it had not yet borne fruit? The incident is obviously symbolic. The day before the cursing of the tree was Palm Sunday, the day of Jesus' Triumphal Entry into Jerusalem, when, in fulfillment of Zechariah 9:9, He presented Himself to the people and their leaders as the Messiah....

Although some individuals accepted Him, the nation as a whole rejected Him.... Subsequently, less than forty years later, in A.D. 70, God judged the Jews by destroying their city and *scattering them throughout the civilized world.*

...**The two incidents are linked together.** The cursing of the tree was a picture of the judgment that would soon fall on Israel because Israel had rejected their Messiah.

...When the memory of the withered fig tree was still fresh in their minds, Jesus spoke the parable in question. He said that when the church sees the fig tree leafing out again, it will know that "it is...at the doors."

What the parable means, therefore, is that when the nation of Israel revives after its coming disintegration and death in A.D. 70, *the return of Christ will be imminent.*[186] (Emphasis added)

The fig tree bloomed in 1948. Jesus said the days of Noah would soon follow. And, He said, it would be *that* generation that would see "all these things happen." Of course, Jesus was speaking of all the things that He had just expounded upon in Matthew 24—right up to the gathering of the elect by the angels, accompanied by a trumpet blast from heaven.

We are *that* generation—the first generation to see the literal return of Israel.

And now, we're living right in the middle of the blooming of a number of events described by Jesus in Matthew 24 as "those things."

34

To the Exact Season

Is this simply a mere fluke of the facts of botany and the facts of history—colliding—to perfectly match Jesus' apparent meaning of the fig tree parable?

CONSIDER THIS: IN THAT FIG TREE PARABLE, JESUS MENTIONED THAT IT WOULD put forth its earliest shoots *in the spring*. Then, summer's fullest fruit was soon to follow. Now have a look at the following.

International Standard Bible Encyclopedia:

> When the young leaves are **newly appearing**, *in April*, every fig-tree which is going to bear fruit at all will have some *taksh* ("immature figs") upon it, even though "the time of figs" (Mark 11:13 the King James Version), i.e. of ordinary edible figs— either early or late crop— "was not yet."[187] (Emphasis added; parentheses in the original)

Facts about Israel—Truths about our Future: The Mystery of Israel the Fig Tree:

> **The common or edible fig** is native to the Mediterranean/Israel region, where it can produce three crops per year. Breba figs[188]

develop in the spring (May) **on the previous year's shoot growth.**
They are generally inferior to the main crop and are often dis-
carded to encourage growth of the main crop. **Two main crops
follow** in July-November, with pollinated figs in August-Sep-
tember.[189] (Emphasis added; parenthesis in the original)

Amazingly, the actual fig trees in Israel begin their first growth each
year in April–May, during the spring. Was it a mere coincidence that the
revenant nation of Israel was officially reborn into new life on May 14,
1948?

That historical birth of a brand-new nation occurred just as the fig
trees were beginning to put forth their new shoots in the Middle East…
an unprecedented and globally relevant event that precisely mirrored
Jesus' words in the fig tree parable!

Wouldn't Jesus Christ, the One who created everything and through
whom all things hold together (Colossians 1), also have known that this
specific event would occur on a date that corresponded with His parable? Of course!

There is also the fact that several monumental historical events
occurred in *April* of 1948 as well, just a few weeks before Israel's official
rebirth. Those events were, in the first place, instrumental in making
possible the May 14 revival of Israel. The "fig tree" Israel was producing
its first growth, as Jesus described in the parable, precisely during April-
May of 1948.[190]

Wow!

What do we say about these scientific and historical truths? Is all of
this simply a mere fluke of botany mingled with a coincidental collision
of the facts of history, which just happened to perfectly match Jesus'
meaning of the fig tree parable? I highly doubt it.

In the spring of 1948, the fig tree bloomed, just as Jesus said it would.
That now-thriving *tree* still commands the daily attention of practically
every nation under the heavens.

Also, just as Jesus said it would.

35

Two Resurrections

These were two promised, and fulfilled, resurrections that
completely altered the course of human history
as well as eternally significant cosmic events.

AFTER JESUS GAVE HIS DISCIPLES THAT LIST OF PROPHETIC EVENTS WE FIND IN Matthew 24 and after He gave the revelatory clue of the fig tree parable, He immediately offered another key piece of information.

He once again invoked the "days of Noah" as a sign of the approaching last days.

As it was in the days of Noah, so it **will be at the coming of the Son of Man.**

For in the days before the flood, people were eating and drinking, marrying and giving in marriage, up to the day Noah entered the ark; and they knew nothing about what would happen until the flood came and took them all away.

That is how it will be at the coming of the Son of Man. (Matthew 24:37–39; emphasis added)

Comebacks That Changed the World

No doubt the countdown clock of Satan's ultimate demise began with *the promised resurrection of Jesus Christ.* This truth is the central theme of the New Testament gospel message.

And, according to Jesus' fig tree parable, the countdown clock that would most definitively point toward His Second Coming would start with *the promised resurrection of the nation of Israel.*

These two formerly dead "things"—a person and a nation—completely altered the course of human history, both fulfilling major biblical prophecies. We're the first generation to be living on the fulfilled side of both events!

And both prophecies are found *only* in the Bible. Both are declared to be divine signals delivered from the throne of Yahweh, testifying to the nations that He alone is God and Satan is not. No other "religious" book in the entire human existence has ever dared to include in its writings a single word concerning the bodily resurrection of Jesus Christ and/or the geographical return of the nation of Israel.

Foretold Before They Even Entered

Many students of the Bible are shocked to learn that the scattering and the eventual return of Israel in the last days were *first* foretold by Moses even *before* the children of Israel had set foot on a single square inch of the Promised Land! Those prophecies are recorded in the book of Deuteronomy.[191]

Then, as we continue from Deuteronomy, moving through the remaining pages of the Old Testament, we find this recurring theme: *Israel will return to the land as a geographical nation in the last days, and the presence of that nation will serve as a witness to the nations of the world that the Lord is God and that His kingdom is soon to come.*

Following are only a few of several passages in Scripture where that promise is made. And these are from just two of the Old Testament prophets who pointed to this miraculous national resurrection. There are many more like them.

> This is what the Sovereign Lord says: I will take the Israelites out of the nations where they have gone. **I *will gather them* from all around and *bring them back into their own* land.**
>
> I will make them *one nation in the land*, on the mountains of Israel. *There will be one king over* all of them and **they will never again be two nations** or be divided into two kingdoms. (Ezekiel 37:21–22; emphasis added)

> **And so I will show my greatness and my holiness, and I will make myself known in the sight of many nations.** *Then they will know that I am the Lord.'* (Ezekiel 38:23; emphasis added)

> **When I have** *brought them back from the nations* and have gathered them from the countries of their enemies, I will be proved holy through them in the sight of many nations.
>
> **Then they** *will know that I am the Lord their God*, for though I sent them into exile among the nations, **I will gather them to their own land**, not leaving any behind. (Ezekiel 39:27–28; emphasis added)

> "However, the days are coming," declares the Lord, "when it will no longer be said, 'As surely as the Lord lives, who brought the Israelites up out of Egypt,'
>
> But it will be said, '**As surely as the Lord lives, who brought the Israelites up** out of the land of the north and *out of all the countries* where he had banished them.' **For I will restore them to the land I gave their ancestors.**" (Jeremiah 16:14–15; emphasis added)

I myself will gather the remnant of my flock out of all the countries where I have driven them and will bring them back to their pasture, where they will be fruitful and increase in number. (Jeremiah 23:3; emphasis added)

"I will be found by you," declares the Lord, "and will **bring you back from captivity. I will gather you from all the nations** and places where I have banished you," declares the Lord, "and will bring you back to the place from which I carried you into exile." (Jeremiah 29:14; emphasis added)

See, I will bring them from the land of the north and **gather them from the ends of the earth**....

They will come with weeping; they will pray **as I bring them back**....

"**Hear the word of the** LORD, **you nations**; proclaim it in distant coastlands: '**He who scattered Israel will gather them and will watch over his flock like a shepherd.**'" (Jeremiah 31:8–10; emphasis added)

Truly incredible is that while God's people waited for Israel's return to the land, many centuries passed. Yet the resurrection of that nation didn't happen during any of those generations. Thus, numerous biblical scholars through the ages surmised that this impossible prophetic event could only happen *after* the literal return of Jesus, when He would finally set up His physical Kingdom on the earth. Some even deduced that this prophecy must only refer to a "spiritual" Israel, meaning the birth and advancement of the "church," and not a physically revived nation of Israel situated in their original homeland in the Middle East.[192]

But then it happened—precisely as the Word of God had foretold.

The Land of Miracles

From May 14, 1948, forward, more than eight million Jews from all over the world have streamed back to their homeland. And they continue to return, even as you read this book.

As of this writing, there are now more Jewish people living in the returned Israel than in any other nation on the planet. By the day of Israel's seventy-second Independence Day, Israel's total population, including non-Jews, was more than nine million. This is more than a tenfold increase since Israel's founding.[193]

Israel is now a major world player among the nations and is an international military might with which to be reckoned. It is unquestionably the almost-daily focus of geopolitical and world attention, as well as the central player in day-to-day Middle East affairs.

Israel is also among the world's most accomplished leaders in the arts and sciences, as well as computer and medical technology. Since 1966, twelve Israelis have received the Nobel Prize—giving that nation more recipients of that award per capita than the United States, France, and Germany. It has more laureates, in real numbers, than India, Spain, and China. That's quite an achievement for a nation that, as of this writing, is only seventy-two years old.[194]

Never doubt. The long-prophesied resurrected nation of Israel is back. And as we've already discovered, in the last twenty-eight hundred years of human history, we are the only generation to see Jesus' prophecy of the budding fig tree fulfilled.

We're also the only generation to see the ancient city of Jerusalem finally restored as the rightful and legally recognized capital of that returned nation. Both of these facts are a clear sign that we are now in the last days, rapidly approaching the days of Noah.

The figs are getting ripe. The parabolically prophetic *summer* is just around the corner.

At this point in history, there really is no reasonable way to dispute the matter.[195]

36

Because of the Gentiles

*Once again, a large part of the church of the
last days is being duped.*

THE NEXT BIBLICAL FACT WE'LL EXAMINE ADDRESSES THE OFT-HEARD argument that the Israel of today's Middle East can't be the "real" Israel of prophecy. The detractors make this assertion because they claim Israel was reformulated as a nation only by the political maneuvering of several Gentile nations and international institutions of influence. The argument is that Yahweh would "never" use Gentile nations and institutional powers to accomplish the return of Israel.

Yet, Isaiah told us more than 2,800 years ago that this is exactly how God declared it would happen:

> Thus says the Lord GOD: "Behold, I will **lift up my hand to the** *nations* [Gentiles], and raise my signal **to the peoples; and** *they* [the Gentiles] *shall bring* **your sons in their arms,** and your daughters shall be *carried on their shoulders.*" (Isaiah 49:22; emphasis added)

This clear truth has never been lost on the classical scholars. Once again, a large part of the church of the last days is being duped.

The Cambridge Bible for Schools and Colleges:

The first of the three short oracles describes **the restoration of** [Israel] as **a spontaneous act** of homage **on the part of the Gentiles.**[196] (Emphasis added)

The Pulpit Commentary:

It is usual to expound this and parallel passages (Isaiah 60:4; 66:20) of **the return of the Jews to their own land by favor of the Gentiles.**[197] (Emphasis added)

Jamieson-Fausset-Brown Bible Commentary:

The Gentiles shall aid in restoring Israel to its own land (Isa 60:4; 66:20).[198] (Emphasis added)

Too Small

Others insist that the Israel in today's Middle East cannot be the genuine one, because it is simply too small; it doesn't faithfully represent the Israel of old. Shockingly, Isaiah 49 addresses this objection as well, asserting that the physically returned nation of the last-days Israel would be much smaller than the original. It also reveals that the returned nation would feel "closed in" by the surrounding nations and would publicly express its concerns about the resulting situation. The words of that prophecy have now been fulfilled to the letter—again, only in our generation.

Though you were ruined and made desolate and your land laid waste, now **you will be too small for your people**, and those who devoured you will be far away.

The children born during your bereavement will yet say in your hearing, "*this place is too small for us; give us more space to live in.*" (Isaiah 49:19–20; emphasis added)

What do current statistics say about Israel being *too small* for its people? In 2015, Reuters news agency reported on the matter. It's almost as if its reporter had read Isaiah 49 before writing the piece:

Today's [Israeli] population of 8.4 million is forecast to reach 15.6 million by 2059 and 20.6 million in a high case scenario, *meaning the small country* **could simply run out of room.**[199] (Emphasis added)

The *Times of Israel* also reported on the situation, again echoing Isaiah's words in a prophecy that, for 2,800 years, sounded rather strange and confounded biblical commentators. Now, we no longer have to wonder. The prophecy is being fulfilled before our eyes.

The government [of Israel] plans to build 1.5 million new homes by 2040, mostly in the **crowded center,** but critics say housing without infrastructure won't work, **call to develop Negev, Galilee.**
    [By 2050] Israel's population—the fastest-growing in the developed world, increasing by two percent annually—is set *to almost double* from the current nine million to 17.6 million, according to the Central Bureau of Statistics. And that's *in a dot of a country*, just a little bigger than New Jersey.[200] (Emphasis added)

And how can we ignore a dramatic headline like this one printed in *The Jerusalem Post*? "Racing Toward Disaster: Israel's Unsustainable Population Bomb." The headline itself declares the prophecy of Isaiah 49, apparently without its writer even knowing it.

The publication of a report by an august body such as the National Economic Council reflects *the new kind of thinking* that is required in Israel, if it is not to collapse under the weight of *a populace too numerous for a small*, fragile, promised land to sustain.[201] (Emphasis added)

Too Narrow

All of this is not to mention US President Barack Obama's May 2011 insistence that Israel should return to its 1967 borders.[202] This directive was issued based upon Obama's hope to create a "Palestinian State" in the Middle East, partially using land that was within Israel's borders. Israel's Prime Minister Netanyahu flatly rejected Obama's aspiration, stating, "We can't go back to those indefensible lines." In other words, Netanyahu was effectively asserting: If we were to do that, our land would be too narrow. We would be unable to properly defend it.[203]

We read it, we watch it, and we discuss the details of it in our daily news reports. But the majority of today's prophetically slumbering church misses most, if not all, of the words of Isaiah that are popping to life right before us…even as you are reading the words of this sentence. Yet, these prophecies have only been fulfilled in our historical generation.

Think of how many times since the opening pages of this book we have cataloged certain prophetic events and had to declare, "We are the only generation to see this happen."

The clock of the *last days* is ticking toward the soon-coming "days of Noah."

And there is no stopping that divine timer.

37

In the Day of Salvation

The coming of Jesus, then the return of Israel,
are indeed bound up together.

EVEN THE GENERAL TIME FRAME OF ISRAEL'S ULTIMATE RETURN IS PROPHESIED
in Isaiah 49. It's like a hidden gem waiting to be discovered.

This is what the LORD says:

> **In the time of my favor** I will answer you, **and in the day of**
> **salvation** I will help you; I will keep you and **will make you to**
> **be a covenant** for the people, **to restore the land** and to reassign
> its desolate inheritances **to say to the captives, "Come out,"** and
> **to those in darkness, "Be free!"**
> They will feed beside the roads and find pasture on every
> barren hill…. He who has compassion on them will guide them
> and lead them beside springs of water. (Isaiah 49:8–10; empha-
> sis added)

God declares that He will implement Israel's return in the "time of
His favor," which He also designates to be "in the day of salvation." The
English word "salvation" is translated from the Hebrew word *yeshua*.[204]
Yeshua, of course, is the Hebrew name for…*Jesus!*[205]

So, when we take a closer look at Isaiah 49, we discover that God declares—in the Hebrew language—that He will accomplish the return of Israel *in the day of Yeshua*. These words are literally present in the Hebrew text. And there is no greater fulfillment of true "salvation" coming to the earth than in the personal presence of Jesus Christ.

During the Days of the Gospel

The period that encompasses the crucifixion and resurrection, the birth of the church, and the preaching of the gospel in the last days can be called "the day of Jesus" or, as our English texts have it, the "day of salvation." The text also identifies that "day" as the "year" of God's favor.

Of course, the words "day" and "year" in this context are meant to symbolize sweeping segments of time. This is made clear by the fact that the two words are used synonymously within the same verse. These terms, in this case, represent epochs in which a certain spiritual reality is the main emphasis. Thus, from the time of Jesus' crucifixion on, the human race has been living in God's merciful "day of salvation."

Paul Understood This Truth as Well

Paul understood all of these truths we've discovered thus far. He even quotes this passage from Isaiah 49.

In the closing words of 2 Corinthians 5 and in the opening words of chapter 6, Paul interprets Isaiah 49:8 to be about a distinctive prophecy concerning God's timing of revealing Yeshua to the world.

We implore you on Christ's behalf: Be reconciled to God. God made him who had no sin to be sin for us, **so that in him we might become the righteousness of God. As God's co-workers we urge you not to receive God's grace in vain...**

For he says, "**In the time of my favor** I heard you, and
in the day of salvation [*Yeshua*] I helped you" [Isaiah 49:8].
I tell you, *now is the time* of God's favor, *now is the day of
salvation* [*Yeshua*]. (2 Corinthians 5:20–21, 6:1–2; emphasis
added)

In that same passage of Isaiah 49:8, in some undisclosed year, *after*
the *day of salvation* had commenced, God promised He would restore
the nation of Israel—the blooming fig tree:

I will keep you and **will make you to be a covenant** for the people, **to restore the land** and to **reassign its desolate inheritance.**
(Isaiah 49:8; emphasis added)

A number of the classical scholars understood these truths; notice
how they, too, connected Isaiah 49:8 to the coming of the days of Jesus,
and even to the corresponding return of Israel.

The *Pulpit Commentary* hearkens to those great New Testament passages of Revelation 13:8 and 1 Peter 1:20, declaring that God's plan
of salvation to the nations, wrought in the person of Jesus Christ, was
planned before the foundation of the world:

[Isaiah 49] Verse 8.—**In** *an acceptable time*; literally, in a time of
good pleasure; i.e. **the** *time fixed* by my good pleasure *from the
creation of the world.*[206] (Emphasis added)

Keil and Delitzsch Biblical Commentary on the Old Testament makes
the point that the coming of Jesus, then the return of Israel, are indeed
bound together in this prophecy from Isaiah 49:

It must not be forgotten, moreover, that throughout these
prophecies the *breaking forth of salvation*, not for Israel only, but
for all mankind, is regarded as *bound up* with the termination of

the captivity; and from this its basis, the *restoration of the people who were then in exile, it is never separated.*[207] (Emphasis added)

Keil and Delitzsch also sees the clear meaning of the words of Isaiah 49 in the "days of salvation—Yeshua":

> **We call to mind here Jeremiah 1:5; Luke 1:41; Galatians 1:15, but above all the name Immanuel,** which is given by anticipation to the Coming One in Isaiah 7:14, **and the name Jesus,** which God appointed through the mouth of angels, when the human life of Him who was to bear that name was still ripening in the womb of the Virgin (Matthew 1:20–23) ....*And is not this a sign that prophecy is a work of the Spirit, who searches out the deep things of the counsel of God?*[208] (Emphasis added)

Barnes' Notes on the Bible, commenting upon Isaiah 49, agrees with all the points we've just made and acknowledges that the apostle Paul declared the same truths:

> In a time of favor; in a time that shall be adjudged to be the best fitted to the purposes of salvation, Yahweh will be pleased to exalt the Messiah to glory, and to make him the means of salvation to all mankind.
>
> And in a day of salvation—In a time when I am disposed to grant salvation; *when the period for imparting salvation shall have arrived.*
>
> **Have I helped thee**—Have I imparted the assistance which is needful to accomplish **the great purpose of salvation** to the world. **This passage is quoted by Paul** in 2 Corinthians 6:2, and **is by him applied to** the *times of the Messiah.*[209] (Emphasis added)

In the next two verses of prophecy, found in Isaiah 49:9–10, we see even more language that beckons our spirit to behold the New Testament gospel message through Jesus Christ. In these verses we also envision shades of the Twenty-Third Psalm:

> That you may say to the prisoners, Go forth; to them that are in darkness, Show yourselves. They shall feed in the ways, and their pastures shall be in all high places.
>
> They shall not hunger nor thirst; neither shall the heat nor sun smite them: for he that has mercy on them shall lead them, even by the springs of water shall he guide them. (Isaiah 49:9–10, KJV)

Once again, the *Keil and Delitzsch* commentary elucidates:

> The "servant of Jehovah," in this central sense, is the heart of Israel. **From this *heart of Israel* the *stream of salvation flows out*,** first of all **through the veins of the people of God,** and thence through the veins of the nations generally.... *The history of Israel is coiled up* as into a knot for a further **and final development,** in whom **Israel's world-wide calling to be the Saviour of mankind,** including Israel itself, *is fully carried out [in Jesus Christ].*[210] (Emphasis added)

It now should be quite clear that Isaiah was speaking to the fact that sometime *after* the church was born, and when the gospel was in the process of sweeping the planet (all of this also known as the *day of Yeshua*), God would finally bring Israel back. The blooming of the fig tree, Israel's return in 1948, would have been just a few more than a thousand years after the birth of the church.

At this point in our journey, without attempting to pinpoint a specific date of Yeshua's return, we can now say with a high degree of assurance that we are living in the historical period nearing the closing of the last days.

It's time for the slumbering church to wake up.

38

Heralds

*How can it be that so much of
today's church still fails to see?*

THE EXISTENCE OF ISRAEL—AS GIGANTIC A LAST-DAYS SIGN AS IT IS—ISN'T THE
only clue that we've moved into the days of Noah. Other vital signals
were also decreed to appear during that age.

Consider the following verse from Matthew 24. In it, Jesus listed
one of the most certain signs of the last days:

And this **gospel of the kingdom will be preached** in the whole
world as a testimony to all nations, **and then the end will come.**
(Matthew 24:14; emphasis added)

International Bible Encyclopedia:

It is definitely predicted that the preaching of the gospel to all the
nations not only must happen before the end, but that *it straight-
way precedes the end*: "Then shall the end come" (Mt 24:14).[211]

191

To the Whole World

When Jesus spoke these words, the fullest revelation of the gospel wasn't yet complete. Jesus hadn't gone to the cross; He hadn't risen from the grave or ascended into heaven. The church had not been born. The Holy Spirit had not been given. The Great Commission of reaching the world with the gospel had not been decreed.

Also consider that humanity hadn't even explored and settled the rest of the *whole world* when Jesus spoke that prophecy. The technology to take the gospel to the entire planet wasn't available. Regardless, Jesus claimed that when a certain generation finally sees the completed gospel reaching the entire planet, ostensibly through massive information and communication technologies, then we will know that the coming of the Son of Man is near.

We are the only generation in the last two millennia to witness this prophecy's fulfillment. In fact, we've only had world-reaching communications technologies available within the last several decades. Today, the gospel is going out to the entire world. The book you're reading is even a small part of the greater fulfillment of that prophecy. The clock continues to tick—and the bigger picture becomes increasingly clearer.

Revelation Technologies

Along these lines, many passages in the Bible also speak of astounding technologies that couldn't have been imagined when they were written, including the ability for the whole world to observe things together, at once, instantly—and even to hear the gospel collectively. And don't forget the various forms of the miracles of modern transportation that have enabled the scattered Jews from all over the world to rapidly return, *en masse*, to Israel.

These prophecies also take into account a worldwide marking system that the Antichrist will use in the last days to determine who can buy, sell, and work. All of these inventions were nonexistent when the biblical writers first spoke of them. At the time, they would seem to have been utter impossibilities, even science fiction. But today we don't give them a second thought, because we live in a world where all of these high-tech wonders are commonplace.

To once again repeat our familiar refrain: *We're the only generation to see these things happen.* Yet they were described in the Bible thousands of years in advance. How can it be that so much of today's church still fails to see?

Malevolent Tribes

We must not leave out the astonishing prophecies of Ezekiel 38 and 39 that speak to a specific alignment of malevolent nations. This international association will be brought together for the presumed purpose of destroying a "resurrected Israel."

These prophecies, written more than 2,500 years ago, refer to new alliances involving what are now the nations of Russia, Iran (Persia), Turkey, and Libya, along with other Middle Eastern and African nations that are told to finally join together and attack Israel in the last days.

Each of these nations today is either predominantly Muslim or deeply involved and allied with Muslim nations. Of course, Islam didn't exist when the prophecies were written; it wouldn't emerge until some 1,300 years afterward.

The Ezekiel 38–39 prophecy declares that Israel will be robust and back in the land when this attack happens. We've now experienced a returned and powerful Israel. Even now—according to many prophecy watchers, Jew and Gentile alike—the predicted enemy nations are beginning to form their alliances. And as they breathe out their threats, they continue to amass devastating weapons for the stated purpose of one day attacking Israel.[212]

Again, we are the first and only generation to see even the remotest possibility of these prophecies being fulfilled. The clock is no longer merely ticking. The clanging sound of the midnight alarm of the ages is nearing its approach.

Conclusion

Noah understood what it meant to preach prophetic end-time truths in his day as he beseeched the people to repent. He too was mocked. He too was ignored. Yet God's Word was fulfilled in spite of the mocking, and the mockers ultimately perished because of their unbelief.

When we speak to the unbelieving world of the soon-approaching judgment of God, we certainly shouldn't do so with glee, but with broken hearts and a sense of urgency. We understand that a number of those metaphorical *fish* living at the deepest levels of the ocean's chasms could not even fathom another world of physical reality just above their heads. Therefore, they will not believe it. But their unbelief doesn't negate the unalterable truth.

Let us, as believers, take comfort in and be encouraged by the fact that the Lord will soon return. When He does, the end of the present vile human rule will come crashing down upon an anti-Christ world. The beginning of Jesus' glorious reign of righteousness will commence. Therefore, let us encourage one another with these certainties (2 Peter 3:2).

How Then Must We Live?

On one hand, we should live our day-to-day lives as though Christ's return might not come for another thousand years, yet always with keen awareness of the prophetic times in which we're living. We still have to mow the grass, pay the bills, and plan for the future. So I say we should enjoy every day of life the Lord grants us. We're not guaranteed another single day.

Yet, on the other hand, we must also courageously proclaim our faith and reach out to the world around us with the zeal and passion that comes from knowing that Jesus could return at any moment.

We're not allowed to attempt to discern the exact date of His return, but we've been given distinct markers and signs so that we might know where we're located within the general course of history. In other words, we *are* to recognize the seasons. In so doing, *that day* will not overtake us, His children, like a thief in the night.

> [Jesus]…said unto them, when it is evening, ye say, it will be fair weather: for the sky is red. And in the morning, it will be foul weather today: for the sky is red and lowering.
>
> O ye hypocrites, ye can discern the face of the sky; but can ye not discern the signs of the times? (Matthew 16:2–3, KJV)

> But ye, brethren, are not in darkness, that that day should overtake you as a thief.
>
> Ye are all the children of the light, and the children of the day: we are not of the night, nor of darkness. (1 Thessalonians 5:4–5, KJV)

Darkness is coming, perhaps soon. But never forget…*we have the light*. Don't let the Bible critics convince you to dim it or extinguish it altogether. Instead, let us be faithful to shine the light of the gospel message straight into the face of the soon-coming darkness.

This is our calling. This is our destiny. This is our purpose for living…

…especially since we're moving so much closer to the "second" days of Noah.

❖

PART SIX

A Generational Phenomenon

The wise will be put to shame; they will be dismayed and trapped. Since they have rejected the word of the LORD, what kind of wisdom do they have?

—JEREMIAH 8:9

39

Summoning the Flood

The very first institution ordained among humanity from the throne of God itself was struck down...

THE PROGRESSION THAT WILL BE LAID OUT OVER THE NEXT SEVERAL PAGES IS A biblical and historical schematic. It describes how the first huge crashing waves of the current prophetic outpouring began. In reality, these days have been slowly building ever since Noah's Flood. And the waters have been steadily rising since the prophetic return of Israel. But these last several decades of humanity's story have been exceptionally prescient.

Warning: The next three short chapters of this section might first appear to be a bit political in nature. I assure you that is *not* their greater message.

Rather, the following information is presented as a faithful recounting of the verified facts of history, especially as they relate to only two American presidential cycles. However, what you will see next should flick on a spiritual light bulb, revealing what's really been happening not just in the political realm, but, most importantly, in the unseen realms.

The Crucial Hour

In October of 2012, an aged Dr. Billy Graham only had a little more than five years to live in this earthly dimension. In that same month, Dr. Graham's son, Franklin Graham, the heir of his father's global ministry, penned an article titled, "This Could Be America's Last Call." Apparently, he saw the same things that so many of us who pay attention to the times were seeing as well. The article was written a month before the United States would elect Barack Obama as president for his second term.

Franklin Graham, whether he knew it or not at the time, seems to have been used as a prophetic voice to America and to the world. I think you will find his 2012 words especially poignant considering what has transpired since then and what we continue to see unfold before us, particularly relating to the most current geopolitical and societal upheavals.

Here are a few excerpts from Franklin Graham's article:

This is a crucial hour for our nation. Above all, this is a time for deep, intercessory prayer on behalf of our great country, which is in grave danger unless we repent of our sins and turn back to the God of our fathers....

When America's leaders actively promote and legislate immorality, restrict the religious freedoms that our country was founded on, and are openly hostile to men and women of faith, then I believe we are ripe for God's judgment.

So pray and then vote on November 6, asking God for His mercy and grace upon our land. **There's still time to turn** from our wicked ways **so that He might spare us from His wrath against sin.**[213] (Emphasis added)

Welcome to Obamaland

The day after Barack Obama won the 2012 presidential election, the younger Graham wrote again. This time, he issued yet another prophetic warning. It was even more ominous, and had a particular ring of urgency:

> **If we are allowed to go down this road** in the path that this president wants us to go down, **I think it will be to our peril and to the destruction of this nation.**
>
> **Unless we're willing to repent for our sins,** we will stand in his judgment **I want to warn America: God is coming around. He will judge sin, and it won't be pretty.** We have God's blessing as a nation. **Scripture is clear.** God blesses countries, but **God also brings bedlam when countries turn their back on him.** If we don't obey his laws, **he will withdraw his hand of protection.**[214] (Emphasis added)

The Big Five

The prophetic explosions that have taken place in the United States and around the world since that election—and continuing until the very day you're reading these words—are simply too numerous to recount here.

However, an essential short list of the opening harbingers would at least include the five most obvious elements of the Obama-promised "fundamental changing of America." Each is an undeniable assault upon the Word of God. Each constitutes a direct violation of biblical "borders." And the ramifications of each have affected the entire planet.

Harbinger #1—Borders of Marriage

On June 26, 2015, a shockingly prescient biblical date,[215] the Supreme Court of the United States, the world's indisputably acknowledged

bellwether nation, voted to do away with the historical and biblical definition of marriage. To do so, the High Court actually went against its
own words from two years earlier wherein it had proclaimed—with the
identical *agreeing and dissenting* justices voting—that the definition of
marriage belonged *only to the states* and not to the federal government.
SCOTUS also said that for it to comment on the definition of marriage
would be an unprecedented and illegal act.[216]

Regardless of the acknowledgment of constitutional law and precedent, the first institution ordained among humanity from the *throne of
God* itself was struck down in the one Gentile nation that had been, in
recorded history, the most blessed by God. That unprecedented agenda
was pushed, prompted, and openly promoted by Barack Obama, even
though he had campaigned on the promise to the Christian community
that he would uphold the traditional view of marriage as being between
one man and one woman only.

Even *Time* recorded the hypocritical atrocity:

Barack Obama misled Americans for his own political benefit
when he claimed in the 2008 election to oppose same sex marriage for religious reasons....

[However] As a state senate candidate in 1996, Obama filled
out a questionnaire saying "I favor legalizing *same-sex marriages*,
and would *fight efforts to prohibit* such marriages."

But 12 years later as a candidate for president, Obama told
Rick Warren's Saddleback Church that marriage *could only
extend to heterosexual couples*.

"*I believe that marriage is the union between a man and
a woman*," Obama said at the time. "Now, for me as a Christian—for me—for me *as a Christian, it is also a sacred union.*
God's in the mix."[217] (Emphasis added)

That was just the beginning.

Harbinger #2—Borders of the Womb

The abortion holocaust, brought on with *Roe v. Wade* in 1973, continued to be vigorously supported during the entire eight years of the Obama administration. Obama pushed the agenda, even at the risk of putting legitimate mainstays of American companies on the street— especially if those businesses and organizations were "faith-based." The diabolic agenda of wanton abortion had just been slammed into a blistering overdrive

One of the most visible examples during the Obama administration's abortion tyranny was the travails of Hobby Lobby—a devoutly Christian-owned company.

Forbes reported in January of 2013:

Welcome to Obamaland where our inalienable rights are being gradually degraded.

Hobby Lobby faces looming fines of up to $1.3 million per day for refusing to abide a spurious provision of the Affordable Care Act, aka Obamacare. Hobby Lobby's owners object to **being forced to finance certain drugs**, Plan B and Ella (or the "morning-after" and "week-after" pills), which the FDA notes **can terminate pregnancy** after conception.

Over forty legal challenges have contested the contraception mandate. Churches have largely been exempted, but faith-based hospitals and universities face similar predicaments.[218] (Emphasis and parenthesis in original)

But there were still more borders that Obama and his administration would attempt to leave in shambles before his term in office was up.

40

A Flood of Border-Busting

*Obama was ultimately going to side with
the Arab world over Israel.*

IT WAS ALSO DURING THE OBAMA YEARS THAT THE DEFINITION OF GENDER identity was forever blurred within our culture. This blasted deep inside the heretofore sacred institutions of public education, and even within the halls of several mainline denominations of the Christian faith.

Harbinger #3—Borders of Gender

Early in May 2016, with that same spirit in mind, and in yet another unprecedented maneuver, Obama's Departments of Justice and Education's respective civil-rights divisions issued directives to schools about transgender students. America's public institutions of education at all levels were instructed to allow "transgender students" to shower and dress together if they happened to be in the process of *reassuring* their preferred gender identity. No medical examination or documentation of gender at birth was required.

The *New York Times* reported the unparalleled decree:

> The Obama administration is planning to issue a sweeping
> directive telling every public school district in the country to

allow transgender students to use the bathrooms that match their gender identity.

A letter to school districts will go out Friday…. The declaration—signed by Justice and Education department officials—**will describe what schools should do** to ensure that none of their students are discriminated against.[219] (Emphasis added)

Under the Obama administration, the assault on the foundations of God's Word relentlessly continued, almost unabated. The entire agenda appeared to have been orchestrated in the dark, demonic, unseen realm of Satan's lair. Again, a number of prophecy watchers were convinced we were entering, during those days, a new chapter in human history… perhaps the prophesied demonic incursion of the last days.

Harbinger #4—Borders of Israel

The Obama presidency also appeared on more than one occasion to vehemently oppose almost everything constructive having to do with the prophetically returned nation of Israel.

In December 2010, the Middle East upheaval, now known by historians as Arab Spring, proved to be a huge test and a definitive revelation as to where Obama's "fundamentally changed" world was headed—especially as that worldview was related to Israel. Even the *New York Times*, while often standing firmly in Obama's corner, let the cat out of the bag: Obama was ultimately going to side with the Arab world over Israel.

Mr. Obama, during a tense telephone call the evening of Feb. 1, 2011, had just told Mr. Mubarak [president of Egypt] that his speech, broadcast to hundreds of thousands of protesters in Tahrir Square in Cairo, had not gone far enough. Mr. Mubarak had to step down, the president said.

Minutes later, a grim Mr. Obama appeared before hastily summoned cameras in the Grand Foyer of the White House.

The end of Mr. Mubarak's 30-year rule, Mr. Obama said, "must begin now." With those words, **Mr. Obama upended three decades of American relations** with its most stalwart ally in the Arab world, **putting the weight of the United States squarely on the side of the Arab street.**[220] (Emphasis added)

As Arab Spring continued to boil over, spilling its anti-Israel rhetoric and threatening to bring its devastation upon that nation, Prime Minister Benjamin Netanyahu chastised Obama's policies that appeared to be fueling the monumental uprising.

Great Britain's *Guardian* reported:

When [Netanyahu] cautioned Barack Obama…against backing the revolt against Hosni Mubarak's regime, he was told [by Obama] he failed to understand reality. [Netanyahu replied] "I ask today, who here didn't understand reality? Who here didn't understand history?"[221]

Then, in May 2011, Obama formally endorsed a policy calling upon Israel to return to its original borders, the ones that existed before the 1967 Middle East war. Here again was an unprecedented presidential directive with Israel's sovereignty firmly sighted in the crosshairs.

In apparent support of the Obama agenda in this regard, CNN reported the biblical atrocity:

"We believe the borders of Israel and Palestine should be based on the 1967 lines with mutually agreed swaps, so that secure and recognized borders are established for both states," Obama continued.

Political opponents also criticized Obama, with possible Republican presidential candidate Mitt Romney saying *the president had "thrown Israel under the bus."*

"*He has disrespected Israel* and undermined its ability to negotiate peace," Romney said in a statement. "He has also violated a first principle of American foreign policy, which is to stand firm by our friends." [222] (Emphasis added)

Obama's goal was to promote the rise of a legitimate Palestinian state, right in Israel's backyard and at its front doorsteps—another hugely prophetic *no-no*.

Harbinger #5—Borders of the Nation

In February 2016, the Federation for American Immigration Reform lamented:

> Since 2009, the Obama administration has systematically gutted effective immigration enforcement policies, moved *aggressively against State and local governments that attempt to enforce immigration laws*, and stretched the concept of "prosecutorial discretion" to a point where it has *rendered many immigration laws meaningless.* [223] (Emphasis added)

God's Word has something ominous to say in regard to national borders. Read the next two passages. Pay special attention to the second one, as God tells Israel that because they had rejected His Word, He would use weakened borders as an *act of judgment* against their rebellion.

- God invented national borders:

When the Most High **gave the nations their inheritance**, when he divided all mankind, **he set up boundaries for the peoples** according to the number of the sons of Israel. (Deuteronomy 32:8; emphasis added)

- God uses encroachment upon sovereign national borders as judgment upon disobedient nations:

The foreigners who reside among you will rise above you higher and higher, but you will sink lower and lower. They will lend to you, but you will not lend to them. They will be the head, but you will be the tail.

All these curses will come on you. They will pursue you and overtake you until you are destroyed, because you did not obey the Lord your God and observe the commands and decrees he gave you. They will be a sign and a wonder to you and your descendants forever.

Because you did not serve the Lord your God joyfully and gladly in the time of prosperity, therefore in hunger and thirst, in nakedness and dire poverty, you will serve the enemies the Lord sends against you. He will put an iron yoke on your neck until he has destroyed you. (Deuteronomy 28:43)

Could all of this really be mere coincidence? Those who knew the Word of God saw something far more sinister than a quirk of happenstance. This appeared to be out-and-out spiritual warfare, and it was unfolding before the eyes of the world. Oddly enough, the focus of the cosmic war was laser-centered on *borders*. Consider the prophetic implications of that. It all began in the Garden of Eden, when Satan—and Adam and Eve—violated every border set before them.

———

Think about the five harbingers we just examined. Even though we largely looked at them from the perspective of the United States—the global bellwether nation—they are also universal sins. Each represents the worldwide spirit of our times.

1. Abortion (the seed of the womb of the woman[224]) is the world's number-one cause of death, and has been so for decades.[225]

2. The worldwide border and immigration crisis is now in unprecedentedly dangerous territory.[226]

3. The God-ordained institution of marriage between one man and one woman is currently in a drastic and shocking state of universal decline.[227]

4. With the advent of the international scourge of computer porn, the sex-slave industry and pedophilic behavior have skyrocketed. Concurrent with those atrocities have also come a rise in drug and alcohol addiction, unprecedented abuse of women and children, and a global spike in the number of people diagnosed with depression disorders. That's not to mention corresponding increases in systematic brain alteration and dysfunction, sexual dysfunction, suicide rates, homosexual behavior, and gender dysphoria.[228]

5. The nations of the world continually express their disdain, even blatant hatred, for the presence and the prominence of the resurrected nation of Israel in the Middle East.[229]

There you have it: *the Big Five*.

They're now a worldwide phenomenon for the first time in humanity's history. A flood of filth. An outpouring of demonic intrusion. The corruption of all flesh and the continual loss of global sanity. They are all the symptoms of a *worldwide giving-over* to a depraved mind, just as prophesied in Romans 1 more than two thousand years ago:

> Furthermore, since they did not see fit to acknowledge God, He gave them up to a depraved mind, to do what ought not to be done.
>
> They have become filled with every kind of wickedness, evil, greed, and depravity. (Romans 1:28–29)

Sadly, most of America's collective church appears to be oblivious to the prophetic nature of our times. They're too busy "eating and drinking" and "giving in marriage."

41

The Shift That Triggered

It appeared to a number of believers that the withdrawing of the hand of God had begun.

AFTER FUNDAMENTALLY CHANGING THE DEFINITION OF MARRIAGE AND gender, then taking multiple stands supporting wanton abortion, serious students of God's Word knew America, and the world, had to be on the brink of some real trouble.

However, when Donald Trump was elected president in 2016, he solemnly promised to stand firm with Israel. In fact, he quickly signed the Jerusalem Embassy Act, which all of his predecessors had refused to sign even after assuring in every single election cycle that they would sign it.[230] Trump then, within the first two years of his brand-new administration, declared Jerusalem the legally recognized capital of Israel. This was yet another unprecedented move towards specific prophetic fulfillment.

Then came another stand against the halls of hell. Trump's position against the America abortion holocaust was another much-ridiculed element of his campaign. However, it was a platform he firmly commanded right up to the day of his election and beyond.

Donald Trump declared that overturning the landmark Supreme Court decision giving women the right to abortion would happen "automatically"[231] if he were elected president and had the opportunity to appoint justices to the High Court.

> *"I am pro-life,"* Trump said during Wednesday night's presidential debate when asked whether he wanted that decision, Roe v. Wade, reversed by the Supreme Court.
>
> Trump said that if the ruling were to be reversed, laws on the legality or illegality of abortion would "go back to the individual states" to decide, which was the case prior to *Roe v. Wade.*[232]

Trump was also a strong proponent of traditional biblical marriage, a fact acknowledged by the Human Rights Campaign, a vehement supporter of homosexual marriage.

> Trump has been a consistent opponent of marriage equality. He said that he opposed it because he was a "traditional" guy, choosing to support domestic partnership benefits instead. Trump later reversed himself and said he also opposed civil unions.
>
> Despite a brief flirtation with "evolving" in 2013, **Trump has consistently maintained his opposition to marriage equality**, sometimes by citing polling and making an analogy to his dislike of long golf putters.
>
> **After the Supreme Court ruling**, Trump said the court had made its decision and, although he disagreed with the ruling, he did not support a constitutional amendment that would allow states to re-ban marriage equality. **He later said he would appoint Supreme Court judges who would be committed to overturning the ruling.**[233] (Emphasis added)

President Trump then rescinded Obama's transgender bathroom order, as we see reported by NPR:

The Trump administration is rescinding protections for transgender students in public schools.

The move by the Justice and Education departments **reverses guidance the Obama administration publicized** in May 2016, which said a federal law known as Title IX protects the **right of transgender students to use restrooms and locker rooms that match their gender identities.**[234] (Emphasis added)

Of course, President Trump's most well-known promise was to shore up our own national borders and repair America's burgeoning immigration nightmare.

A Triggered Swamp

Each of the "Big Five" harbingers—those atrocities outlined in the pages of Scripture—were either eliminated entirely by the Trump administration or were in the midst of the painfully slow political process of bringing about the promised reversal. And that's when the "swamp" came to life.

Before his first term was over, the newly elected president, along with the nation he served, was forced to endure the morale-grinding ordeals of a worse-than-Watergate spying scandal involving the deepest of the deep state. The chasm-like depths of the political and criminal outrages of forged documents, fake spy reports, and lying to federal FISA courts went all the way to the top. The ties were connected to formerly long-respected federal law enforcement agencies, esteemed seats on the federal courts, and even key people in the previous presidential administration.[235]

All of this was the foundation for the Mueller investigation, which lasted several long years. And right behind that failed and nationally exhausting investigation came a surreal, and at times almost laughable, House impeachment proceeding.

Immediately after the conclusion of the ultimately failed impeachment process came the chaotic and panic-filled months of the global pandemic of COVID-19. Even that viral crisis became politically weaponized to be used against the Trump administration and a large part of his base—*America's churches.*

All of this was immediately followed by pandemonium, fiery riots, pillaging, looting, and the wanton killing of citizens and police officers across America. These events sprang up in the wake of the tragic death of George Floyd.[236]

During those days, a number of US cities began defunding and dismantling their respective police departments.[237] And while massive rallies and demonstrations were taking place in almost every major city in America and in other major cities around the world, the leftist mainstream media sat idly by, not saying a word about the COVID-19 pandemic "dangers" that might be involved. Yet they, at the same time, chastised and derided law-abiding citizens for returning to work and church. Trump supporters were continually disparaged for attending his massive campaign rallies.[238]

Clearly, a spirit of lawlessness, depravity of mind, and truth being thrown to the ground was beginning to sweep the nation—and the planet. Throughout that time, a recurring question could be heard in almost every conversation among various groups of people from all over the world: *"When will all this end?"*

A Word of Perspective

Please understand. As stated from the outset of this section, I am not suggesting that Barack Obama was/is somehow the personification of evil. Nor am I suggesting that Donald Trump is some kind of an angel from heaven sent to deliver the world from evil.

What I am saying in these chapters is that something ominously prophetic has been happening to America and to the world, and it has

occurred within just a few short years—most of it during the administrations of only two of this nation's presidents.

The Bible assures us that the Lord maneuvers kings and nations in
accordance with His will and His ultimate end-time plans.[239] However, I
am pointing out that we're currently watching the prophetic assurances
of God's Word come upon the international scene with an intensity
unlike anything the world has ever seen.

As previously acknowledged, Franklin Graham's portentous message
written just a few years before the turbulent times of 2020 now have an
especially revealing ring to them, wouldn't you agree? Look at his words
again:

> [God] will judge sin, and it won't be pretty. We have God's bless-
> ing as a nation. Scripture is clear. God blesses countries, but *God
> also brings bedlam* when countries turn their back on him. If we
> don't obey his laws, *he will withdraw his hand of protection.*[240]
> (Emphasis added)

It appeared to a number of believers that the *withdrawing of the hand
of God* had finally begun.

⊰◈⊱

PART SEVEN

The Days of Noah

We are living in a time when states and cities can indefinitely mandate draconian "face coverings" on our own mouths and noses, along with a full panoply of restrictions on life, liberty, and property.

Putting everything together, the courts of Sodom and Gomorrah believe there is a right for a man to play female sports, a right for a man to secure a taxpayer-funded castration…but no right to open your business or walk freely without a cloth on your own mouth and nose.[241]

—DANIEL HOROWITZ, THE *CONSERVATIVE REVIEW*, AUGUST 2020

The Lord saw how great the wickedness of the human race had become on the earth, and that every inclination of the thoughts of the human heart was only evil all the time.

—GENESIS 6:5

42

Just Like This

*I never truly understood the gravity of this passage
until I had spent more than three decades in
ministry in a single church and community.*

NOW WE COME BACK TO JESUS' PRECISE WARNING CONCERNING THE END-TIMES
days of Noah.

The following is the text of Luke 17. As we have seen, a similar
discourse is also given in Matthew 24. Especially note the words emphasized in bold.

> [26] Just as it was in the days of Noah, so also will it be in the days
> of the Son of Man.
> [27] People were *eating, drinking, marrying and being given
> in marriage* up to the day Noah entered the ark. Then the flood
> came and destroyed them all.
> [28] It was the same in the days of Lot. People were eating and
> drinking, buying and selling, planting and building.
> [29] But the day Lot left Sodom, fire and sulfur rained down
> from heaven and destroyed them all.
> [30] *It will be just like this* on the day the Son of Man is
> revealed. (Luke 17:26–30)

First, notice the term "just" in verse 26. In this context, there's not much wiggle room in that word. Jesus didn't say those days would be "kind of like," "similar to," or "almost the same." He didn't say He was speaking parabolically or metaphorically. He emphasized the word "just," having only seconds before used the words "so also *will it be.*"

Think of what Jesus is highlighting.

Eating and drinking. Celebrating marriage. Conducting the daily affairs of all aspects of business. Nothing is evil about any those activities in and of themselves. They are all the stuff of everyday life.

But in this admonition concerning the last days, Jesus is defining a pervasive worldview. He is foretelling the immersive and exclusively secular approach to life that will ultimately have little to no regard for the spiritually binding forces of righteousness, truth, faithfulness, and integrity.

The Question

I have to admit that I never truly understood the gravity of this passage until I had spent more than three decades in ministry in a single church and community. Then, after observing several generations and their reactions to major prophetic events that moved through the timelines of those generations—*it hit me.* Once the events had passed and the anxiety of those immediate days had waned, they simply got on with the routine affairs of life. They quite often slipped right back into their take-it-or-leave-it attitudes regarding the Word and ways of God, especially their consistent involvement among the family of God.

That same attitude, Jesus said, would deeply infect the world's population in the last days. This is exactly what occurred in Noah's day, such that he and his family became the last living souls on the planet who still loved Yahweh and His ways.

But how could that happen again?

Remember that question. You'll soon discover the answer for yourself, and it will probably be quite shocking when the gravity of its truth hits you.

Let's begin by remembering the ominous words of the prophet Hosea. They speak of the central reason the Lord was bringing His judgment and rebuke upon His own dear children. They had rejected His Word, and the priests of God had shirked their responsibility of warning them.

> **My people are destroyed for lack of knowledge**: because thou hast *rejected knowledge*, I will also reject thee, that thou shalt be no priest to me: seeing thou hast *forgotten the law of thy God*, I **will also forget thy children.** (Hosea 4:6, KJV; emphasis added)

The Beginning of the Answer

Think of the last several generations that have grown up in this present darkness. They've been steeped in a cavernous mire of fake information when they've had no real familiarity with the full truth of God's Word. As a result, their entire thought processes are influenced and characterized by abject fakery.

Consider the institutions of education, entertainment, and "science," as well as the currently hallowed halls of information and communication technologies and a huge portion of the visible institution of the "church." All have been thoroughly distorted from the inside out, infested by demonic influence and manipulation to one degree or another.

Apparently, the apostle Paul saw our own days when he spoke of those "later times."

> The Spirit clearly says that **in later times some will abandon the faith and follow deceiving spirits and things taught by demons.** Such teachings come through **hypocritical liars,** whose

consciences have been seared as with a hot iron. (1 Timothy 4:1–2; emphasis added)

Think about the long-lasting and far-reaching implications of it all. Deceiving spirits. Demonic outpouring. Hypocritical, duplicitous liars. Fake news. Deep-fake videos. Deep-fake audios. Artificial (fake) intelligence. Fake governments. Fake "science." Fake medical industry "information." Fake "information" on fake "social" interaction communication venues. Fake marriage. Fake genders. Fake relationships. Fake governments. Fake religions. Phony philosophies of life. On and on the list goes.

As you read the prophetic words of the New Testament—most coming out of the mouths of Jesus, Paul, Peter, and John—remember that these attitudes and markers of our own vile human sin nature have *always* been among the human race. The difference however, when these prophecies are examined in context, is that in the last days there will be something pervasively universal about the infestation.

Just like in Noah's day, chicanery will permeate practically every heart on the planet. Unless one is genuinely born again, every soul will get caught up in its worldwide web.[242]

For false messiahs and false prophets will appear and perform great signs and wonders to deceive, if possible, even the elect. (Matthew 24:24)

The coming of the lawless one will be accompanied by the working of Satan, with every kind of power, sign, and false wonder, and with every wicked deception directed against those who are perishing, because they refused the love of the truth that would have saved them. (2 Thessalonians 2:9–10, Berean Study Bible)

The last-days flood of lunacy will be borne upon the wings of the demonic realm, largely working through an amped-up and never-before-seen explosion of *signs and wonders*—both technological and supernatural.

Again, I ask you to contemplate the sheer deluge of the "doctrines of demons" and the resulting deception and depravity that has followed. And think of the current crop of younger citizens of this planet who will have only known this kind of diabolical fakery for their entire lives. They truly believe this current world system is *normal.*

Who will tell the next generation otherwise? Not the government. Not the entertainment industry. Certainly not our educational realm or the world of modern "science." And sadly, a scant amount of contextually connected biblical truth is taught from most of America's pulpits. Thus, few of our homes and families—which have now been completely redefined by our culture—will teach the biblical truth either.

Just like every generation before us that absorbs the vain philosophies of their times as "normal," so will the young people behind us. It's no longer unthinkable to imagine people "lining up" to take *the mark* (Revelation 13).

They'll all want to make certain they are sitting at the cool kids' table. That's what they learned was important. And they'll surely want to be "saved" from the latest coming calamity, along with the pre-planned "fear-demic" that will accompany it. How would they know of any other way to respond?

And that's the way it was in the days of Noah, as well as in the days of Lot.

The planet is finally there again—for the first time since the days written of in Genesis.

43

The Great Brainwashing

Is there any wonder that so much unbridled
confusion reigns across the planet?

As I write these words, only 10 percent of America's population claims to even come close to attempting to live according to a biblical worldview. If the trend continues, that number will fall even more drastically in the next few years. Among Millennials, the percentage already drops to just 4 percent.[243]

It's not difficult to see where all this is headed. We're at least at the edges of the days of Noah, as well as of the days of Lot—and we're in fact probably way beyond the mere edges. And if America—the largest "Christian" nation in global history—is already at that prophetic precipice, we can be reasonably certain that the rest of the planet is far ahead of us.

Of course, there are exceptions in every generation. God will always have His ambassadors of truth—*Noahs* of every age.

But, by and large, the majority of the generations we're speaking about have grown up, for example, believing that Israel is to be hated, dismantled, and turned over to the Muslim world. They have been taught that the prophetically returned nation of Israel is only a "fake" Israel, filled with "fake Jews" who are merely the evil "occupiers" of the land.

Think of what you've already discovered concerning Israel's presence in today's world as being a sign to the "nations" that Yahweh is the God of creation. Yet, entire Christian denominations are helping spread the outpouring of that evil brand of hatred against Israel.[244]

Cosmic Accident

Large segments of those same generations have also been brainwashed into believing that their lives are the consequence of a purely accidental cosmic explosion. They're convinced they are a mere fluke of an impersonal evolutionary process that began in a coincidentally converged sludge pond of randomly appearing chemical concoctions. They believe that the very brainpower they possess to support this mythological, pseudoscientific dribble is the result of a twist of fate. The madness of that reasoning is mind-boggling. But they have no idea there's anything wrong with their demonically influenced thought processes. It's all they've ever known.

They're convinced that government is their savior and that politically correct truisms are the ultimate and indisputable *facts* of life. If the government or the fake news media tells them something is true...they will simply believe it, and comply. But what else *should* they think? They've had almost every vestige of a biblical worldview pulled from their public life and awareness. And, if they've gone to church at all, they've heard little, if any at all, of things that you're reading right now.

Additionally, if these citizens were born since the early 2000s, all they've ever known is the "herding" mentality of their culture,[245] as well as a dangerous *social media depression syndrome*,[246] with a huge dose of gender and sexual *dysphoria* thrown in the mix.[247] All of these factors have, more than likely, contributed to the pervasive use of illicit drugs, pornography, and all manner of open doors to the demonic spirits of mental and psychological depravity, and even suicide.[248]

This is all they are familiar with. This is what they understand about "life" on planet earth. This is their daily "normal." And they will pass these traits to their children, and to their children's children—as generational curses.[249]

The Question Answered

We've now answered the question we asked in the previous chapter: How is it that the last-days generation will become so completely ambivalent to the prophetic times in which they live?

Now you know. Is it any wonder that unbridled confusion reigns across the planet? Is there any wonder that in 2020 the global powers were, for the first time ever, practically 100 percent successful in closing down the church? What kind of *world to come* is being numinously cobbled together by this flooding torrent of filth, deception, and outright fraud?

Actually, the Bible gives us these answers as well. Everything is hurtling toward the kingdom reign of the *man of lawlessness* and the days of anarchy. It will be a repeat of what life was like during the days of Noah just before the return of the Lord Jesus Christ.

> **The coming of the lawless one will be in accordance with how Satan works.**
>
> He will use all sorts of displays of power through signs and wonders that serve the lie, and all the ways that wickedness **deceives those who are perishing.**
>
> **They perish because they refused to love the truth and so be saved.**
>
> For this reason **God sends them a powerful delusion** so that they **will believe the lie** and so that **all will be condemned who have not believed the truth but have delighted in wickedness.**
> (2 Thessalonians 2:9–12; emphasis added)

[The beast] **prospered in everything** it did, **and truth was thrown to the ground.** (Daniel 8:12; emphasis added)

All of the preceding are only the *attitudes* and lifestyle *norms* that mark the depths of those coming days of Noah. However, the book of Genesis has even more to say about the specific *happenings* of those days. They also figure into the total equation.

44

The Sons of God

This appears to be the breaking point of the "why"
for the necessity of the Flood.

WHAT WAS GOING ON IN THE DAYS OF NOAH THAT APPARENTLY WILL AGAIN converge and collide within a singular period of generational history?

As we examine the prevailing issues of that time exactly as the Scriptures describe, remember that these features were *globally* established. That is to say, they were global as far as wherever humans had settled in those early days of earth's history.

So, for the end times to be "just like" the days of Noah, the requirement would have to be the same, but on a much grander scale. The traits would have to possess a recognizable worldwide presence. Because of the now universally pervasive and exponentially increasing technological abilities, no generation before ours could have accomplished such a feat. But *we* are the first. We have done it. We are living it.

Something Evil This Way Comes

The account of the Flood begins in Genesis 6. In the first two verses of that chapter are some of the most hotly debated words in that book and

229

perhaps in the entire Bible. I've written about this topic before in several of my previous books; however, since this is the central theme of the days leading up to Noah's Flood, we'll dive back into the subject here.[250]

When human beings began to increase in number on the earth and daughters were born to them:

> The sons of God saw that the daughters of humans were beauti-ful, and they married any of them they chose...
>
> **The Nephilim** [giants][251] were on the earth in those days—and also afterward—when *the sons of God* went to the *daugh-ters of humans* and had children by them. They were the heroes of old, men of renown.
>
> **The Lord saw how great the wickedness of the human race had become on the earth,** and that every inclination of the thoughts of the human heart was **only evil all the time.** (Genesis 6:1–2, 4–5; emphasis added)

The narrative we find here is presented in the text as being the *last straw*—the thing that caused Yahweh to push the "reset" button and destroy everything that had breath. Something "extra-normally" evil took place. Otherwise, God destroyed multitudes of people and started the whole thing over simply because they didn't "marry properly." That notion seems a bit far-fetched. And, as you will soon see, the original language of Genesis doesn't even come close to allowing that spurious, but modernly popular, interpretation.

Bene Elohim

Most of the debate revolves around the question: "Just who are these *sons of God*?" Only three serious choices are commonly proposed:

1. High-ranking noblemen of the time
2. The sons of Seth (from the line of Cain, the first murderer)

3. Divine beings—*angels* (translated this way in the Jewish Septuagint[252])

Charles Ellicott offers an excellent summary of these three options in his exposition on Genesis 6. He concludes with the following salient observation concerning the "sons of God" being either nobles or Sethites:

> **But no modern commentator has shown** how such marriages could produce "mighty men...men of renown;" or how strong warriors could be the result of the intermarriage of pious men with women of an inferior race, such as the Cainites are assumed to have been.[253] (Emphasis added)

That last point is the toughest one to overcome, even though some scholars (including Ellicott himself) try to do so with all their might.

It's a tough point of fact, because if these beings are not divine, the problem really goes to the only other two options, both of which have the "sons of God" as mere humans. But whether they are men of nobility or ignobility doesn't really matter. *They're just men.*

So here's the question: How in the world can a marriage between mortal men (good *or* evil ones) and mortal women (good *or* evil ones) produce offspring that turn into killer-freak monstrosities—especially a whole world full of them? How does marrying "only" for the desire of a beautiful woman—even if it's a particularly lustful desire—bring about universal venality to the point that the entire planet is filled with terror, violence, corruption of all flesh, and all other manner of evil...to the point that God decided to destroy them all?

Ellicott is absolutely correct. Not a single modern commentator of any credibility at all has been able to demonstrate how "improper marriages" between human men and human women could result in a world that became infested with Nephilim—*terrorist giants.*[254]

Accordingly, we're left with the only sensible third choice. The "sons of God" were divine beings—perhaps of a class of angels that existed prior to the Flood.

Moreover, since that Hebrew phrase—*bene elohim*—is used only a handful of times in the Bible, and in *every single* case the beings are identified *only* as entities from the unseen realm, it makes sense that we would interpret Genesis 6 in the same manner. Nothing in Genesis 6 would cause us to change the context of the translation of *bene elohim*. Neither is anything else there that would cause us to even search for another meaning.

So, it would seem that the interpretation of "sons of God" in Genesis 6 could be easily agreed upon by biblical scholars—right?

Think again.

45

Killer Angels

*You can now understand why the passage is
the subject of so much modern scholastic angst.*

WITH THE INFORMATION FROM THE PRECEDING CHAPTER IN MIND, FOLLOWING
is how a number of well-known biblical scholars describe the terminology "sons of God" as it is used elsewhere in the Old Testament, as well as
how the ancient Jewish interpreters understood the context.

Dr. C. Fred Dickason, in his book, *Names of Angels*, explains it like
this:

> *Bene elohim* is a technical term *for angels* and is probably the
> sense in which "the sons of God" in Genesis 6 is used—Bene
> Elohim—*refers to angels* as a class of mighty ones or powers. It
> is used of angels in Job 1:6; 2:1; 38:7. Some say that this term is
> also used of God's own people; but close inspection of the pas-
> sages usually listed (Deuteronomy 14:1; Hosea 1:10; 11:1) will
> show that *the exact term is not bene elohim.*[255] (Emphasis added;
> parentheses in original)

There really is no reason to try to sanitize the passage to make it fit
our more modern and theologically delicate age. We simply need to let

the Bible mean what it means—especially when the context calls for that approach.

Following are several more explanations from three different genres of renowned biblical researchers—ancient, classical, and modern.

Cambridge Bible for Schools and Colleges:

This is one of the most disputed passages in the book [of Genesis]. But the difficulty, in a great measure, disappears, if it is frankly recognized, that the verse must be allowed to have its literal meaning.... Intermarriages took place between Heavenly Beings and mortal women.

"The sons of God" are not "sons of gods," in the sense of being their children, but "sons of Elohim" in **the sense of *belonging to the class of super-natural, or heavenly, beings*.**[256] (Emphasis added)

Jamieson, Fausset, and Brown Commentary:

The **term Nephilim**...is commonly traced to [Hebrew] *naapal*, to fall, and considered to signify either *fallen ones*, apostates, or falling upon others. In the first sense **many of the fathers** [ancient scholars of the first several centuries] *applied it to designate fallen angels*.[257] (Emphasis added)

Keil and Delitzsch:

[That "sons of God" in Genesis 6 means divine beings] may be defended on two plausible grounds: first, the fact that the "sons of God," in Job 1:6; Job 2:1, and Job 38:7, and in Daniel 3:25, *are unquestionably angels* (also יוב סילא in Psalm 29:1 and Psalm 89:7); and secondly, the antithesis, "sons of God" and "daughters of men." ...these two points *would lead us most naturally* to regard the "sons of God" *as angels*, in distinction from men and the daughters of men.[258] (Emphasis added; parentheses in original)

Guzik Bible Commentary:

The sons of God saw the daughters of men: It is more accurate to see the sons of God as either demons (angels in rebellion against God) or uniquely demon-possessed men, and the daughters of men as human women....

The phrase "sons of God" clearly refers to angelic creatures when it is used the three other times in the Old Testament (Job 1:6, 2:1, and 38:7). The translators of the *Septuagint translated sons of God as "angels."* They clearly thought it referred to *angelic beings, not people* descended from Seth.[259] (Emphasis added; parentheses in the original)

Barnes' Notes on the Bible (on the term "sons of God" from Job 38:7):

The sons of God—*Angels*—called **the sons of god** from their resemblance to him, or their being created by him.[260] (Emphasis added)

Matthew Poole's Commentary (on the term "sons of God" from Job 38:7):

The sons of God; *the blessed angels*; for man not being yet made, **God had then no other sons;** and *these are called the sons of God,* partly because they had their whole being from him, and partly because they were made partakers of his Divine and glorious image.[261] (Emphasis added)

The academically acclaimed biblical language professor and Bible scholar, Dr. Michael Heiser, who has an MA in ancient history and

Hebrew studies, along with a PhD in Hebrew Bible and Semitic languages, has this to say about the language of Genesis 6:

> **It might seem unnecessary to mention this,** given the enthusiasm many Bible readers have today for tapping into the Jewish mind to understand the words of Jesus and the apostles. **When it comes to Genesis 6:1–4,** though, that enthusiasm often sours, since **the result doesn't support the most comfortable modern Christian interpretation.** *The truth is* that the writers of the **New Testament know nothing of the Sethite view,** *nor of any view that makes the sons of God in Genesis 6:1–4 humans.*[262] (Emphasis added)

Myriad other prominent scholars have similar views of this passage. The interpretation of what we are looking at in the text of Genesis 6 is fairly undeniable. You can now understand why the passage is the subject of so much scholastic angst.

This interpretive anxiety is why most of the scholarly translations use the direct conversion from Hebrew to English and simply place the words "sons of God" in the text. In that way, the translators simply leave the matter up to the preachers, teachers, and scholars to battle—or ignore entirely, which, sadly, is often the case.

However, at least a few of the more modern translations dare to let the text speak for itself. I respect them for their academic courage. Have a look at a couple of examples:

International Standard Version:

> Some **divine beings** noticed how attractive human women were, so they took wives for themselves from a selection that pleased them.[263] (Emphasis added)

Good News Translation:

Some of the **heavenly beings** saw that these young women were beautiful, so they took the ones they liked.[264] (Emphasis added)

The New International Version:

The sons *of God* saw that the daughters *of humans*.[265] (Emphasis added)

Notice that the NIV doesn't use the term "angels" or "divine beings" for "sons of God." However, that translation does describe the women as the daughters *of humans*, which is faithful to the context of the original Hebrew. A clear juxtaposition is presented by the manner in which the translators of the NIV chose to render it. It is the same distinction that the ISV makes with its translation. At least nine of the top twenty scholarly translations of Scripture also make this distinction by using the word "humans."[266]

Abject Evil

If you've never explored this topic before, you probably just had the breath sucked out of your lungs.

In all fairness, I must tell you that there are other scholars who disagree with these explanations. However, I can also say that their arguments, in my studied opinion, are exegetically and linguistically feeble compared to those presented here. Again, as several scholars have noted, if we simply let the text say what it says in its proper context, the answer is right before us.

The long and short of it is this: Whatever was actually going on before the Flood, there can be no question that the exploits of those days held a level of wickedness unlike anything the newly created planet and human race had experienced. And, somehow, the fallen and rebellious angelic realm was directly responsible for that flood of malevolence that eventually permeated the entire global population.

Jesus said it will happen again.

46

Pervasive Degradation

*The result of that horrendously sweeping degradation
was that the earth itself had become ruined.*

THE NEW INTERNATIONAL VERSION OF THE BIBLE TRANSLATES THE HEBREW words in Genesis 6:13 in the following manner:

> So God said to Noah, "I am going to put an end to **all people**,
> for **the earth is filled with violence because of them**. I am surely
> going to destroy both them and the earth." (Emphasis added)

The phrase *all* "people" doesn't properly translate the fullness of the meaning of the Hebrew word used in the verse or the completed context of the rest of the account. And without those elements, we miss a key piece of information about the days of Noah. The word in question is *basar,* which most accurately translates as "flesh."[267]

All Flesh

In the Scriptures, *basar* is used to speak of either humans or animals—or, as the Genesis Flood narrative presents—*both* humans *and* animals.

Sometimes the word is used interchangeably within the same verse or adjacent verses.

Such is the case with Genesis 6:13. Just a few verses later, in Genesis 7, the context is more fully borne out. The same word *basar* is used:

> *Every* **living thing** [*basar*] that moved on land perished—birds, livestock, wild animals, *all* **the creatures** that swarm over the earth, *and* **all mankind**. *Everything* **on dry land that had the breath of life** in its nostrils died.
>
> *Every living thing* **on the face** [*basar*] of the earth was wiped out; *people and animals* and the **creatures that move along the ground and the birds** were wiped from the earth. Only Noah was left, and those with him in the ark. (Genesis 7:21–23; emphasis added)

This fact is why almost all of the more than two dozen top translations of the Bible translate Genesis 6:13 as God declaring that He is going to destroy *all* flesh, *every* living creature, or *everything* that has breath.[268]

To be sure, the Flood was in fact sent to eradicate the earth's human population. However, it was also designed to destroy every other living thing as well—except, of course, Noah, his family, and whatever animals God chose for the purpose repopulation.

What This Means

Understanding this important bit of information brings us to another huge clue as to the wickedness wrought by the rebellion of the fallen angelic realm. Whatever they were trying to accomplish, the planet had ultimately collapsed into a state wherein "all flesh" had become "corrupt." Therefore, "their ways" had become corrupt as well.

The Hebrew word represented in the English as the phrase "their *way*" is *derek*. That word means "to depart from the *natural order* of things," or "to depart from the acceptable 'manner' of life."[269]

The Hebrew word for "corrupt" is *shachath*. It means "to be marred or ruined," or, "to become spoiled—*defiled*."[270]

> And God **saw the earth**, and behold, **it was corrupt**, for **all flesh had corrupted** *their way* on the earth. (Genesis 6:12; emphasis added)

The word "corrupt" derives its original meaning from the Latin roots *cor*, "altogether," and *rumpere*, "break." In other words, God said that all life on earth had been "altogether broken."[271]

Putting the definitions of these words together in context communicates something along the lines of: "All flesh had become altogether broken and spoiled, thus everything that had breath, animal and human, had departed from the natural order that God had originally set for them."

Think of the implications of these discoveries. The result of that horrendously sweeping degradation was that the earth itself had become ruined and was filled with violence "because of the defilement of all flesh."

Something indescribably malevolent had been produced at the hands of the demonic interference spoken of in the opening words of Genesis 6. That demonic interference had been gladly accommodated by the degenerate humans of Noah's day. The entire creation was now culpable before its Creator.

This is certainly not the mere children's bedtime story often presented in today's church.

However, there's still another vital question we have yet to address.

47

The Elephant in the Room

And the angels who did not keep their positions of
authority but abandoned their proper dwelling.
—JUDE 1:6

THE NATURAL QUESTION THAT SHOULD FOLLOW FROM OUR STUDY THUS FAR might be stated as: "Precisely how *was* human flesh, as well as animal flesh, 'spoiled' or corrupted beyond hope? And did fallen divine beings actually engage in sexual relationships with human women?"

The honest conclusion is that the Bible doesn't give us a detailed answer. Genesis 6:2 only identifies that the *corruption* occurred through the rebellious interaction of the fallen angelic realm in conjunction with an element of cooperation from the human realm.

Also remember that, apparently, these two distinctive realms most likely weren't yet separated by the "invisibility" we now experience. It's a reasonable assumption that the two realms would have at least been entirely familiar with each other from before the time of the Fall in the Garden of Eden.

The topic we're currently investigating is difficult to consider, to be sure. Numerous scholars have struggled mightily with these same questions. Could it be that a certain class of angels was capable of sexually reproducing with humans before the days of the Flood? It *could* very well have been. We have no way of knowing, other than what the rather plain language of Genesis 6 appears to convey.[272]

Jude

Regarding this topic, we also have to deal with a couple of New Testament passages that a sizable number of highly respected scholars believe address the days of Noah, especially the unspecified "sin of Genesis 6."

First, let's have a look at Jude:

> **And the angels** who did not keep their positions of authority but **abandoned their proper dwelling**—these *he has kept* in darkness, bound with everlasting chains for judgment on the great Day. (Jude 1:6; emphasis added)

Meyer's New Testament Commentary:

> What Jude says of the angels corresponds with the doctrine of the angels[273] contained in the Book of Enoch.[274]
>
> Jude [speaks of] **a *definite class of angels*,** to whom, in agreement with the Book of Enoch, **he refers Genesis 6:2. This is correctly observed** by Hofmann, Wiesinger, and Schott, with whom Brückner appears to agree.[275] (Emphasis added)

Please take a moment and see my endnote regarding the Book of Enoch.[276] That noncanonical book—a work that is quoted, as well as being alluded to in the New Testament—presents the fallen angels of Genesis 6 as having had sexual relationships with certain human women. We also see this view reflected in the work of several renowned biblical scholars, as well as in the writings of a number of the most respected Jewish sages.

Gill's Exposition of the Entire Bible:

The Jews make this [sexual union with earthly women, before the Flood] to be **a sin of theirs** [the angels], and **so interpret Genesis 6:2.**[277] (Emphasis added)

Here is what the *Pulpit Commentary* has to say about Jude's declaration:

The sin alleged as the reason for the penalty which the writer recalls to the minds of his readers is that they **failed to keep...their proper habitation**; by which latter clause a descent to a **different sphere** *of being* is intended.... The reference, therefore, is taken to be to **the Jewish idea** *that amatory passion is not limited to the creatures of earth, and that some angels, yielding to the spell of the beauty of the daughters of men* [Genesis 6], *forsook their own kingdom, and entered unto unnatural relations with them.*[278] (Emphasis added)

Lange's Commentary on the Holy Scriptures: Critical, Doctrinal, and Homiletical asserts:

Their own habitation, *not heaven in general,* but **their own dwelling of light** [original bodies] assigned to them by the Creator. Their fall and guilt seem to have been the consequence of their **leaving that habitation** and arbitrarily going beyond the sphere allotted to them.

...*They made themselves at home on earth* and exchanged the power belonging to their vocation in heaven with an earthly exhibition of power *usurped for the sake of selfish sensual indulgence* [Genesis 6:2].[279] (Emphasis added)

It certainly appears that some type of reproductive interaction with the first vestiges of humanity might have been available to at least a *certain class* of the pre-Flood angelic realm.

However, there's still more that we need to examine.

48

The Sins of the Angels

*Much more than a faint hint...it's more akin to
an ear-piercing clap of thunder.*

IN THE BOOK OF 2 PETER, NOTE THAT PETER ALSO TIES THE "SINS OF THE angels" to the days of Noah, as well as to the days of Lot and the sins of Sodom and Gomorrah. He then ties *all of that* to "the corrupt desire of the flesh and the despising of authority."

Remember, Peter wouldn't have pulled this understanding from mere "tradition," and certainly he wouldn't have conjured it up from his own imagination. He lived and walked with Jesus for three full years, and was anointed to be the first pastor of the first church. Therefore, it seems quite likely that Peter received this information from the Lord Himself.

After all, Peter had been there when Jesus used the days of Noah and the days of Lot as an example of "how it would be" in the last days. He was also present when Jesus proclaimed that the last-days' judgment would be more tolerable for Sodom and Gomorrah on the day of judgment than for the wicked generation of Jesus' days on earth (Matthew 10:15; 11:24).

Following is Peter's explanation:

For **if God did not spare angels when they sinned**, but sent them to hell, putting them in chains of darkness to be held for judgment;

if he did not spare the ancient world when he brought the flood on its ungodly people, but protected Noah, a preacher of righteousness, and seven others;

if he condemned the cities of Sodom and Gomorrah by burning them to ashes, and made them an example of what is going to happen to the ungodly;

and if he rescued Lot, a righteous man, who was distressed by the depraved conduct of the lawless

(for that righteous man, living among them day after day, was tormented in his righteous soul by the lawless deeds he saw and heard)—

if this is so, then the Lord knows how to rescue the godly from trials and to hold the unrighteous for punishment on the Day of Judgment.

This is especially true of those who follow the corrupt desire of the flesh and despise authority. (2 Peter 2:4–10; emphasis added)

What do scholars say about Peter's declaration? Have a look at a few examples.

Cambridge Bible for Schools and Colleges:

[For if God spared not the angels that sinned] Here the nature of the sin is not specified. We may think either of **a rebellion of angels headed by Satan**…or of **the degradation of their spiritual nature** *by sensual lust, as in Genesis 6:2.* Looking to the more definite language of Jude, 2 Peter 2:6–8, where **the** *guilt of the angels is placed on a level with that of Sodom,* it **seems probable that** *the Apostle had the latter in his thoughts.*[280] (Emphasis added)

International Standard Bible Encyclopedia:

Most scholars…interpret "sons of God" as referring to supernatural beings in accordance with the meaning of the expression
in the other passages.

**The intention of the original writer…was to account for
the rise of the giant race of antiquity** by *the union* of demigods
[supernatural beings] with human wives.[281] (Emphasis added)

While *Peter Pett's Commentary on the Bible* is quite lengthy, it is well
constructed, and relates 2 Peter to several other passages. His conclu-
sions are remarkable:

The first example is **the angels who sinned before the Flood**
(Genesis 6:1-4). **They had followed "lascivious ways."** They
"saw that the daughters of men were fair, and took all whom
they chose" (Genesis 6:2).

It is clear that these are the angels described as "sons of God"
in Genesis 6:1–2 for a number of reasons. Firstly because *Peter
appears to be listing his illustrations in Biblical order*, thus angels
that were imprisoned because of their sin (2 Peter 2:4 compare
Genesis 6:1–2).

1. There is *no other mention* in Genesis of angels sinning.
Note also in respect to this how it is emphasized that both the
past destruction of the Flood and *the coming destruction by fire*
will affect "the heavens" as well as the earth (2 Peter 3:5; 2 Peter
3:7).

2. **Noah and the Flood of water** that destroyed the earth
(2 Peter 2:5 compare Genesis 6:5 to Genesis 8:22). Note also in
respect to this 2 Peter 3:5–6.

3. **Lot and the Destruction by fire** of Sodom and Gomorrah (2 Peter 2:6–8 compare Genesis 18–19). Note also in respect
to this 2 Peter 3:7; 2 Peter 3:10.

Thus three incidents in Genesis are given [by Peter] in order, and **in Genesis** there is **only one reference to angels sinning**.[282] (Emphasis, numerals 1–3, and brackets added; parentheses in the original)

The following is from the writings of the early church scholars. The article is titled *Fathers of the Third and Fourth Centuries—Lacantius*. It concerns the "sin of the angels" spoken of by Peter. These scholars wrote during the first few centuries of the early church's nascent beginnings.

When, therefore, the number of men had begun to increase, God in His forethought…sent angels for the protection and improvement of the human race; and inasmuch as He had given these a free will, He enjoined them above all things not to defile themselves with contamination from the earth, and thus lose the dignity of their heavenly nature.

He plainly prohibited them from doing that which He knew that they would do, that they might entertain no hope of pardon.

Therefore, *while they abode among men*, that most deceitful ruler of the earth, by his very association, gradually enticed them to vices, and *polluted them by intercourse with women*.[283]

And lastly, we look at *Meyer's New Testament Commentary*:

The nature of the sin is not stated; otherwise in Jude. What sin the apostle refers to is only *faintly hinted at* by the circumstance that the example of *the flood immediately follows*.[284]

I certainly agree with Meyer's final assessment of the matter, except… I would assert that the sin highlighted in Genesis 6—as we have now seen—appears to be much more than a faint hint.

It's more akin to an ear-piercing clap of thunder…for those with ears to hear.

49

Genesis 6 and Sodom

The similarities and the contextual connections between Jesus' words in Luke 17 with Genesis 6, Genesis 19, Jude 1, and 2 Peter 4 are uncanny.

WHEN WE EXAMINE THE GENESIS 19 ACCOUNT OF SODOM AND GOMORRAH, we discover that its focal point is sexual perversion of all kinds—especially the desire of the wicked men of the city of Sodom to engage in acts of sexuality with—*wait for it*—the angelic visitors.

Here we are forced to ask: Is the comparison of Sodom with Genesis 6 a mere coincidence in Peter's account, or is it something that he's using to highlight the focus of his teaching?

The importance of this line of questioning is further punctuated when we consider the fact that, in Noah's day, God found *only eight righteous people* to whom He would show mercy before He brought the Flood. All were from Noah's family. Likewise, in Sodom, God eventually demonstrated that there were *not even ten righteous people* still left in the city. Those were comprised of only Lot's family—Lot, his wife, and his two daughters. Lot tried to convince his two sons-in-law of the coming wrath, but they thought Lot had lost his mind. Their mockery cost them their lives.

Sound familiar?

To top it off, this is exactly how Jesus characterized *the last* of the last days. He said that those days would eventually become "just like" the days of Noah…*and* the days of Lot.

The similarities between Jesus' words in Luke 17 with Genesis 6, Genesis 19, Jude 1, and 2 Peter 4 are uncanny. I believe they are without coincidence.

Hey Jude

Jude, just like Peter, also makes the connection between the sin of the angels and the sin of Sodom and Gomorrah. In so doing, he ties the sin of the angels all the way back to Genesis 6.

Here's what Jude proclaimed:

And the angels who did not keep their positions of authority but abandoned their proper dwelling—these he has kept in darkness, bound with everlasting chains for judgment on the great Day.

In a similar way, **Sodom and Gomorrah** and the surrounding towns **gave themselves up to sexual immorality** and perversion. *They* **serve as an example** of those who suffer the punishment of eternal fire. (Jude 1:6–7; emphasis added)

Now, let's examine what several commentaries say about this passage. *Expositor's Bible Commentary*:

"Like them." [In a similar way] i.e. the fallen angels. **The two judgments are similarly joined…**

In the case of the angels the *forbidden flesh* (lit. "Other than that appointed by God") refers to the *intercourse with women;* [Genesis 6—*the only place* in the Bible where this is laid forth] in the case of Sodom to the departure from the natural use (Romans 1:27).[285] (Emphasis added; parentheses in the original)

Cambridge Bible for Schools and Colleges:

The words [of Jude 1:7] describe the form of evil for which the cities of the plain have become a byword of infamy. In saying that *this
sin was like that of the angels*, it is clearly implied that in the latter
case also there was a degradation of nature, such as is emphasized
in the words that "*the sons of God went in unto the daughters of men*"
(Genesis 6:4). *Impurity…is thought* of as *the leading feature in the
fall of the angels.*[286] (Emphasis added; parenthesis in the original)

International Standard Bible Encyclopedia:

This interpretation [sons of God = angelic beings] accords
with…Jude 1:6, where the unnatural sin of the men of Sodom
who *went after "strange flesh"* is compared with that of the angels
(compare 2 Peter 2:4 ff). (See Havernick, Introduction to the
Pentateuch; Hengstenberg on the Pentateuch, I, 325; Oehler,
Old Testament Theology, I, 196 f; Schultz, Old Testament Theology, I, 114 ff; Commentary on Genesis by Delitzsch, Dill-
mann, and Driver.)[287] (Emphasis added)

In my opinion, the *Pulpit Commentary's* explanation regarding Jude
offers the most logical grammatical way to interpret the Greek words of
the text. Also, it addresses those who attempt to sanitize Jude's words to
make them more palatable to preach from modern pulpits.

Pulpit Commentary:

This example [of Jude 1:7] is closely connected with the immediately preceding [Jude 1:6] by the way in which the verse opens;
which phrase expresses a likeness between the two cases, to wit,
between the reservation of those angels in bonds for the final
judgment, and the fate of those cities as subjects of the penal
vengeance of God.

The sin charged against these cities is stated in express terms to have been *the same in kind with that of the angels*—the indulgence of *passion contrary to nature*. They are described as having in *like manner with these* (that is, surely, *in like manner with these angels just referred to*; not, as some strangely imagine, with these men who corrupt the Church) *given themselves over to fornication*, and gone after strange flesh.

The verbs are selected to bring out the intense sinfulness of the sin—the one being a strong compound form expressing unreserved surrender, the other an equally strong compound form denoting a departure from the law of nature in the impurities practiced.[288] (Emphasis added; parenthesis in the original)

Detractors Have Trouble

Even though *Gill's Exposition* seems to prefer not to connect the "sin of the angels" with that of the people of Sodom and Gomorrah, as noted in a previous chapter, it still has to admit that this was indeed the prevailing interpretation of the most ancient of the Jews, right up until the time of Jesus and beyond.

Gill's Exposition of the Entire Bible:

The Jews make this [Sodom's sexual immorality] to be a sin of theirs [the angels], and so interpret Genesis 6:2.[289] (Emphasis added)

Meyer's NT Commentary appears to grapple with the same problematic position as *Gill's*. Consequently, author Heinrich Meyer also has that the similarity of Sodom to the sin of the angels did not exist, and he goes through great linguistic gymnastics to try to arrive at that conclusion. However, Meyer finally admits a rather inconvenient fact:

This interpretation was indeed understood by a number of the respected scholars of his day as the correct one:

> [The opening words of verse 7: "In the same manner"] *must refer to the angels* who, according to the Book of Enoch, **sinned in a similar way** as the inhabitants of those cities (**Thus say [the biblical scholars] Herder, Schneckenburger, Jachmann, de Wette, Arnaud, Hofmann,** *and others*).[290] (Emphasis added, parentheses in original).

The plain fact is that a number of non-Jewish scholars to this day have a tough time with Genesis 6, as well as with any suggestion that Jude and Peter lend understanding to its interpretation. So, they merely eliminate the original Jewish thought, then substitute the more "genteel" and "sophisticated" Gentile interpretation.

This is where a lot of the sanitizing and Scripture-scrubbing makes its way into today's pulpits, thus watering down the declaration of the abject evil that brought the Great Flood upon the earth.

Satan has to love it. It has taken a while, but the doctrines of his demons are finally taking hold in the greater part of today's church. Therefore, the depraved depths of the wickedness of our day escape its notice.

And God's people perish for a lack of knowledge.

50

Organic Manipulation

*Once again we find ourselves realizing that we are the very
first human generation to develop these techno marvels.*

I HAVE LONG BELIEVED THAT WE SHOULDN'T RULE OUT THE PRESENCE OF SOME
type of bio-manipulation processes that might have also (or *instead of*)
been used by the fallen ones spoken of in Genesis 6. Of course, the Bible
doesn't actually proclaim these ideas, at least not in today's terminology.

However, the truth is, we simply don't know—nor do we have any
way of knowing—exactly what knowledge the fallen realm might have
had before the Flood. And don't forget: From the beginning, it was a
certain "knowledge of good and evil" that Satan offered Adam and Eve.
He promised them that if they would only partake of that knowledge,
they could be "like the gods," or even like God Himself.[291]

It could have been that, with their superior knowledge of creation,
these fallen beings were involved in some type of human/animal genetic
manipulation experimentation. They might have been a part of Satan's
diabolical plan to biologically reengineer or reverse engineer what God
had originally designed. Perhaps they were attempting to create the
world's first human/animal *chimeras*?[292]

This potentiality certainly helps explain the description of those
days in Genesis 6:

The Lord saw how great the wickedness of the human race had become on the earth, and that every inclination of the thoughts of the human heart was only evil all the time. (Genesis 6:5)

Again, taking Jesus' clue about the last days as being "just like" the days of Noah, and then comparing those days to what's actually happening in our own day, it makes this possibility much easier to contemplate.

Remember, if Jude and 2 Peter really do refer to the fallen angels of Noah's day, as the preponderance of scholars suggest, then whatever they participated in was mind-blowingly evil. In case you're inclined to doubt that, think of the abject wickedness that currently prevails among the fallen ones. Now consider the fact that God still allows them a certain sphere of freedom in which to operate, until the Day of Judgment. Obviously, their current depravity doesn't even compare to what their counterparts did during Noah's day.

Now, there's something to reflect upon!

Unimaginable Evil

Then again, what Genesis 6 speaks about could also have been a mixture of both possibilities—antediluvian angel-to-human breeding, as well as some sort of demonic brand of genetic manipulation. We just don't know. We can only speculate.

However, whatever it was, the pertinent truth is that the demonic realm is most likely influencing today's technological uptick in the unnatural genetic engineering of humans and animals as well. After all, I can't imagine that humans alone have "discovered" these genome manipulation processes while the demonic world stands around scratching their collective heads in astonishment, saying, *"Gee! I never knew that! I'm so glad they showed us how to accomplish these technological wonders!"*

Demonically Manipulated

Think of today's relatively new CRISPR-cas9 technologies,[293] along with the aforementioned human/animal chimera (chimeras) technologies, as well as the human embryonic manipulation techniques that we have only recently acquired. While each of these technologies, and others of the same class, certainly holds great promise for producing useful procedures that could alleviate certain elements of suffering, they also have the potential for some of the vilest evil one could imagine. And, it's already beginning to happen. Even renowned medical schools, scientists, and doctors are beginning to speak out concerning the unthinkable evil that might be lurking right around the corner.[294]

Once again we find ourselves realizing that we are *the first human generation* to develop these techno marvels. It seems we are actually living out the resultant evils of the days of Noah, exactly as described in Genesis 6—the corruption of *all flesh* is right over the horizon of our own existence.

Let me remind you again of a portion of the *Guzik Bible Commentary* that we previously examined. I believe it lays out the only two real possibilities that make any sense, as far as our limited knowledge allows, as to how this evil might have begun within the pre-Flood days:

> Concerning… The sons of God saw the daughters of men: It is more accurate to see *the sons of God* as either demons (angels in rebellion against God) or uniquely demon-possessed men.[295] (Emphasis added; parenthesis in original)

Could this be at least a part of what Paul was warning about in his letter to Timothy?

> Now the Spirit expressly states that in later times some will abandon the faith to follow deceitful spirits and the teachings of

demons, influenced by the hypocrisy of liars, whose consciences are seared with a hot iron. (1 Timothy 4:1–2, Berean Study Bible)

What If It Were You?

The Bible tells us that Noah and his family were the only humans who had not been defiled or drastically altered by the demonic outpouring that had flooded the land.

To get a better perspective of the magnitude of that truth, imagine that our present earth age was finally at its end. What if you and your family were the only humans left on the entire planet who loved the Lord?

Further, what if your world openly comingled with those in the demonic realm, engaging in all kinds of perversions that were channeled through occult rituals and physical "contacts" made with the unseen realm? What if that kind of unspeakable wickedness and depravity were as commonplace as a tree growing on the side of the road? Welcome to Noah's world. And welcome to the raw edges of our own.

With these truths in focus, I would venture to say that the only "righteous family" that would be left upon the earth in the last days might be the genuine blood-bought, born-again family known as the *true Church*. You know…the one that Satan is now in the process of trying to shut down, and *shut up*.

Close the churches! Cover your mouths! Don't sing! Don't say "all lives matter"! Because they don't!

Don't celebrate the resurrection of Jesus! Don't celebrate the birth of the church! Going to church is mega dangerous! It's mega deadly! It's "unloving" toward your fellow humans for you to gather in worship!

Riots are okay. Casinos are just fine. Big-box stores are perfectly safe. Restaurants, bars, liquor stores, and gymnasiums are okay as well.

Just don't go to church!

Is today's world making a bit more sense now?

❖

PART EIGHT

The Visitors

They are demonic spirits that perform signs, and they go out to the kings of the whole world, to gather them for the battle on the great day of God Almighty.

—REVELATION 16:14

51

The Corrupting Visitation

*The falling away would slither its ways through
the halls of theological corruption by way
of deceivingly seductive "spirits."*

THE APOSTLE PAUL WARNS THAT FROM THE DAYS OF THE EARLY CHURCH FORWARD,
the institutional, visible church would be especially susceptible to horrific exploitation. History faithfully records that an ever-pervasive corruption has indeed taken place over the last two thousand years. We are
still watching it rip through the churches of the world like never before.

Paul never relented in trying to prepare the church for this certain
end-time truth.

- "The Spirit clearly says that in *later times* some will abandon the
  faith and follow *deceiving spirits* and *things taught by demons.*"[296]
  (1 Timothy 4:1; emphasis added)
- "For such men are *false* apostles, *deceitful* workers, *masquerad-
  ing* **as apostles of Christ**. And no wonder, for **Satan himself**
  masquerades **as an angel of light**. It is not surprising, then, if **his
  servants** *masquerade* as servants of righteousness." (2 Corinthians 11:13–14, Berean Study Bible; emphasis added)

263

- "The coming of the lawless one will be in accordance with how Satan works. He will use all sorts of displays of power through signs and wonders that serve the lie, and all the ways that wickedness deceives those who are perishing. They perish because they refused to love the truth and so be saved. For this reason God sends them a powerful delusion so that they will believe the lie and so that all will be condemned *who have not believed the truth* but have delighted in wickedness." (2 Thessalonians 2:9–12; emphasis added)

The Weakened Visible Church

However, those are not the only times Paul mentions this demonically induced "falling away." The apostle also emphasized in his letter to the church at Thessalonica that this demonic incursion would penetrate deep within the bowels of the visible church in the last days.

> Let no one in any way deceive you, for that day [the Day of the Lord (v. 2)—the return of Christ] will not come unless **the apostasy** [falling away from biblical truth] **comes first**, and the **man of lawlessness is revealed**, the **son of destruction**. (2 Thessalonians 2:3, NAS; emphasis added)

Between Paul's letter to Timothy and his letters to the churches at Corinth and Thessalonica, we understand that a weak and deceived visible church would be one of the primary characteristics of the last days. The falling away would slither its way through the halls of theological corruption by way of deceivingly seductive spirits.

That demonic power would entice church leaders to ultimately pass along what would amount to nothing less than the teachings of the demonic realm. The result would be the straying of professors, commentators, preachers, teachers, and everyday church members away from God's plain truth and into dark error. Just like in the Garden of Eden. And just like in the days of Noah.

But in 2020, the promised end-time demonic visitation began to get personal.

52

In the Temple of God

*One might have assumed that every church in the world
would have understood this fulfillment of Scripture.*

IN 2 THESSALONIANS 2:4, JUST ONE VERSE AFTER THE PASSAGE WE EXAMINED
in the previous chapter, Paul reminds the church of another last-days
global phenomenon, one that actually happened for the first time, at
least in its beginning stages, in the year 2020.

Have a look at Paul's ominous warning:

> He [the Antichrist, the man of lawlessness, the son of destruc-
> tion] will oppose and **will exalt himself over everything that is
> called God** or is worshiped, so that **he sets himself up in God's
> temple, proclaiming himself to be God.** (2 Thessalonians 2:4;
> emphasis added)

In my previous book, *Masquerade: Preparing for the Greatest Con
Job in History,* I laid out a detailed study of this passage, taking almost
a dozen chapters to do so. In that effort, I demonstrated, through the
works of myriad commentators dating from the first century all the way
into our day, as well as through in-depth Greek word studies, that this

verse has nothing to do with a rebuilt Temple on the Temple Mount in Jerusalem—as it is often interpreted today.

But, here's the inescapable fact: In every New Testament book that Paul wrote, when he used the specific Greek words translated as "temple of God" or "God's temple," he unmistakably was speaking of *the Church*.

Additionally, the apostle used an exclusive Greek word when addressing the topic. (Please see endnotes for further explanation, as well as for a sizable sample of the commentary on this subject. If you've never seen this revelation before, you'll be stunned.)[297] The greater point is that the implications of that revelation are profound, especially for our own day. Think again of the opening chapters of this book. We're now witnessing and living in the midst of the "spirit" Paul warned us about: "He will set himself up in the temple of God, claiming himself to be God."

Do Not Stop Meeting

Notice what the Holy Spirit commands the church regarding the last days, especially when all hell is breaking loose upon the planet:

> And let us consider how we may spur one another on toward love and good deeds, *not giving up meeting together*, as some are in the habit of doing, but encouraging one another—**and *all the more*** as you *see the Day*[298] *approaching*. (Hebrews 10:24–25; emphasis added)

This is the time when we are to be the most vigilant in continuing to assemble as the church, the one against which Jesus proclaimed that the gates of hell would not prevail. We are *not* to give in to fear. We are *not* to stop worshiping together, even if we have to do it "underground," as our brethren all over the world have done for centuries.

Worship Us or Don't Eat

By late July 2020, China, home to the second-largest Christian population in the world,[299] was again cracking down on believers—this time
with a particularly insidious vengeance.

The *Daily Wire* issued the dire news with this headline, "China
Forces Christians to Renounce Faith, Destroy Christian Symbols or Be
Cut off from Welfare, Reports Say."

> The Chinese Communist Party (CCP) is reportedly forcing
> people of faith to renounce their beliefs and replace religious
> symbols and imagery with portraits of Chairman Mao and Pres-
> ident Xi Jinping.[300]
>
> A local pastor, one targeted by the Chinese government,
> explained, "The government is trying to eliminate our belief
> *and wants to become God instead of Jesus.*"[301] (Emphasis added)

The basic message of the Chinese government to the tens of millions
of its Christian citizens was: *Acknowledge your government as God, or you
won't eat.* In other words, the government of China was setting itself
up in the "temple of God," proclaiming itself to "be God." This wasn't
much different, at least in spirit, than what was happening across the
United States of America, even in the heart of the Bible Belt, beginning
in 2020.

Think of it. We've already listed and referenced the number of
times the globalists have asserted the promise and power of their
desired COVID-19 *vaccine solution.* It's always coupled with the assertion that once they've distributed the vaccine on a large enough scale,
they can then begin "biologically monitoring" who's had the vaccine
and who hasn't, and where we can and cannot go without it. They'll
do it with special "scanning" equipment. So, if those global masters
decide you have to take a vaccine in order to go to church, who will
monitor everyone coming in and out of our church facilities, services,

programs, and mission excursions? You guessed it. "They" will be the "ones."

Nothing to see here. *Right?*

The "Man" of Lawlessness

In 2020, the "spirit" of *the man of lawlessness* genuinely set itself up as "God" over the churches of the world and demanded that we obey. And the vast majority of the churches did so. This was a time of testing. This was a time of sifting. They will soon demand even more of God's people—even a "mark" (Revelation 13–14).

One might have assumed that every church in the world would have understood this pervasive new spirit to be a prophetic disclosure dropped right in their laps. However, since we're living in the days of Noah, hardly a soul noticed. Most preachers never mentioned what was happening to our Chinese brothers and sisters, much less to our own churches. Most simply went on eating and drinking. A large number of Christians actually celebrated the church's downtime that was ushered in by the *fear-demic* of our time.

The church had been duped. This was probably because a number of them had been taught all their lives that Paul's warning of the man of lawlessness "setting himself up in the temple of God" had something to do with a rebuilt Third Temple in Jerusalem, and *not the last-days' church.*

So, a large portion of the world's churches fell dangerously susceptible to the delusion of our day. As a result, Christians turned against Christians in the midst of the chaos and media-driven fear.

And that's how it happens.

53

The Day of Evil

We will either choose to stand against the evil
that comes to us, or we succumb to it.

EVEN THOUGH THE GENERAL UNDERSTANDING OF PAUL'S WARNING TO THE church in the sixth chapter of Ephesians is enormously helpful regarding our everyday Christian life, this is not the central concern of his instruction.

In that passage, Paul is actually emphasizing a particular day. Verse 13 identifies it as "the day of evil." Have a look:

Finally, **be strong in the Lord** and in his mighty power.

Put on *the full armor of God*, so that you can **take your stand** against the devil's schemes.

For our struggle is not against flesh and blood, but against the rulers, against the authorities, against the powers of this dark world and against the spiritual forces of evil in the heavenly realms.

Therefore put on *the full armor of God*, so **that when the** *day of evil* **comes,** you may be **able to stand** your ground, and after you have done everything, to stand.

Stand firm then, with the belt of truth buckled around your waist, with the breastplate of righteousness in place,

and with your feet fitted with the readiness that comes from the gospel of peace.

In addition to all this, take up the shield of faith, with which you can extinguish all the flaming arrows of the evil one.

Take the helmet of salvation and the sword of the Spirit, which is the word of God.

And pray in the Spirit on all occasions with all kinds of prayers and requests. With this in mind, be alert and always keep on praying for all the Lord's people. (Ephesians 6:10–18; emphasis added)

The Day of Evil

Have a look at what several of the most renowned classical scholars have to say regarding the "day of evil" phrase:

Meyer's New Testament Commentary:

The *evil day* here *manifestly appears* as a *peculiar* and still *future* day…. Hence also *not: every day*, on which the devil has special power; but the emphatic designation [in the Greek language] could suggest to the reader only a single, morally evil, day well known to him, and that is the day in which the *Satanic power puts forth its last and greatest outbreak.*[302] (Emphasis added)

Expositor's Greek Testament:

The times immediately preceding the Parousia [the Second Coming of Jesus]…and the searching day of the future in which the *powers of evil will make their last and greatest effort.*[303] (Emphasis added)

Cambridge Bible for Schools and Colleges:

Some expositors see here a reference to *the final conflict of the Church*.[304] (Emphasis added)

McLaren's Exposition asserts that this passage also connects the meaning of "the day of evil" to the times in which Jesus and Paul spoke concerning the very last days just before the Second Coming of the Lord.

McLaren accomplishes this goal by using the well-known phrases "when we look not for it" (Matthew 24:24) and "at what hour the thief would come" (Matthew 24:43). Both, in their original contexts, are direct connections to the return of Jesus, and are spoken by Jesus Himself.

For these reasons, then, because **the "evil day" will certainly come,** because **it may come at any time,** and because it is **most likely to come "when we look not for it,"** it is the dictate of plain common sense to be prepared.

If the good man of the house had known at what hour the thief would have come, he would have watched; but he would have been a wiser man if he had watched all the more, because he did not know at what hour the thief would come.[305] (Emphasis added)

The Daily Battle

Suffice it to say, the general teaching of Ephesians 6 truly applies to *every age,* and to every Christian's specific journey through life. Our lives are filled with many "days of evil" against which we must take our stand. We will either choose to stand against the evil that comes to us or we will succumb to it. If we are to successfully stand against it, we must stand in the power of the name of Jesus Christ and be suited up in the *armor of God.*

However, it appears to be obvious that this warning speaks of the last days and the outpouring of wickedness that will come upon the earth in that epic period of human history, the likes of which we have never seen before.

It speaks of the days when the fallen ones will be ripped from their numinous spheres of cloaked operations.

In that "day" the curtains will be opened.

It will truly be *the day of evil.*

54

Casting Down

He was hurled to the earth, and his angels with him.
—REVELATION 12:9

REVELATION 12 IS A PANORAMIC VISION GIVEN TO JOHN WHILE HE WAS ON THE island of Patmos. The imagery of that chapter covers from the opening pages of Genesis—the fall of humanity wrought by the wiles of Satan—through to the very last days—that period known as "the days of evil."

In fact, the purpose of Revelation 12 is to set up the fullest understanding of Revelation 13. That chapter famously reveals the horrific, demon-possessed days of Antichrist, the days that are to fall upon the earth just before the return of Jesus Christ. That time of human history and the years leading up to it will be the epitome of the "days of evil" spoken of by the apostle Paul in Ephesians 6.

Have a look at the following segment of Revelation 12. Notice how often we are told that Satan and the demonic realm will "come down" to be among us:

The great dragon was hurled down—that ancient serpent called the devil, or Satan, who leads the whole world astray. He was hurled to the earth, and his angels with him.

Then I heard a loud voice in heaven say: "**Now have come the salvation** and the power and **the kingdom of our God, and the authority of his Messiah.** For **the accuser** of our brothers and sisters, who accuses them before our God day and night, *has been hurled down*.... But **woe to the earth** and the sea, because **the devil** *has gone down* **to you! He is filled with fury,** because **he knows that his time is short."** (Revelation 12:9, 10, 12; emphasis added)

Now, have a look at several commentaries' understanding of that passage:

Barnes' Notes on the Bible:

He was cast out into the earth...was cast down to the earth, where he is permitted for a time to carry on his warfare against the church.... This refers to the period when there were indications that God was about to set up his kingdom on the earth.

And his angels [demons] were cast out with him...the followers in the revolt shared the lot of the leader, and that **all who rebelled** *were ejected* from *heaven* [all of the dimensions that are unseen and unreachable by earthbound humanity].[306] (Emphasis added)

In the following,[307] the day of evil is equated with that period specified in Revelation 12.

Arno Gaebelein's Annotated Bible:

The Scriptures clearly teach that there is a vast dominion of darkness over which Satan is the head and that, as the god of this present age, he has rulers over this world and a large army of wicked spirits in the heavenlies....

But a day is coming when the old serpent, called the devil and Satan, will be *cast out into the earth and his angels with him*....

This will happen according to the Apocalypse (Revelation 12:1–17)… Then the heavenlies will be cleared of their wicked and unlawful occupants. *They will be forced to the earth*, where Satan for a brief period will exhibit his great wrath and institute the great tribulation…. All this we know from God's revelation, and it is a solemn revelation.

The rulers of darkness of this world, the wicked spirits, do all in their power to keep a lost world, *with its supposed progress and scientific discoveries*, in ignorance and darkness about themselves.[308]

It seems we've uncovered yet another clear biblical truth that, to the ultimate detriment of today's church, is seldom discussed in Bible studies or preached from our pulpits.

But, this matter goes much deeper than you might imagine.

55

The Shaking

*It is one universal shaking of all this our world and the
heavens over it, of which the prophet speaks.*[309]

THE "CASTING DOWN" OF THE DEMONIC REALM INTO THE HUMAN WORLD IN
the last days is a subject that stretches from the Old to the New Testaments. And it certainly seems to correspond with everything we've
learned about the original days of Noah as well.

Let's explore an example of this type of prophetic connection that
carries that message. Our illustration comes from the Old Testament
book of Haggai.

Seen but Unknown

The prophet Haggai is warning the people of his time that soon the
Lord would discombobulate their world until it became a thing beyond
their recognition. This divine shaking would involve powers that were
being influenced by diabolical influencers of iniquity for the purpose of
affecting Israel's ultimate overthrow.

As previously noted, in this passage we again find what theologians
call a *compound prophecy*, a relatively common biblical phenomenon.[310]

In other words, the Lord of Hosts is using the current events of the prophet's own lifetime to also leave a word of prophecy for those of the Church Age in the last days. What was happening in Haggai's time, as horrific as it was, would only be a microcosm of what was ultimately to come at the end of the ages.

Take special note of Haggai's use of the word "shake," because we'll see it again throughout the New Testament.

> For thus says the Lord of hosts, "Once more in a little while, I am going to *shake the heavens* and the earth, the sea also and the dry land. **I will shake *all* nations**, and *what is desired by all nations will come*, and I will fill this house with glory," says the LORD Almighty. (Haggai 2:6–7; emphasis added)

Barnes' Notes on the Bible gives further understanding of the ultimate shaking to which Haggai refers:

> It is one universal shaking of all this our world and the heavens over it, of which the prophet speaks.
>
>   He **does not speak only of Luke 21:25** "signs in the sun and in the moon and in the stars," which might be, and yet the frame of the world itself might remain. *It is a shaking,* **such as would *involve the dissolution of this our system*,** as Paul draws out its meaning; **Hebrews 12:27**.[311] (Emphasis added)

Barnes' Notes confirms how other prophecies in the Old Testament that follow a similar nature of Haggai's have a much farther vision than just the prophet's own time.

> **Prophecy, in its long perspective,** uses a continual foreshortening, **speaking of things in relation to their eternal meaning and significance,** as to that which shall survive, when heaven and earth and even time shall have passed away.

It blends together the beginning and the earthly end; the preparation and the result; the commencement of redemption and its completion; our Lord's coming in humility and in His Majesty. *Scarcely any prophet but exhibits things in their intrinsic relation, of which time is but an accident.*[312] (Emphasis added)

This phenomenon—concerning the prophets themselves often being unaware of all the details regarding the distant future—is precisely what the apostle Peter told us:

Concerning this salvation, the prophets, who spoke of the grace that was to come to you, searched intently and with the greatest care, trying to find out the time and circumstances to which the Spirit of Christ in them was pointing when he predicted the sufferings of the Messiah and the glories that would follow....

It was revealed to them that they were *not serving themselves but you,* when they spoke of the things that have now been told you by those who have preached the gospel to you by the Holy Spirit sent from heaven. Even angels long to look into these things. (1 Peter 1:10–12; emphasis added)

Above all, you must understand that **no prophecy of Scripture came about by the prophet's own interpretation of things.**

For prophecy never had its origin in the human will, but prophets, though human, **spoke from God as they were carried along by the Holy Spirit.** (2 Peter 1:20–21; emphasis added)

It would seem that Haggai was not only shown the prophetic outcome of his own day, but apparently, he saw our days as well. However, he wasn't the only one who was allowed that glimpse.

56

Falling Stars

Now when we read passages about stars
falling from the heavens, the meaning
of the phrase ought to be rather obvious.

THE NEW TESTAMENT ALSO EMPLOYS THE LANGUAGE OF "SHAKING" TO REFER
TO the last days, just before the return of Jesus. Even the writer of the
New Testament book of Hebrews quotes from that passage in Haggai,
relating it to the "shaking" of the last days.

> And His voice shook the earth then, but now He has promised,
> saying, "**Yet once more *I will shake* not only the earth, but *also*
> *the heaven*.**" (Hebrews 12:26–27; emphasis added)

There is no doubt that at the end of all current earthly things and the
beginning of the state of the ultimate restored paradise, everything will
be made new. This will include the earth, the literal heavenly bodies, and
all that has been corrupted by Satan's presence among them. However,
these "shakings" spoken of throughout the Scriptures also have another
significant meaning.

First, have a look at a couple of other fairly well-known New Testament passages. Notice again the use of the word "shaken." Practically all

of the most reliable scholars believe these two passages are speaking of the same event—the days just before the return of Jesus Christ, the days of Noah.

Matthew 24:29:

Immediately after the distress of those days the sun will be darkened, and the moon will not give its light; the *stars will fall* from the sky, and *the heavenly bodies will be shaken.* (Emphasis added)

Mark 13:25:

The stars will fall from the sky, and the heavenly bodies *will be shaken.* (Emphasis added)

Luke 21:26:

Men fainting from fear and the expectation of the things which are coming upon the world; for *the powers* of the heavens *will be shaken.* (Emphasis added)

The Scholars Speak

Here's what several scholars have to say about these verses:
Bengal's Gnomen:

Those firm inter-chained and **subtle *powers of heaven* (distinct from the stars) which are accustomed to influence the earth.** [The demonic realm]… are thus denominated by Matthew, Mark, and Luke….

A *number of the earliest commentators*, and *many that followed* them, took this passage to refer to *the cosmic battle* in the heavenly realms. *The fallen ones* in the *last days* will ramp up their assault against the throne of God.[313] (Emphasis added; parenthesis in the original)

Meyer's New Testament Commentary:

The interpretation of Olshausen, who follows Jerome, Chrysostom, Euthymius Zigabenus, in supposing that **the trembling in the *world of angels* is referred** to (Luke 2:13).[314] (Emphasis added; parenthesis in the original)

Pulpit Commentary:

We must notice the *spiritual application* of this prediction, as it has obtained a wide acceptance. "The powers of the heavens" are the *hosts of the prince of the power of the air,* "the *spiritual wickedness in high places;*" the stars are all that exalt themselves, who shall be consumed and vanish at the brightness of the cross.[315] (Emphasis added)

Thayer's Greek Lexicon:

These heavens are opened by being cleft asunder, and from the upper heavens, or *abode of heavenly beings, come down upon earth*—now the Holy Spirit, Matthew 3:16; Mark 1:10; Luke 3:21; John 1:32; *now angels,* John 1:51 (52); and now in vision *appear to human sight* some of the *things within the highest heaven,* Acts 7:55; Acts 10:11, 16; through the aerial heavens sound voices, which are uttered in the heavenly abode: Matthew 3:17; Mark 1:11; Luke 3:22; John 12:28; 2 Peter 1:18.[316] (Emphasis added)

Cambridge Bible for Schools and Colleges (Luke 21:26):

The powers of heaven, i.e. the "bright dynasts"—**the Hosts of the Heavens** [denoting the cosmic war of all the angelic powers of heaven, obedient and fallen.][317] (Emphasis added)

Thayer's Greek Lexicon (Luke 21:26):

[Gk. Dunamis] Power consisting in or resting upon *armies, forces, hosts,* hence, the *host of heaven, hebraistically* [stated as] *the stars*: Matthew 24:29; Luke 21:26; and, Mark 13:25.[318] (Emphasis added)

The Fallen Ones

From now on when we read passages about stars falling from the heavens, the meaning of the phrase ought to be obvious. If we let the Bible interpret the Bible first, our task is made much easier.

Have another look at that "shaking" verse from Mark 13. Notice what it says about the "stars."

The stars will fall from the sky, and the heavenly bodies will be shaken. (Mark 13:25; emphasis added)

Where else do we hear that language concerning the "stars"? We see it several times in the book of Revelation. And in these instances, the text itself tells us what the *stars* actually represent.

- "**The mystery of the seven stars** that you saw in my right hand and of the seven golden lampstands is this: **The seven** *stars are the angels* of the seven churches" (Revelation 1:20; emphasis added).
- "His tail swept *a third of the stars* **out of the sky** and *flung them to the earth*.... The great **dragon was** *hurled down*—that

ancient serpent called the devil, or **Satan**, who leads the whole world astray. **He was** *hurled to the earth, and his angels* [the fallen stars] **with him**" (Revelation 12:4, 9; emphasis added).

- **"The fifth angel** sounded his trumpet, and I **saw** *a star that had fallen* from the *sky to the earth*. The **star** *was given the key* **to the shaft** of the Abyss. *When he* [the star, or fallen angel] opened the Abyss, smoke rose from it like the smoke from a gigantic furnace" (Revelation 9:1–2; emphasis added).

Here's the takeaway. In the last days, angelic warfare will erupt in the dimensions of the heavenly realms like never before. Fallen angels will be flung down to the earth among humanity. Satan himself will be among them.

Whether these fallen ones will be made physically manifest to humanity or remain largely cloaked as they are now is yet to be revealed. Regardless, the "casting down" of an unprecedented demonic outpouring in the last days cannot be denied. All of this, once again, reflects the imagery of Genesis 6 and the original days of Noah.

However, every day that passes during that coming time will bring the evil one that much closer to his ultimate demise.

He will be filled with rage because of it.

57

From The Heart of the Earth

The pronouncement of the event is so powerful,
and made so often, that we must take it
to mean something unprecedented.

YET ANOTHER PORTENTOUS PASSAGE ALSO COMES FROM THE BOOK OF Revelation. Scholars connect it to the same *last-days* manifestations that are referenced in Revelation 12, as well as the other New Testament passages we examined in the last chapter.

I am now referring to the abyss of Revelation 9. Consider the defining portions of that passage and notice the personification of a fallen "star":

> The fifth angel sounded his trumpet, and I saw a star that had fallen from the sky to the earth.
>
> **The star was given the key** to the shaft of the Abyss. **When he opened the Abyss,** smoke rose from it like the smoke from a gigantic furnace.
>
> The sun and sky were darkened by the smoke from the Abyss. **And out of the smoke** *locusts came down on the earth* and were given power like that of scorpions of the earth....
>
> They had *as king over them the angel of the Abyss,* whose name in Hebrew is Abaddon and in Greek is Apollyon (that is, *Destroyer*). (Revelation 9:1–3, 11; emphasis added)

Locust Imagery

Let's see what a number of respected scholars have to say about this passage. Notice again, we are introduced to an unthinkable demonic manifestation. These are specifically last-days manifestations of a ferociously demonic outpouring.

Expositor's Greek New Testament:

The dense smoke resolves itself into **a swarm of *infernal demons*** in ***the form of locusts*** but rendered more formidable by **their additional power** of stinging like scorpions.[319] (Emphasis added)

Ellicott's Commentary for English Readers (Revelation 9:3):

Their power to torment men is the prominent idea. The locusts are ***not literal locusts*....** The scorpion-like power seems to depict ***a malicious energy***, as the locusts depict a ***devastating multitude*.**[320] (Emphasis added)

Matthew Henry's Concise Commentary:

Out of this smoke there came a swarm of locusts, *emblems of the devil's agents*, who promote superstition, idolatry, error, and cruelty.[321] (Emphasis added)

Geneva Study Bible:

A description of the ***malignant spirits invading the world***, taken from their nature, power, form and order.... For our battle is not here with flesh and blood, **but with powers Ephesians 6:12.**

   This place of *the power of the devils*, generally noted in this verse, is particularly declared afterwards in Revelation 9:4–6.[322] (Emphasis added)

Ellicott's Commentary for English Readers (Revelation 9:11):

The great battle is not on the surface only, the invasions, revolutions, tyrannies, which try and trouble mankind, **involve *spiritual principles*** [fallen angels] and are but tokens of the great conflict between the spirit of destruction and the spirit of salvation, between Christ and Belial, God and Mammon, the Prince of this world and the Prince of the kings of the earth.[323] (Emphasis added)

Meyer's New Testament Commentary:

An express contrast between Apollyon the Destroyer, and Jesus the Saviour, **can be found only by those who understand the former as Satan himself.**[324] (Emphasis added)

The *Commentary Critical and Explanatory on the Whole Bible* also makes a direct connection of Revelation 9 with Revelation 12 and Isaiah 14:

This is **a connecting link** of this fifth trumpet **with Revelation 12:8 Revelation 12:9 Revelation 12:12,** "Woe to the inhabiters of the earth, for **the devil** is come down," &c. **Compare Isaiah 14:12,** "How art thou **fallen from heaven, Lucifer,** son of the morning!"
     The *locusts are supernatural instruments* [demons and demon-possessed humans] **in the hands of Satan** to torment.[325] (Emphasis added)

Inter-Varsity Press New Testament Commentary Series:

The "authority" or power is that of scorpions (v. 3), and the strange *demonic locusts* that wield this authority use it precisely **to harm or injure human beings** (v. 4).[326] (Emphasis added)

Expository Notes of Dr. Thomas Constable:

Probably *these are demons* who assume some of the characteristics of locusts. [Note: Moffatt, 5:406; Mounce, p194; Ladd,
p131.] **Spirit beings later appear as frogs** (Revelation 16:13).[327]

Pulpit Commentary:

"The angel" evidently, points to the star of ver. 1, **who is *Satan
himself*. ...He is the "destroyer,"** the one who causes "perdi-
tion" to mankind. Reference the words of our Lord given by St.
John (John 8:44), **"He was a murderer from the beginning."**[328]
(Emphasis added)

Thayer's Greek Lexicon:

The Abyss: The *abode of demons*, Luke 8:31; Revelation 9:1;
Revelation 9:11; Revelation 11:7; Revelation 17:8; Revelation
20:1, 3.[329] (Emphasis added)

According to the Word of God, in the last days, during the days of
unmitigated evil, there will be a great "dislodging" in the unseen realms
of iniquity. In addition to the shaking of the heavens above, in Revelation 9 we're also told that the earth itself is opened up and the demonic
within it arise. That demonic appearance would then become a type
of manifestation on earth unlike anything humanity has ever experienced, at least since the times of Noah's day—and it would occur in
those "days" right before the return of Jesus.

Notice the emphasized words in the following:

- **"If those days** had not been cut short, no one would survive, but
  for the sake of the elect those days will be shortened" (Matthew
  24:22; emphasis added).

- **"For in those days** there will be tribulation unmatched from the beginning of God's creation until now, and never to be seen again" (Mark 13:19, Berean Study Bible; emphasis added).
- **"Men's hearts failing them for fear**, and for looking after those **things which are coming on the earth**: for the powers of heaven shall be shaken" (Luke 21:26, KJV; emphasis added).
- **"There will be a time** of distress **such as has not happened from the beginning of nations until then"** (Daniel 12:1; emphasis added).
- **"But mark this**: There will be *terrible times* **in the last days"** (2 Timothy 3:1; emphasis added).
- **"As long as it is day**, we must do the works of him who sent me. **Night is coming**, when no one can work. While I am in the world, I am the light of the world" (John 9:4–5; emphasis added).

The difference between the end-time repeat of the "days of Noah" and the original event that commenced in Genesis 6 is that in the last days, the fallen "sons of God" don't willfully and rebelliously cross their boundaries in order to "come down" among humanity. This time they are cast down to the earth and summoned up from the unseen realms.

In those horrific "days" and the years leading up to them, how are we to stand? And with *what* exactly should we be equipped in order to take that stand?

Now, we enter into the realm of the armor of God.

58

Clothed in Power

This had to have been the passage from which Paul,
a former Pharisee and Jewish rabbi, was bringing
forth the metaphor for the early church.

TWICE IN EPHESIANS 6:10–14 WE ARE TOLD TO PUT ON THE "ARMOR OF GOD."

That same passage also asserts that if we will wear the true armor of God, we will be equipped to "take our stand" against that unprecedentedly ominous day of evil. This promise is repeated four different times.

So what is the "armor of God" of which Paul speaks? When examining Ephesians 6 by itself, a sizable number of the major commentaries speculate that he must have been describing the armor of a Roman soldier.

Meyer's New Testament Commentary:

The Roman soldiery wielded the power in all the provinces, Paul himself was surrounded by Roman soldiery…the term [armor] could not but call up the thought of the Roman soldier.[330]

Expositor's Greek Testament:

No doubt the Roman soldier is particularly in view. Paul, the Roman citizen, would think of him, and it was the Roman military power that filled the eye where Paul labored and wrote.[331]

At first glance, that Roman armor assumption seems logical. But, according to Scripture itself, this is not the imagery upon which Paul based his exhortation to the church. He didn't say "put on the armor of the Roman legions." He didn't say "put on the armor of the gladiators." He was emphatic in his command; he asserted twice that it is *God's armor* with which we are to adorn ourselves.

The Answer

There is a striking passage in the Old Testament, found in Isaiah 59, wherein Yahweh declares that He is adorning Himself with certain articles of armor for a uniquely specific purpose. He's preparing Himself to engage in a righteous battle.

This had to have been the passage from which Paul, a former Pharisee and Jewish rabbi, was bringing the metaphor for the early church's edification.

The Lord looked and was displeased that there was no justice. **He saw that there was no one**, he was appalled that there was no one to intervene; **so his own arm achieved salvation** for him, and **his own righteousness** sustained him.

He [the Lord] put on righteousness as his breastplate, and the helmet of salvation on his head; he put on the garments of vengeance and wrapped himself in zeal as in a cloak.

According to what they have done, so will he repay wrath to his enemies and retribution to his foes; he will repay the islands their due.

From the west, people will fear the name of the Lord, and from the rising of the sun, they will revere his glory. **For he will come *like a pent-up flood*** that the breath of the Lord drives along.

The Redeemer will come to Zion, to those in Jacob who repent of their sins. (Isaiah 59:15–20; emphasis added)

I love verse 20 of Isaiah 59! It foretells the coming of Jesus Christ, "the Redeemer" who will come first to Israel (i.e., Zion and Jacob). *Benson Commentary*:

Isaiah 59:20–21. And, or, moreover, **the Redeemer** shall come to Zion — To Jerusalem, or to his church, often signified by Zion, **namely**, *Christ shall come*, of whom the apostle expounds it, Romans 11:26.[332] (Emphasis added)

Scholarly Attestation

Now, have a look at what several of the classical commentators say about Isaiah 59 in relation to the armor of Paul's instructions in Ephesians 6.[333]

Lange's Commentary on the Holy Scriptures: Critical, Doctrinal, and Homiletical:

This is the original source of the Apostle Paul's extended description *of the spiritual armor*, Ephesians 6:14; Ephesians 6:17. Also in 1 Thessalonians 5:8 there underlies the *same representation of the equipment* required by Christians.[334] (Emphasis added)

Ellicott's Commentary for English Readers:

The close parallelism with…Ephesians 6:14-17 suggests a *new significance* for St. Paul's *"whole armor of God."*[335] (Emphasis added)

Cambridge Bible for Schools and Colleges:

The fully developed image of His arming Himself with His own attributes has no exact parallel in the O.T. (cf. however, Ch. Isaiah 11:5). *It is reproduced* and *further elaborated* in the N. T.

it suggests *the figure of the Christian armor* (Ephesians 6:14 ff.;
1 Thessalonians 5:8).[336] (Emphasis added)

Barnes' Notes on the Bible:

Paul (in Ephesians 6:14–17; compare 2 Corinthians 6:7) has
carried it out to greater length, and introduced more particu-
lars in the description of the spiritual armor of the Christian.[337]
(Emphasis added)

Gill's Exposition of the Entire Scripture:

The apostle has *borrowed these phrases* from hence, and *applied
them to the* Christian armor, Ephesians 6:14.[338] (Emphasis added)

Biblical Illustrator:

Just as in Ephesians 6:1–24. The manifold self-manifestations of
the inner life of the soul are symbolized under each of **the different pieces of armour.**[339] (Emphasis added)

John Trapp Complete Commentary:

Christ did; and so must every Christian, [Ephesians 6:14] where
the apostle Paul soundeth the alarm, and describeth his weapons as here, *defensive and offensive, alluding likely to this text.*[340]
(Emphasis added)

As Trapp rightly asserts, one of the most significant takeaways from
the comparison of Isaiah 59 and Ephesians 6 is that we have an even
fuller understanding that the Christian—when up against the day of evil,
and suited in the "armor of God"—is then equipped for both defense
and offense. In other words, God's people are not to sit idly by and allow

the enemy to advance on all fronts. We're in a deadly, winner-takes-all battle. This is warfare at its ugliest and darkest—*spiritual warfare* that is also played out in the physical realm.

In the middle of the suffocating days of Noah, we are called to be soldiers in Yahweh's army. Suited in *His armor,* we are to stand solely upon the truth of God's Word, while the world leans upon its own understanding and the ever-shifting sands of politically correct catchphrases and slogans. We are also to be *wrapped in righteousness*, while the world is plunging itself into ever-descending depravity. We must endeavor to *live in faith* and encourage our brothers and sisters to do likewise while the world lives in abject panic, depression, and hopeless fear.

We are like Daniel, Shadrach, and Abednego before us, who were living in the bowels of Babylon's godlessness, and like Noah and Lot, each living through days of abject wickedness and depravity. And, just like God's people in our present world—especially those living in lands that are insanely hostile to the biblical faith—we too must be prepared to take our stand. The day of evil is plunging upon us.

We are to be the faithful carriers of the *gospel of salvation* in the face of the spirit of Antichrist and his demonic gospel of compliant obedience. Our *sword* is the Word of God. Our *shield* is the Eternal One Himself. He alone is our Rock and Deliverer, our God in whom we trust.

We are not to sit by and just "let it come." We are not called to take a defeatist attitude. Rather, we are instructed to be the salt and the light. We are armed with the spiritual weapons enabling us to loyally fulfill the important role of serving as heaven's agents of change and power.

We are to resist the ploys of the *evil one* whenever we have the opportunity to do so. We are specifically called to affect the culture around us in a *proactive* manner, not from a position of weakness and unquestioned compliance.

> You are the salt of the earth. But if the salt loses its saltiness, how can it be made salty again? It is no longer good for anything, except to be thrown out and trampled underfoot. (Matthew 5:13)

We are the true Church, the same one about which Jesus declared:

On this rock I will build my church, and the gates of Hades will not overcome it. (Matthew 16:18)

We are uniquely equipped to win this war—because we will be wearing *the armor of God!*

❖

PART NINE

Preparing the Ark

Do your best to present yourself to God as one approved, a worker who does not need to be ashamed and who correctly handles the word of truth.

—2 TIMOTHY 2:15

59

The Eternal Pattern

*The lesson here is not what happened to the generations of
Noah and Lot, but what is going to happen to all the world
and the generation that abides when the Lord shall come.*[341]

DO YOU WANT TO KNOW WHAT JESUS TAUGHT CONCERNING HOW THE END
times will unfold? Suffice it to say, our Lord didn't leave us in the dark.

It might surprise some to learn that the pattern revealed in this chapter was the *only* prevailing systematic view of end-time events for the first
three hundred years of the church's history. To this day, it is also considered to be the most biblically literal view.[342]

From the opening pages of this book, our focus has been upon the
words of Jesus, wherein He asserted that the coming of the Son of Man
would be "just like" the days of Noah and the days of Lot. It was in those
specific words where Jesus revealed the precise pattern of the last days.
We know this because the pattern—*and its four defining elements*—is
identical in the lifetimes of both Noah and Lot and is easily discernable
from the Scriptures.

The Pattern of the Days of Noah and Lot

Element 1. Each of their "worlds"[343] grew increasingly wicked with every passing year. Finally, both Noah and Lot found themselves living within the heart of the most tumultuous and wicked days their worlds had ever known, until that time.

- **Noah's Day:** "The Lord saw how great the wickedness of the human race had become on the earth, and that every inclination of the thoughts of the human heart was only evil all the time" (Genesis 1:5).

- **Lot's Day:** "The Lord said, 'The outcry against Sodom and Gomorrah is so great and their sin so grievous'.... Before they had gone to bed, all the men from every part of the city of Sodom—both young and old—surrounded the house. They called to Lot, 'Where are the men who came to you tonight? Bring them out to us so that we can have sex with them'" (Genesis 18:20, 19:4–5).

Element 2. Both Noah and Lot were *chosen* by Yahweh Himself to live in those abominable periods of time as ambassadors of God's Word. God preserved these faithful families, even in the midst of the horrific evil of their day (2 Peter 2:4–10).

Element 3. In each example, Noah and Lot weren't "taken out" until just before the destructive wrath of God fell upon the wickedness of their worlds. That *wrath* was the flood waters in Noah's time and the fire from heaven in Lot's. Right up to the second of the respective outpourings of God's wrath, the two men and their families remained in their worlds as witnesses.[344]

Tribulation vs. Wrath

Before moving to the fourth point, we need to establish another important biblical fact. Simply stated, there is a marked difference between "tribulation" [345] and God's "wrath." [346] Contextual scrutiny makes this fact clear, and so do the Greek lexicons.

> The word *tribulation* is never equated with the *wrath* that God Himself brings upon *the world*. For detailed proof of this assertion, I urge the reader to please see my endnotes, wherein every single use of the New Testament Greek word *tribulation* is listed—including the only three times that the specific phrase *great tribulation* is mentioned. [347]

In the three times that the phrase "great tribulation" is used, two instances indicate the same meaning. But the third time the phrase is used, the expression denotes something entirely different. (See the endnotes for a thorough explanation of the grammar and context of the original Greek for "tribulation" and "great tribulation.") However—and this is a vital distinction—"tribulation" is always connected to the persistent trials and the consequences of sin suffered by Christians who are living in a fallen world—throughout *all ages*. Following are examples:

> These things I have spoken unto you, that in me ye might have peace. *In the world ye shall have tribulation*: but be of good cheer; I have overcome the world. (John 16:33, KJV; emphasis added)

> Confirming the souls of the disciples, and exhorting them to *continue in the faith*, and *that we must through much tribulation enter into the kingdom of God*. (Acts 14:22, KJV; emphasis added)

For verily, when we were with you, *we told you before that we should suffer tribulation*; even *as it came to pass*, and ye know. (1 Thessalonians 3:4, KJV; emphasis added)

The Family of God

There is a fourth element to this divine pattern, as demonstrated in the lives of Noah and Lot.

Element 4. If there is any genuine symbolism in these two periods to which Jesus refers, it would have to be that Noah's and Lot's families represent the church of the last days. In their respective days, their families were the only ones who escaped the wrath of God, yet they still lived and thrived in the midst of the unmitigated turmoil.

The church is indeed a *family*. We are the "called-out ones," the *ecclesia*.[348] And, the born-again, called-out ones are the only "family" or "household" that will escape the coming wrath of God.

Therefore, as we have opportunity, let us do good to all people, especially to those who belong to the family of believers. (Galatians 6:10)

Now therefore ye are no more strangers and foreigners, but fellow citizens with the saints, and of the household of God. (Ephesians 2:19; KJV)

For this reason I kneel before the Father, from whom his whole family in heaven and on earth derives its name. (Ephesians 3:14–15)

I write so that you will know how one ought to conduct himself in the household of God. (1 Timothy 3:15, NASU)

For it is time for judgment to begin with the family of God; and if it begins with us, what will the outcome be for those who do not obey the gospel of God? (1 Peter 4:17)

Both the one who makes men holy and those who are made holy are of the same family. So Jesus is not ashamed to call them brothers. (Hebrews 2:11)

First and Last

Noah represents the picture of the "first world's" days of tribulation, culminating in God's flooding wrath. However, Lot represents the "last-days" world, which will be consumed in fire (see 2 Peter 3:5–12). The period of the last days will also be one, like Lot's, wherein God's people will be gathered to Him by His angels (see Matthew 24:29–31).[349]

This is not to mention the fact that Jesus spoke of Sodom and Gomorrah as pointed examples of the certainty of the last-days judgment (Matthew 10:15, 11:24; Luke 10:12, 17:29). The apostles Paul, Peter, and Jude leave us with the same message in this regard (Romans 9:29; 2 Peter 2:6; Jude 1:7).

There's no doubt. Noah's and Lot's worlds each hold the same easy-to-discern pattern for how everything will ultimately unfold before the return of Jesus Christ.

Concluding Observations

A number of renowned scholars, both classical and modern, assert that Jesus used the examples of Noah and Lot precisely because each *lived through* the final days of their "worlds," right up until God's wrath fell. Following are only a few of the many examples:

The IVP New Testament Commentary Series (Luke 17):

In other words, *if you identify with God, suffering and persecution may result, but God will redeem you.* If you fear the rejection of persecution, you will not come to Christ, but neither will you be redeemed by God. Again **the point is,** *expect suffering but persevere with patient faith.* Redemption comes, and so does God's vindication.[350] (Emphasis added)

Coffman's Commentary on the Bible:

The fact that Jesus selected these two great physical phenomena from the Old Testament, making them comparable to the Second Advent, is a clear word that the Second Advent will also be…a cataclysm of unbelievable and unprecedented destruction; and that in the midst of the Great Disaster, the Son of man will appear in order to redeem the faithful from the earth, who shall be caught up with the "Lord in the air" (see 1 Thessalonians 4:13–18).

Men either believe this or they don't; and this writer, *striving to read the word of the Lord aright,* believes it, *with no pretensions* whatever of being able to explain it.

The lesson here is not what happened to those generations, but *what is going to happen* to all the world and *the generation that abides* when the Lord shall come.[351] (Emphasis added, parenthesis in the original)

Matthew Poole's English Annotations on the Holy Bible:

So it would be *before* the final ruin of the world. *Till the very days came,* and men felt it, the generality of men would not believe it, nor make any preparation for it. But in our Lord's propounding these two great examples to them, *he also lets them know their duty and wisdom,* viz. **to watch,** and **be upon their guard,** *with Lot to get ready to go out of Sodom, with Noah to prepare an ark* upon this admonition which he gave them.[352] (Emphasis added)

The greater point is this: No matter what view of the precise unfolding of the last days one might hold—every element of *any* interpretation must ultimately be filtered through the eternal pattern Jesus set forth concerning the days of Noah and Lot. Remember, this is exactly what the early church did for more than three hundred years after it was born, and it's what most serious exegetical biblical scholars continue to do, to this day.

"It will be *just like* this…as it was in the days of Noah, *so shall it be.*"

60

The Closed Door

The world is standing at the brink of God's patience.

SOME OF THE MOST SOBERING WORDS IN THE GENESIS ACCOUNT OF THE FLOOD are found in chapter 7:

> Then **the LORD closed** the door behind them. (Genesis 7:16, NLT; emphasis added)

When that door finally closed, apparently even Noah and his sons could not budge it back open until the ark had safely rested again upon dry ground. The closing of the door represented the chosen family's safety and their ultimate salvation. Those who are truly "in Christ" through a genuine, born-again relationship are eternally secure. He is the door.

However, for those who despised God's prophets and God's Word, the *closed door* represented their ultimate doom. God's grace, mercy, and patience had come to an end for them. The end of that "age" was over. The same principles hold true for our own generation.

Matthew Henry's Concise Commentary:

> When God put Noah into the ark, and so when he brings a soul to Christ, the salvation is sure: it is not in our own keeping, but

in the Mediator's hand. But *the door of mercy* will shortly *be shut against those that now make light of it.* Knock *now*, and it shall be opened, Luke 13:25.[353] (Emphasis added)

The same truth is asserted in the last book of God's Word:

These are the words of [Jesus] who is holy and true, who holds the key of David. *What* [Jesus] *opens no one can shut*, and *what he shuts no one can open.* (Revelation 3:7, emphasis added)

And we know what Jesus said about *that door* as well:

[Jesus said to them] *I am the door.* **If anyone enters by me, he will be saved** and will go in and out and find pasture. (John 10:9; emphasis added).

God was patient with the people of Noah's day. He gave them 120 years to repent. Ever since the cross, the resurrection, the birth of the church, and the subsequent preaching of the gospel, God has given humanity a little more than two thousand years to repent and turn back to Him. But His mercy will not be extended forever.
Benson Commentary:

So far **mercy prevailed**, that **a reprieve was obtained** for *six-score years* [120 years]; and **during this time Noah was preaching righteousness** to them, and, to assure them of the truth of his doctrine, was preparing the ark.[354] (Emphasis added)

Keil and Delitzsch Biblical Commentary on the Old Testament:

"Therefore his days shall be 120 years:" this means, not that human life should in future never attain a greater age than 120 years, but that *a respite of 120 years should still be granted to the human race* [during Noah's day]. This sentence, as we may gather from the context, was made known to Noah in his 480th year, to be *published by him as "preacher of righteousness"* (2 Peter 2:5) to the degenerate race.[355] (Emphasis added)

Jamieson-Fausset-Brown Bible Commentary:

Yet his days shall be an hundred and twenty years—it is probable that the corruption of [Noah's] world, which had now reached its height, had been long and gradually increasing, and *this idea receives support from the long respite granted.*[356] (Emphasis added)

When God's patience had reached its limit, He shut and sealed the door. There were no second chances. There was no reopening of the door.

One Last Nail

Once again we find ourselves like Noah and Lot as the world stands at the brink of God's forbearance. It appears that the last nail is about to be hammered into place. Yet, most people still scoff at God's Word and insist upon mocking those of us who love Him—just like the Scriptures declared.

Above all, you must understand that **in the last days scoffers will come,** scoffing and following their own evil desires. They will say, **"Where is this 'coming' he promised?** Ever since our ancestors died, everything goes on as it has since the beginning of creation."

But they deliberately forget that long ago by God's word the heavens came into being and the earth was formed out of water and by water. *By these waters also the world of that time was deluged* and destroyed. (2 Peter 3:3–6; emphasis added)

So, in our own days, they get up from their beds every morning and go on with their lives as though tomorrow will be just another day—ridiculing God's promises as they go.

They eat and drink…eat and drink…eat and drink…

Until—in the twinkling of an eye—it's too late.

61

The Value of a Name

How precious to me are your thoughts, God!
How vast is the sum of them!
—Psalm 139:17

In my estimation, it would be unthinkable to write a book on the topic of Noah without also laying out the following astounding revelation.

The shortened form of the study that follows was published by a man I considered a valued friend, Dr. Chuck Missler. After teaching many years at Calvary Chapel Costa Mesa, Dr. Missler (1934–2018) founded the renowned worldwide Bible and prophecy ministry known as Koinonia House.

After being made aware of a project I was working on back in 2014, Dr. Missler graciously provided material for what turned out to be a book that is still being powerfully used by the Lord. That book is titled *The Rabbi Who Found Messiah: The Story of Yitzhak Kaduri.*[357]

The Gospel in Genesis

In 1996, Dr. Missler published an article titled "The Gospel in Genesis: A Hidden Message."[358] The revelation he presented absolutely thrilled the Christian world and confounded a number of biblical antagonists as well.[359] It was what many believed to be a significant last-days disclosure, unfurled around the genealogy of Noah as found in the book of Genesis.

By taking the names of each of the patriarchs that make up Noah's lineage, Dr. Missler studied them out in the Hebrew language to see if their names carried any significance. He demonstrated this to be the case with a number of biblical Hebrew names.

What Dr. Missler found amazed him. If you've never seen this revelation before, I believe you'll also be excited by what you'll see next.

The Family Tree

In the fifth chapter of Genesis, a total of ten names listed comprise Noah's genealogy: Adam, Seth, Enosh, Kenan, Mahalalel, Jared, Enoch, Methuselah, Lamech, and of course Noah.

Examining the original root meanings of the names, Dr. Missler discovered a hidden message buried within the first pages of Genesis since Moses first recorded the words.

Dr. Missler explained the challenge of his search:

The meaning of proper names can be a difficult pursuit since a direct translation is often not readily available. Even a conventional Hebrew lexicon can prove disappointing. A study of the original roots, however, can yield some fascinating insights.[360]

As of this writing, Dr. Missler's detailed study is still posted on his ministry website. There, he thoroughly explains the meanings of each of the ten names, as well as some of the slight variations associated with a few.

For ease of our study here, I have reproduced the names and their meanings in table format, similar to how they appear on Dr. Missler's page.

The Genealogy of Noah

Hebrew	English meaning
Seth	Appointed
Enosh	Mortal
Kenan	Sorrow
Mahalalel	The Blessed God
Jared	Shall come down
Enoch	Teaching
Methuselah	His death shall bring
Lamech	The Despairing
Noah	Rest, or comfort

When putting together the meanings of the names, from first to last, the following coherent message emerges, as reported from Dr. Missler's presentation:

Man (is) appointed mortal sorrow; (but) the Blessed God shall come down teaching (that) His death shall bring (the) despairing rest.[361] (Emphasis in original)

I can't think of anything more profound to say about this discovery than by repeating what Dr. Missler has already said:

You will never convince me that a group of Jewish rabbis conspired to hide the Christian Gospel right here in a genealogy within their venerated Torah!

The implications of this discovery are more wide spread than is evident at first glance. It demonstrates that in the earliest chapters of the Book of Genesis, God had already laid out His plan of redemption for the predicament of mankind. It is a love story, written in blood on a wooden cross which was erected in Judea almost 2,000 years ago.

The Bible is an integrated message system, the product of supernatural engineering. Every number, every place name, every detail, every jot and tittle is there for our learning, our discovery, and our amazement. Truly, our God is an awesome God."[362] (Emphasis added)

At this point, we must agree in awe with the Psalmist:

How precious to me are your thoughts, God! How vast is the sum of them! Were I to count them, they would outnumber the grains of sand—when I awake, I am still with you. (Psalm 139:17–18)

62

Kingdom Builders

*I find it absolutely breathtaking to
consider the glory of it all.*

Here we are!

These are the last few pages of our journey together.

But we're not yet finished. I've got one more perspective-boosting biblical truth to share with you. This is the one that keeps me going strong and staying enthusiastic, even in the midst of our generation of crazier-than-ever world events.

Think about this one last revelation with me....

From the beginning, the Lord knew that *our* specific days would come. He also knew that you and I would be living in them!

In fact, the Word of God says that He actually positioned *us* to live in this precise time, and in our various places of responsibility. He is trusting *us* to faithfully "build the ark" of the last days! He is counting upon *us* to testify of His glory, to expose the darkness, and to one last time warn the lost world of the soon coming flood of His wrath.

Have a look at a Scripture passage that pinpoints this marvelous truth. In the seventeenth chapter of Acts, we see that Paul is preaching to the Athenians when he gives the stunning revelation:

The God who made the world and everything in it is the **Lord of heaven** and earth and **does not live in temples** built by human hands. And he is **not served by human hands**, as if he needed anything. Rather, **he himself gives everyone life and breath and everything else.**

From one man he made all the nations, that they should inhabit the whole earth; *and he marked out their* [each person who makes up each nation] *appointed times in history* and *the boundaries* of their lands [and where each should live out their days].

God did this so that *they would seek him* and perhaps *reach out for him and find him*, though he is not far from any one of us.

For *in him we live* and **move and have our being.** (Acts 17:24–28, emphasis added)

He Knows Where You Are

The scholars have noted this truth for ages. Consider some of their observations:

Robertson's Word Pictures in the New Testament (Acts 17:26):

[God's] hand appears in the history *of all men* as well as in that of the Chosen People of Israel. Thus there is *an interplay between God's will and man's activities*, difficult as it is for us to see *with our shortened vision.*[363] (Emphasis added)

Matthew Poole's English Annotations on the Holy Bible:

This doctrine was preached by Moses, who tells the people, that **God is** *their life*, and *the length of their days*, that they might love him, and obey his voice, and cleave unto him, Deuteronomy 30:20.[364] (Emphasis added)

Gill's Exposition of the Entire Bible also explores the wondrous depths of the revelation about which Paul was speaking in Acts 17. I find it spectacular to consider the glory of God's wisdom and foreknowledge.

Please! Don't skip over any of this next excerpt! I believe that its truth will deeply inspire you; it moves me every single time I read it.

As you read it, notice how *Gill* also acknowledges Noah's place in our own heritage and future:

All [human beings] belong to **one family**, and **are of one man's blood, whether Adam or *Noah*:** of whom are all nations of men, for to dwell on all the face of the earth; for from Adam sprung a race of men, which multiplied on the face of the earth, **and peopled the world before the flood**; these being destroyed by the flood, *and Noah* **and his family saved, his descendants were scattered all over the earth**, and *re-peopled it:* and *this is the original* of all the nations of men, and *of all the inhabitants* of the earth…

And [Yahweh] hath determined the times before appointed; how long the world he has made shall continue; and the several distinct periods, ages, and generations, *in which such and such men should live*, such and such nations should exist, and such monarchies should be in being….

Here's the really good part! Feast upon its truth:

Which are so bounded, and kept so distinct in their revolutions, as not to interfere with, and encroach upon each other; and likewise the several years, months, and days of every man's life…. and how long they shall continue there the age or distinct period of time, in which every man was, or is to come into the world, is fixed and determined by God;

Nor can, nor does anyone come into the world sooner or later than that time; and also the particular country, city, town, and spot of ground where he shall dwell; and the term of time how long he shall dwell there, and then remove to another place, or be removed by death....

To which may be added, the times of the law and Gospel; the time of Christ's birth and death... the time of antichrist's reign and ruin, Revelation 13:5, and of Christ's personal coming, and the day of judgment, 1 Timothy 6:15, and of his reign on earth for a thousand years, Revelation 20:4. **All these are appointed times, and determined by the Creator and Governor of the world.**[365] (Emphasis added)

Phew!

Those beautifully attested biblical truths take my breath away. They give a whole new meaning to "God has a plan for your life," don't they?

Paul reveals that our appointed time was "marked out" for us by Yahweh. Before any human being even thought about you and me, Yahweh already knew us, and He knew just when and where He would place us. *Our* appointed time is *now*...in the advent of the final days of Noah.

As stunning as this great truth is, it really should come as no surprise, because God's Word has been telling us these marvelous truths for more than three thousand years:

- **"Your eyes saw** my unformed body; *all* **the days** *ordained* [planned out] **for me** were *written in your book before one of them came to be.* How precious to me are your thoughts, O God! How vast is the sum of them!" (Psalm 139:16–17; emphasis added).
- "Before I formed you in the womb I knew you, before you were born I set you apart; I appointed you as a prophet to the nations" (Jeremiah 1:5).

Even though Psalm 139 was written by David and the book of Jeremiah was divinely recorded by the prophet himself, the truths of which they speak are eternal. They are from the Holy Spirit. And they apply to you as well.

Think of the gravity of this biblical assurance! *You are here on purpose.* You are here *for* a purpose!

If you truly are a born-again child of God, then you are a *Noah* of this age. And, in this prophetic era of pervasive communication technologies right at your fingertips, it's not a stretch at all to agree with God's Word…you've also been tapped to be an important *voice to the nations*, proclaiming the love of Jesus to a world that continues to unravel at the seams.

The snapping has already happened. Next comes *the shaking*. And it's all soon to be followed by the glorious restitution of all things!

Thank you so much for joining me in this journey. I am honored that you've done so. I look forward to the day when we can meet in person, in the presence of His Glory. Together, as redeemed sons and daughters of the Most High, we will then celebrate the grace and mercy of our Creator—our Lord and Savior—Jesus Christ, the One who redeemed us by His blood.

I'll look for you there, somewhere around the Crystal Sea.

It'll be encircled by the elders, the living creatures, and ten thousand times ten thousand angels singing "Holy is the Lamb Who was slain!"

What a service of worship that will be.

Thank you Oh Lord, for trusting us with your Kingdom's advancement, right in the middle of these uniquely prophetic times! I pray that we always have eyes to see.

Even so, come Lord Jesus, come….

And come quickly.

Epilogue

So then, dear friends, since you are looking forward to this, make every effort to be found spotless, blameless and at peace with him. Bear in mind that our Lord's patience means salvation…

Therefore, dear friends, since you have been forewarned, be on your guard so that you may not be carried away by the error of the lawless and fall from your secure position.[366] But grow in the grace and knowledge of our Lord and Savior Jesus Christ.

To him be glory both now and forever! Amen.

—2 PETER 3:14–15, 17–18

Addendum

The Preparation

Are you ready to shelter in place—perhaps for months, and maybe longer?

Should Christians always obey the government? Doesn't the Bible say we *must* do that?

Should a Christian really be a prepper? Won't people think we're crazy, or overreacting? Would God even honor prepping activity on our part? What about the biblical concept of *living by faith*? Isn't prepping diametrically opposed to that concept?

Does the Bible say that we can, or should, arm ourselves? What would Jesus want us to do? What about turning the other cheek? What about the martyrs, they didn't arm themselves? They didn't fight back. Shouldn't we be like them? If we are not like them in the face of danger, are we then to be seen as people of less faith?

Even if I was going to try and store up certain items, are any particular provisions more important than others? What if I can't afford to store up huge amounts of supplies? How should I even begin to do something like that?

These are some of the most prevalent questions that today's church is asking. Getting biblical, contextually sound, and expertly experienced answers is not as easy as one might think.

The following chapters will answer all of these important questions and more.

I pray the next chapters will prove to be valuable for you, your family, your friends, and your church family.

Enjoy.

Be Thou Prepared

Be thou prepared, and prepare for thyself, thou, and all thy company that are assembled unto thee, and be thou a guard unto them. (Ezekiel 38:7)

In late July 2014, George Barna of the Barna Group[367] revealed the results of a stunning study he had been compiling over the previous two years.[368]

His investigation involved the lack of preparedness and involvement on the part of America's conservative pastors in engaging the American culture concerning vital biblical and societal matters, like the ones we've been exploring throughout this book.

Barna, in a radio interview with American Family Radio, said: "What we're finding is that when we ask them about all the key issues of the day, [90 percent of them are] telling us, 'Yes, the Bible speaks to every one of these issues.' Then we ask them: 'Well, are you teaching your people what the Bible says about those issues?'—and the numbers drop…to less than 10 percent of pastors who say they will speak to it."

Barna went on to say, "So the thing that struck me has been that when we talk about the separation of church and state, it's that churches have separated themselves from the activities of the state—and that's to the detriment of the state and its people."

According to this same report, when asked why they did not engage the culture to which they had been called to minister and why they did not preach the important and often controversial truths of the Bible to their people, the pastors cited fear of losing members, fear of losing financial support, the extremely controversial nature of political subjects, and a lack of familiarity with the details of the issues.

Probably the most telling words of the Barna interview had to do with the lack of preparedness on the part of America's so-called conservative pastors: "When you look at what they get in Bible school or in the seminary, they are not taught to get people engaged in these particular issues. They are taught just to exegete scriptures; they are taught something about the history of where those scriptures came from—but *they are not prepared.*"

Think of it. If the preachers, pastors, and prophets of our day are not spiritually prepared to confront society as it continues to turn from God, who else will do the admonishing? And just as important, if the churches are not preparing their people to *physically* take care of themselves as well as each other as the day of evil approaches…who else will step up to the task?

The Foundation

In the pages that follow, I'll tackle the majority of the most frequently asked questions that I've been addressing regarding biblical "preparedness."

First, just a little about the guy you're getting your information from right now. As I am writing this book, I've had the honor of being the senior pastor of a church on the Gulf Coast of Florida since 1987. Prior to my entry into the full-time ministry of the Kingdom work, I served a little more than ten years in Florida law enforcement. Most of that time I served as a deputy sheriff with two different offices under three sheriffs. In one of those administrations, I conducted several important criminal investigations.

I take seriously the subject of preparedness. Between years of street-level law enforcement experience and pastoring for decades in the center of Hurricane Alley, I've had almost fifty years of experience in these matters—not to mention professional training that goes along with that experience. So I speak to you from that understanding and direct involvement.

It might also be beneficial for you to pick up a copy of my book titled *Be Thou Prepared*.[369] That book covers, in even more detail, the things I'll outline in the coming pages. Additionally, it lays out a sizable amount of other practical resources, illustrations from real-life scenarios, and added biblical instruction for churches, pastors, and teachers. I still receive an enormous amount of communication from around the world about how useful that book has proven to be for so many of God's people.

Must We Obey the Government?

Throughout my entire ministry life, I've been asked if Christians are supposed to obey the laws of the governments to which they are subjected, "no matter what." The question is often asked because of the supposed biblical sticking point of Paul's admonition to the church at Rome in Romans 13, which begins with these words:

> Let everyone be subject to the governing authorities, for there is no authority except that which God has established.
> The authorities that exist have been established by God. Consequently, whoever rebels against the authority is rebelling against what God has instituted, and those who do so will bring judgment on themselves. (Romans 13:1–2)

Paul's exhortation appears to be pretty straightforward. However, the context is supremely important. The message is that the true born-again believer should obey the laws of the land and pay their lawfully expected taxes. Good citizenship is something that God generally honors among His people. It is a fact that the church was not planted upon this earth to become a radical political action committee designed to routinely overthrow ruling governments and political authorities. The Lord of Glory will take care of those weighty matters upon His soon return. That is a solemn promise of Scripture.

However, we must also consider that the people of Paul's day did not have the First and Second Amendment rights we've so long enjoyed in the United States. Neither did they have the ability to vote for their leaders or run for office themselves. Without those privileges, they could not have been expected to bear the weighty responsibilities that go with them. Many, including myself, believe these responsibilities and great blessings of freedom were given to us as a gift from God; and to whom much has been given, much is expected.

Imagine the absurdity of the following scenario: You are living during the Roman times. Because you have no influential voice in your government's affairs or in the selection of your highest rulers, you often find yourself praying, "If only I had the ability to directly impact the government. If only I could choose my leaders and help make a difference concerning which direction our government takes for the future of our nation, and for my children and their children. If only *I* could actually run for office myself, and serve in important government offices!"

Poof! You're instantly transported to the modern-day United States. And there, the gifts for which you so earnestly longed have been given to you on a silver platter. But now, when actually pressed to be involved in the societal and political processes, you respond, "Oh no! We must not speak against our government at all; Romans 13 makes this command clear! In fact, we really shouldn't even get involved in politics at all—especially if you're a *preacher!*"

Do you see how ridiculous many of America's politicians, Christians, and pastors have become in speaking to this biblical matter?

Certainly, we should live in peace with the society around us as much as it is biblically possible for us to do so. This includes living at peace with the governing authorities. Even a poorly run government is better than total anarchy and abject lawlessness. This is why Paul pointed out to his readers that governments are supposed to serve as a restraint against the flood of evil that would surely come if there were no government at all.

However, we are never relieved of our biblical responsibility to be the salt and light of the Kingdom truths, especially as they apply to citizenship and government. Our founding ancestors fully expected that the church would, in fact, be involved in the political and civic processes of our new society. Without that involvement, many of our founders feared our culture would quickly rot to the core. And *wow*...did they nail *that* truth on the head.

Early Rebels

In addition to the preceding facts, the Bible also records instances of Christians refusing to give in to the political whims of the governing authorities of their day, especially when those authorities stepped into the arenas of biblical matters and a person's relationship with the Lord.

Consider the response that Peter and John gave to the Sanhedrin council after being told to renounce the public exercising of their faith in Jesus Christ:

> Then they called them in again and **commanded them not to speak or teach at all in the name of Jesus.** But Peter and John replied, **"Judge for yourselves whether it is right in God's sight to obey you rather than God. For we cannot help speaking about what we have seen and heard."** (Acts 4:18–20; emphasis added)

Remember, it was Peter who would later pen the following words, an admonition similar to Paul's:

> Submit yourselves for the Lord's sake to every human authority: whether to the emperor, as the supreme authority, or to governors, who are sent by him to punish those who do wrong and to commend those who do right. (1 Peter 2:13–14)

The apostle Paul was often jailed, beaten, slandered, or the intended object of a stoning because he refused to kowtow to ecclesiastical authorities or the Roman governmental authorities concerning matters of his biblical faith in Christ.

It seems many of today's Christians have forgotten that four of the New Testament books that Paul wrote were penned from prison! In each case, he was in jail because of his faith in Christ and his refusal to obey the authorities who were trying to silence his witness.

In fact, Nero *executed* Paul after first imprisoning him in Rome for his preaching of the gospel of Jesus Christ. He also executed the apostle Peter, by crucifixion, in order to appease the large swath of Roman citizenry who were quickly turning against Christians. Even the apostle John was sentenced to the island of Patmos, a Roman prison camp, because of his refusal to bow in worship and to offer burnt sacrifices to the emperor of his day.

And don't forget Daniel, Shadrach, Meshach, and Abednego. They were all forced into the king's service in a pagan land. Yet, they faithfully served that government with all the integrity they could muster, while at the same time not denying their faith. They used the wisdom God gave them to do both. They had to be creative at times, but they did not deny their faith in God.

When the day finally came when they were ordered to flatly disavow that same deeply held faith, they respectfully refused to do so. What did their respectful denial cost them? A lion's den and a blazing furnace of fiery death. Yet, they willingly submitted to the lawful punishment.

In both cases, those faithful men were delivered by the hand of Yahweh. And in both cases, the hearts of the king and much of the culture around them were changed for God's glory. It doesn't always end that way. But, in their cases it did. Countless other similar situations have ended in much the same way, down through the ages. Regardless, standing in unrelenting faith in the Lord always ends with the born-again believer being ultimately welcomed into the Kingdom of Jesus Christ by hearing the words, "Well done, my good and faithful servant! Well done!"

We understand that the principle of Romans 13 should be the day-to-day philosophy of every true believer regarding good citizenship and its impact upon our overall witness. However, that principle doesn't come close to commanding that God's people must always obey the government, no matter what. That gross misapplication of Scripture is an absolute violation of the heart of God's Word. Don't let anyone try to convince you otherwise.

Of course, there are consequences for breaking society's laws. One's willingness to face those consequences is between that person, the circumstances of the event, and the person's commitment to the Lord Jesus Christ. But there are also eternal consequences for willfully spurning the lordship of Yahweh and bowing instead to the unholy edicts of godless governmental authorities.

America's authors of the Constitution did not incorporate the First Amendment in the Constitution to *prohibit* Christianity from influencing state-established institutions. They expected our nation to be—generally speaking—Christian in nature (as opposed to Muslim, Hindu, Buddhist, Deist, atheist, or what have you), and they expected our government to reflect that historical predisposition while still providing equal protection for all. This divinely inspired principle was meant to be the defining glory of America. And for centuries, it has been precisely what has set America far apart from the other nations of the world, ever since Noah's Flood.

Accordingly, American Christians must not give up the fight for righteousness. We are called to stay as engaged in the political and civic affairs of the country as much as it remains possible to do so.

> Have nothing to do with the fruitless deeds of darkness, but rather expose them. It is shameful even to mention what the disobedient do in secret. But everything exposed by the light becomes visible—and everything that is illuminated becomes a light. (Ephesians 5:11–13)

As of this writing, we still live in a unique nation, and we are thus in a unique situation. Christian principles founded this nation. The blessings of liberty that we still enjoy, which enable us to take the gospel to the world around us and to exercise our faith without government decreed legal reprisal, were secured for us within those founding principles.

If we do not stay involved and if we give in to fear and threats or simply opt out of our biblical responsibilities of cultural engagement, we may invite similar persecution upon ourselves or upon the generations that will follow. Many believe that we may be on the cusp of those days, even now.

Biblical Prepping

By failing to prepare, you are preparing to fail.
—Benjamin Franklin

Have you ever been called a "crazy prepper?" Well, with the current state of the world, you don't look so "crazy" anymore—*do you?*

Or, perhaps you have constantly shoved to the back of your to-do list the need to make preparations for the days of evil. You've done so out of the concern that your friends or family might think you've truly lost your mind and become "one of *those* people." Well, you're not alone in that regard, I can assure you.

But let me be clear: If you're not making biblical preparations for the times in which we are *now* living, then you are being disobedient to God's Word, plain and simple.

It's as if the Lord has constructed yet another ark right in the middle of *our time.* His Word is clear concerning what lies just ahead. And, as you've already discovered, myriad foretold elements of the last days are actually happening in our lifetime, and *only* in our lifetime. If you are disobedient to the call, the time may soon come when you'll deeply regret your neglectful inactions.

Noah

There's nothing crazy about preparing for the distinct possibility of tough times ahead. *Noah was the world's first prepper!* Shouldn't we also prepare for the "flood" that is surely coming—at least for the days leading up to it?

Think about it. Humanly speaking, we actually owe our lives to Noah's faithfulness. Yet, he too was called crazy. He too was mocked and ridiculed. But, he was right. And his detractors were wrong. Dead wrong.

God revealed to Noah what was soon to come upon the earth. Noah went right to work and prepared. He stored up. He gathered up. He built his boat. He prepared his family, both spiritually and physically. And in the midst of all that, he faithfully preached the Word of God to the lost world around him, imploring people to repent so they too could be saved from the coming day of God's Wrath.

> And God did not spare the ancient world—except for Noah and the seven others in his family. **Noah warned the world of God's righteous judgment**. So God protected Noah when he destroyed the world of ungodly people with a vast flood. (2 Peter 2:5, NLT; emphasis added)

You're in great company if you are a faithful biblical prepper. The Bible speaks of physical prepping from the opening pages of the Genesis all the way through to some of the last New Testament books. Consider a few examples among dozens just like them.

> The prudent see danger and take refuge [prepare], but the simple keep going and pay the penalty. (Proverbs 22:3)

I love the *Good News Bible's* translation of that verse in Proverbs. It states it in more of the style that we might speak it today.

> Sensible people will see trouble coming and avoid it, but an unthinking person will walk right into it and regret it later.

Here's another one, this regarding some of the prepper activity of the early church:

> And they were selling the possessions and the goods, and were
> dividing them to all, as anyone had need. (Acts 2:45, Berean
> Literal Bible)

And what about this one?

> Anyone who does not provide for their relatives, and especially
> for their own household, has denied the faith and is worse than
> an unbeliever. (1 Timothy 5:8)

Surely providing for one's family would include storing up against
the day of famine, disease, and lawless outbursts?

Consider the following truth as well…. We routinely lock away our
valuables. We secure our doors at night while our children are sleeping.
We set the burglar alarms. We might even have a weapon or two stra-
tegically located around the house in case of a home-invasion scenario.
Why would we not also have a supply of clean water and water purification products, along with plenty of food products that might enable us
to shelter in place for months in the event of some sort of calamity? Of
course we should. That, and so much more.

Here's another biblical command to prepare. Or, as Paul puts it, here
is a "rule" among the family of God.

> For even when we were with you, **we gave you this rule**: "The one
> who is unwilling to work shall not eat." (2 Thessalonians 3:10)

We often relate this passage to gainful employment or some other
means of supplying the needs of one's family. A willfully lazy person, and
one who refuses to make certain his own family can eat, should not eat
from someone else's bounty. *We get that.*

But what about the one who doesn't even take the time to prepare for the potential of tough times ahead? What about that one who
doesn't give serious thought and action to make certain his family can

eat and survive in those times? The same rule applies. It's the equivalent principle.

Consider a few more biblical examples of the good company you're in when you are biblically prepping.

Joseph

In Old Testament times, Joseph warned Pharaoh of the coming drought and famine. He could warn his boss because the Lord had first revealed to Joseph the impending disaster in a dream. Joseph helped Pharaoh plan ahead and lay up food and supplies for the coming days of natural disaster.

God even used Pharaoh's preparations, under Joseph's leadership, to eventually provide for the whole family of Jacob, who migrated to Egypt in order to attempt to survive the years of famine (Genesis 41, 45–46). By faithfully making these plans and preparations, Joseph spared millions of lives, and the Lord ultimately received the glory for it all.

Moses

Similarly, more than four hundred years later, when the Israelites were leaving their captivity in Egypt under Moses' direction, God had instructed them to prepare ahead of time for the journey. Amazingly, He had told the Israelites to ask their own captors for their survival supplies! Something supernatural happened in the process when God's people were faithful to follow the Lord's command:

> During the night Pharaoh summoned Moses and Aaron and said, "Up! Leave my people, you and the Israelites! Go, worship the Lord as you have requested. Take your flocks and herds, as you have said, and go. And also bless me."
>
> The Egyptians urged the people to hurry and leave the country. "For otherwise," they said, "we will all die!"
>
> So the people took their dough before the yeast was added, and carried it on their shoulders in kneading troughs wrapped

in clothing. The Israelites did as Moses instructed **and asked the Egyptians for articles of silver and gold and for clothing.**

The LORD had **made the Egyptians favorably disposed toward the people,** and they *gave them what they asked for,* so they plundered the Egyptians. (Exodus 12:31–36; emphasis added)

The Early Church

Reflect upon the many ways in which the early church took measures to meet people's needs. They accomplished that task through special collections, feeding widows, dividing responsibilities among its members, assisting one another in times of persecution, and so on.

Eventually, the early church even developed a network of support, not just to local congregants but also to all Christians across the Roman Empire. They did this through offerings of love, managed and distributed by faithful emissaries, so they could more effectively support one another as well as the unprepared world around them. The examples of the early church in this regard are numerous.

As we have already demonstrated in an earlier chapter, it was the early Christians who faithfully met, worshiped, and then ministered to the plague and pandemic victims of the Roman Empire. They did this on several occasions throughout Roman history.

God honored their efforts and planning. They were preppers.

Always, there were multitudes who came to Jesus Christ as Savior and Lord because of those self-sacrificing efforts and ministries.

And that's really the larger point…isn't it?

The Matter of Self Defense

The biblical context of "turn the other cheek" certainly does not mean refusing to defend one's own life.

Would Jesus truly tell us that it's okay to own firearms, or even to carry a firearm? Would He endorse *using* those weapons, even in a deadly fashion?

It is a fact that Jesus had several meaningful things to say regarding the need to prepare for the possibility of a self-defense scenario. In the Gospel of Luke, He used an illustration from the natural world as He proclaimed specific kingdom truths:

> "When a strong man, *fully armed, guards his own house*," He said, "his possessions are safe. But *when someone stronger attacks* and overpowers him, **he takes away the armor in which the man trusted** and divides up his plunder." (Luke 11:21–22; emphasis added)

Of course, the context of Jesus' statement was strictly spiritual. Jesus was reminding His listeners of Satan's desire to plunder and destroy one's walk with the Lord. He was also reminding us that "greater is He that is in you, than he that is in the world" (1 John 4:4, Revelation 12:11). Satan is the "strong man" of the parable, but the one who is "stronger than Satan" is Jesus Himself, and those who are walking in the power and name of Jesus.

The point is, however, that Jesus used a specific example from everyday life as though arming oneself for personal security and the protection of one's home was a perfectly natural expectation; in other words, it was a self-evident truth.

Home invasion has been around since before Noah's Flood. God's people have never been expected to just let it happen or turn the other cheek in a violent, life-threatening event such as that. That was why

Jesus could use it as such a common-sense analogy. That's also why the crowds could so clearly understand the illustration Jesus employed.

Many Christians believe it is our responsibility—and that it is even our divine duty—to be prepared, to the best of our ability, to protect and defend our loved ones and the sanctity of our homes and churches. Of course, we would often prefer to have a law enforcement officer on the scene handling the situation for us. However, we know this isn't always possible, nor is it always practical. On occasion, the need to defend ourselves is immediate: the police might not be able to respond until long after the time for life-saving action has passed.

Turning the Other Cheek

"But," someone might ask, "what about the command Jesus issued to His followers to *turn the other cheek?*" (Matthew 5:39). This is a fair question, but one that demonstrates the need to understand context when properly handling the Word of God.

With the command to turn the other cheek, Jesus was simply instructing His followers not to become obstinate, disobedient, and lawless in our day-to-day walk with Him.

Ellicott's Commentary for English Readers:

The principle in this matter is clearly and simply this—that the disciple of Christ, when he has suffered wrong, is to eliminate altogether from his motives the natural desire to retaliate or accuse.... But the man who has been wronged has other duties which he cannot rightly ignore. The law of the Eternal has to be asserted, society to be protected, the offender to be reclaimed, and these may well justify—though personal animosity does not—protest, prosecution, punishment.[370]

Barnes' Notes on the Bible:

Christ did not intend to teach that we are to see our families murdered, or be murdered ourselves; rather than to make resistance. The law of nature, and **all laws, human and divine, justify self-defense when life is in danger.** It cannot surely be the intention to teach that a father should sit by coolly and see his family butchered by savages, and not be allowed to defend them. Our Saviour immediately explains what he means by it. **Had he intended to refer it to a case where life is in danger, he would most surely have mentioned it.** Such a case was far more worthy of statement than those which he did mention.[371] (Emphasis added)

In other words, Jesus was teaching that we are to live at peace with those around us as much as it is possible on our part. We are to be generally cooperative and kind in spirit, especially to those in authority over us. We also are to strive to obey the government's laws when they do not directly encroach upon our profession of faith in Christ. If we can go the extra mile or even refuse to retaliate when someone has been unkind to us, that method of daily living becomes a tremendous witness to the world around us.

The biblical context of turning the other cheek certainly does not mean refusing to defend our own life, or the lives of those around us for whom we are responsible.

Think of it. If your home was forcefully entered in the middle of the night, and the plunderer armed with a knife and a baseball bat headed down the hall to your children's bedrooms, should you turn the other cheek and let him have his way with your children? Wouldn't you use every means at your disposal to neutralize the situation and save your kids' lives?

Yes, it is our responsibility—even our heavenly obligation—to judiciously provide for our own security, especially in matters of life and death. Those under our care are depending upon our faithfulness in this matter.

Buy a Sword

Also consider that on Jesus' last night with His disciples, He pointedly instructed them to "buy a sword":

> Then said he unto them, But now, he that hath a purse, let him take it, and likewise his scrip: and he that hath no sword, let him sell his garment, and buy one. (Luke 22:36, KJV)

The context of this verse is exactly what it appears to be. Jesus obviously meant for the command to be taken at face value. He was warning His disciples of potentially tough days ahead for them and their families. *Bengel's Gnomen*:

> [Jesus] permits them to avail themselves of the ordinary helps which minister to the supply of food and to self-defense: and accordingly He informs them of the fact at this time, which was exactly the right time for doing so.[372]

Barnes' Notes on the Bible:

> They were going into the midst of dangers. The country was infested with robbers and wild beasts. It was customary to go armed. He tells them of those dangers—of **the necessity of being prepared** in the usual way to meet them.... great dangers were before them; their manner of life would be changed, and they would need the provisions "appropriate to that kind of life."
>
> The **"common" preparation** for that manner of life consisted in money, provisions, and arms; and he foretells them of that manner of life by giving them directions commonly understood to be appropriate to it.[373] (Emphasis added)

There is no way around it. Jesus actually told His disciples to acquire a sword (the sword of their day was the ancient equivalent of a firearm, a personal protection weapon) and to be ready to defend their families if necessary.

Jesus didn't tell them to overthrow the government or even to attempt to deliver Him from the impending crucifixion. He simply warned them that they may soon need to defend themselves from bodily harm.

Each Wore a Sword

When we see encroaching persecution, when we know that our enemies intend to destroy us, the principle of God's Word is: equip yourself!

Additionally, we must not forget the clear call from other passages in the Bible where God's people were instructed to be ready to defend themselves and their families from the attacks of potentially murderous persecutors.

Recall the days of the man named Nehemiah.

This anointed man of God was charged with the responsibility of rebuilding the walls of the city of Jerusalem after the Persian conquerors had issued a decree allowing God's people to return and begin the work. But enemies—persecutors and terrorists—came heavy against Nehemiah and his people:

> When Sanballat heard that we were rebuilding the wall, he became angry and was greatly incensed. He ridiculed the Jews, and in the presence of his associates and the army of Samaria, he said, "What are those feeble Jews doing? Will they restore their wall? Will they offer sacrifices? Will they finish in a day? Can they bring the stones back to life from those heaps of rubble— burned as they are?"

But when Sanballat, Tobiah, the Arabs, the Ammonites and the men of Ashdod heard that the repairs to Jerusalem's walls had gone ahead and that the gaps were being closed, they were very angry. They all plotted together to come and fight against Jerusalem and stir up trouble against it. (Nehemiah 4:1, 2, 7, 8)

Nehemiah first assessed the reality and the gravity of the matter at hand in order to prepare. He saw that his enemies were dead serious in their intentions to persecute them and even to directly attack them. So, the next thing Nehemiah did, after lifting up his prayers to the Lord, was to arm his workers. They carried weapons while working on the walls!

After I looked things over, I stood up and said to the nobles, the officials and the rest of the people, "Don't be afraid of them. Remember the Lord, who is great and awesome, and **fight for your brothers, your sons and your daughters, your wives and your homes."**

When our enemies heard that we were aware of their plot and that God had frustrated it, we all returned to the wall, each to his own work. From that day on, half of my men did the work, **while the other half were equipped with spears, shields, bows and armor.** The officers posted themselves behind all the people of Judah who were building the wall. Those who carried materials did their work with one hand and **held a weapon in the other, and each of the builders wore his sword at his side as he worked.** But the man who sounded the trumpet stayed with me.

Then I said to the nobles, the officials and the rest of the people, "The work is extensive and spread out, and we are widely separated from each other along the wall. Wherever you hear the sound of the trumpet, join us there. Our God will fight for us!

So we continued the work with **half the men holding spears, from the first light of dawn till the stars came out.** At that time I also said to the people, "Have every man and his helper stay inside Jerusalem at night, **so they can serve us as guards by night** and workmen by day." Neither I nor my brothers nor my men nor the guards with me took off our clothes; **each had his weapon, even when he went for water.** (Nehemiah 4:14–23; emphasis added)

The message is clear. God will fight for us, and He will fight with us. He hears our prayers and blesses the work of our hands, especially when we are involved in His directed work. However, we are to use our brains as well. When we see encroaching persecution, when we know our enemies intend to destroy us, the principle of God's Word is: equip yourself! Pray for God's protection, but be ready to defend yourself if necessary. And never forget: you're also doing God's work when you are equipped and ready to protect those around you who have been entrusted to your care.

Out of Africa

As yet another example, do not forget God's people, the Israelites, on their escape from Egypt and their journey in the wilderness. They were under cruel persecution, simply because they were God's people.

Ultimately the Lord instructed them *to arm themselves* and divide the men into fighting units. They were prepared to defend themselves and their families, as well as the innocent and helpless in their care. As a matter of fact, for the next forty years in the wilderness, they fought numerous battles with hostile tribes who intended to wipe them from the face of the earth.

But the fact remains, Christians will also be persecuted—even martyred—until Jesus returns for His Church.

Jesus pointedly warned His disciples:

Beware of men: for they will deliver you up to councils, and they will scourge you in their synagogues.

...And the brother shall deliver up the brother to death, and the father the child: and the children shall rise up against their parents, and cause them to be put to death.

...And ye shall be hated of all men for my name's sake. (Matthew 10:17, 21–22, KJV)

The time cometh, that whosoever killeth you will think that he doeth God service. (John 16:2, KJV)

In His Olivet Discourse prophecy, Jesus warned the disciples:

Then shall they deliver you up to be afflicted, and shall kill you.... For then shall be great tribulation, such as was not since the beginning of the world to this time, no, nor ever shall be. And except those days should be shortened, there should no flesh be saved. (Matthew 24:9, 21–22, KJV)

Jesus knew what the future held. He did not leave us in the dark. He knew that, just before His return, Christians would endure the most difficult time the world had ever seen. Many of them would be persecuted, even put to death. But it was this same Jesus who also told His disciples: "Buy a sword" (see Luke 22:36) and "flee to the mountains" (Matthew 24:16). There will be some who will fall into the hands of persecutors with little to no opportunity to defend themselves. There will be others, however, who will have the chance to flee, and still others who will be able to fight for life and liberty for themselves and those around them.

But what about those situations when God's people are put in situations of self-sacrifice—even of their own lives?

Great question.

What about the Martyrs?

The truth is that we live in a dangerous world. So we take precautions, we use our common sense, we prepare ourselves.

A man once asked me, "Pastor, if my life is being threatened for my biblical beliefs, should I fight back, flee, or give my life for my faith as a martyr?"

Good question!

I answered, "If the Lord has made it clear to you in that particular situation that you must lay down your life for your testimony, then you must obey the Lord. He will honor your obedience. However, we are also told by Jesus, and other scriptural examples, that in normal situations of day-to-day life, we should be prepared to defend ourselves, or even to flee to the mountains" (see Matthew 24:16).

Then one might also point to the martyrs of old, as well as the current-day martyrs, who refused to fight back, refused to defend themselves, refused to flee. To take that kind of stand is one's personal choice and responsibility before the Lord—especially when your choice involves the lives of others around you.

But remember this as well: Many of those who died as martyrs had no choice. They had no weapons! They had already been disarmed by evil regimes and had been enslaved or brutally repressed. When the time came to fight, they could not. Neither could they flee. They were powerless to resist at all.

This is precisely the situation in North Korea, for example, where most of the world's persecution against Christians currently occurs. I would imagine that many of the North Korean Christians die with heartfelt and bold declarations of faith upon their lips. We are often humbled and inspired to think of their great faith and courage. At the same time, we pray that those kinds of choices and unspeakable horrors don't come to our nation, our churches, or our families.

The Bible also speaks of those who willingly laid down their lives for their faith in God. As we explored in an earlier chapter, many Bible students would immediately think of Daniel or Shadrach, Meshach, and Abednego. Perhaps they would think of Stephen, the apostle Paul, or the martyrs spoken of in Hebrews 11. But most of us fervently pray that we will never be placed in those unthinkable circumstances. If we are, however, the Word of God is clear that God will give us grace in those particular times. Sometimes He even gets in the fire with us or delivers us from the fire—or the lion's den—even in the heat of what we think is impending doom.

> Then Nebuchadnezzar the king was [astounded], and rose up in haste, and spake, and said unto his counsellors, did not we cast three men bound into the midst of the fire? They answered and said unto the king, True, O king.
> He answered and said, Lo, I see four men loose, walking in the midst of the fire, and they have no hurt; and the form of the fourth is like the Son of God. (Daniel 3:24–25, KJV)

However, the clear biblical principle—from Jesus' own lips to the pages of Nehemiah and elsewhere—is that when we can do so, we have an obligation to defend ourselves and our loved ones, as well as those around us who are innocent or unable. Are you prepared to do so?

The truth is that we live in a dangerous world. So we take precautions, we use our common sense, we prepare ourselves—and we trust God with the details of our lives, especially those we cannot foresee and for which we cannot prepare. Ultimately, the Lord is always the final and eternal trust of those who have a personal walk with Him. But we are no less righteous when we use the intelligence God gave us to prepare for the dangers of life around us, including the possibility of direct persecution.

It really is that simple.

The ability to protect ourselves is a God-given right. If God's people had not taken that responsibility in a serious manner through the ages, many suppose the planet, under Satan's domain, would have been rid of Christians and Jews thousands of years ago.

But, the prophetically returned Israel is still here as a magnificent witness to the world, testifying of God's glory and faithfulness. And the Church of Jesus Christ still shines the light of the gospel to the world, beckoning the lost ones to "come out" and be reconciled to their Creator, who is also the soon coming King of Kings. Even in the darkness. Even in the revenant days of Noah, the light still shines.

And it still shines precisely because the Lord Himself, through the ages, in many times and in many ways, told His people to "Be thou prepared!"

Faith Alone

Of course, as believers, we should "trust in God." That should be a given among His faithful children.

Why should I concern myself with preparing? I'm just going to *walk by faith*.

Have you ever heard anyone say that? Have *you* ever said, or thought, that?

Following is another teaching of Jesus that, when not placed in its proper context, has served as a convenient excuse among the more careless or lazy of God's children to not prepare for the future.

Don't Worry. Be Happy!

As we've already discovered from our examination of other passages, i.e.: the wise being prepared, the fool not seeing danger and preparing, the one who doesn't work doesn't eat; and the one who doesn't provide for his family being worse than an unbeliever—we certainly understand that this particular verse cannot possibly mean for us to sit back and do nothing.

Have a look at the passage, spoken by Jesus in the Sermon on the Mount.

> Therefore I tell you, do not worry about your life, what you will eat or drink; or about your body, what you will wear. Is not life more than food, and the body more than clothes?...
>
> So do not worry, saying, "What shall we eat?" or "What shall we drink?" or "What shall we wear?" For the pagans run after all these things, and your heavenly Father knows that you need them. But seek first his kingdom and his righteousness, and all these things will be given to you as well. Therefore do not worry about tomorrow, for tomorrow will worry about itself. Each day has enough trouble of its own. (Matthew 6:25, 31–34)

Here's the context of Jesus' teaching. He's calling the throngs to leave behind the relatively unalterable anxieties of life and follow Him by faith to the higher callings of God's Kingdom. God will provide along the way as He rewards our own hard work, thoughtful preparations, and godly stewardship of the things He has already given us.

Jesus certainly isn't telling His listeners to quit work. Nor is He telling them to not plan for the future. Neither is He saying not to earn a living, purchase clothing, or make certain that food is on the table. Of course not.

Jesus was admonishing His listeners not to become thoroughly worldly people, like the lost world around them. He was saying not to become one of those whose total reason for living is to attain the "high life," a life of luxury and wealth, and be overflowing with plenty. He was warning that a life's pursuit of such things would cause undue and unhealthy anxiety in their lives and rob them of their *faith walk* with God...that daily walk that allows God to surprise us with His occasional holy surprises!

Of course we must work. Of course we must either grow our own food or shop for it. Of course we must clothe ourselves. The point is that, as believers in Christ, we are not to become like the pagans who never even look up to give thanks to the Lord, who is our ultimate provider of all of life's sustenance in the first place.

Pulpit Commentary:

Do not give way to anxiety about the things of life, but look up to God in steady gaze of faith; he will provide.[374]

Matthew Henry's Commentary:

There is scarcely any sin against which our Lord Jesus more warns his disciples, than disquieting, distracting, distrustful cares about the things of this life. This often ensnares the poor as much as the love of wealth does the rich.

Take no thought for your life. Not about the length of it; but refer it to God to lengthen or shorten it as he pleases; our times are in his hand, and they are in a good hand. Not about the comforts of this life; but leave it to God to make it bitter or sweet as he pleases.[375]

Benson Commentary:

For we are not to suppose that our Lord here commands us absolutely to take no thought for our life, food, and raiment; because, in other parts of Scripture, diligence in business is inculcated, and men are commanded to labor with their hands, that they may provide for the supply of their own wants, and also those of others, Romans 12:11; Ephesians 4:28.

What Christ therefore here forbids is, not that thought, foresight, and care which prudent men use in providing sustenance and needful support for themselves, and those dependent upon them; but it is such an anxious care…which prevents our receiving…in the love of God.[376]

Look at it like this. Even those of us who are faithful and biblical preppers can suddenly find ourselves in a situation of utter need. Our storage supply room can burn down or wash away in a flood, or we can be the victims of theft. As believers, regardless of our preparations, we understand that ultimately our lives are always in the hands of our Savior. In the meantime, we are commanded to "be thou prepared." However, to worry about the stuff of life in such a way as to invoke faithless anxiety upon ourselves or those around us is an affront to the Word of God.

Practical and judicious preparation is part of normal everyday life. After all, don't we prepare and think ahead in practically every other area of our life? Of course we do. Why should preparing for the potential of future problems, or even of unthinkable calamities and disasters, be any different?

Consider the following: Do you wear a seatbelt when you drive? Do you strap your children in as well? Do many of our homes have burglar alarms, smoke alarms, and fire extinguishers? Do you have some means of personal protection or home protection? Maybe you own, or even carry, a firearm. Do you carry a spare tire in your car? Do you possess all manner of insurance policies? Do your doors have locks? If you live in an area prone to natural disasters such as hurricanes, tornadoes, or floods, do you have a plan in place in the event of such emergencies?

If you answered "yes" to any or all of these questions, let me ask you another one: *Why in the world do you do these things?* Why not simply "trust in God" in each of these instances? As a matter of fact, why even go to the grocery store— ever again? Won't your food just show up by *faith,* on your front doorstep? Or, do you exercise common sense and prepare for your family to eat by going shopping every now and then?

The truth is, in our everyday activities of living, we are in a constant state of preparing, planning, and protecting. And we never question our own faith in the Lord as we prepare, do we?

The issue of properly prepping is not a matter of having enough faith or trusting God; it is a matter of faithfulness to God's clear instructions in His Word—especially when it commands us to be faithfully prepared and when it also demonstrates how preparedness has been carried out among His people through the ages.

So really, the question is not so much, "*Should* we prepare?"

The focus ought to be, "*How* should we prepare?"

The Seven Basics

The world is extremely unstable, and every indicator is that it is only going to grow worse as it gets closer to the return of the Lord.

What about the possibility of a war coming to our own soil?

This is a horrible thought, to be sure, but many countries live with this distinct possibility every day. September 11, 2001, should have taught us this lesson—or have we forgotten already?

We've already had three major wars take place on the soil of our own nation: the War of Independence, the War of 1812, and the Civil War. Why would we think that this scenario could never present itself again in our nation? Of course, I fervently pray it doesn't. But life simply doesn't hold those kinds of guarantees. The world is extremely unstable, and every indicator is that it is only going to grow worse as the return of the Lord gets closer.

Imagine those living in today's Israel (always under constant threat) saying, "I have made no preparations for my family. We have no food, water, or other emergency supplies. We will just trust in the Lord." Wouldn't you consider them to be abdicating their God-given responsibilities? Wouldn't you even consider them downright foolish?

What do we need to do in the event that we and/or our families have to "flee to the mountains" (see Matthew 24:16)? More importantly, what do we need to do in order to stay put and live in and minister to the world around us, especially when we cannot, or choose not to, flee? In either case, the goal is the same: *survive, if at all possible.*

Seven foundational needs are required to do that: water, shelter, food, clothing, medical supplies, weapons, and tools. In this chapter, we'll start with the first two, which are the two most fundamental.

1. Water

The human body is made up of about 60 percent water. We must have water to survive. Every living cell in our body needs it. Every system in our body depends on it. Without sufficient water, our heart, kidneys, and brain functions eventually shut down. Water is, without a doubt, our number-one need as far as immediate survival requirements go. When disaster strikes, we need to make certain we have plenty of water on hand or ensure that we know how to obtain it.

The human body can go many days without food if necessary, but if we go more than three or four days without water, we're in deep trouble. This is especially true in case of extremely hot or cold weather, or in case of injuries. In these cases, the body's need for water is dramatically increased. We can get water from other fluids, such as juices and milk (the only fluid to avoid entirely is alcohol, because it acts as a fairly potent diuretic).

It is advisable to have emergency water supplies stored in appropriate containers. Most people need between nine and thirteen cups of fluids per day to remain healthy, or about one gallon of water per person per day. We certainly should have adequate supplies of water-cleansing or purifying devices on hand. A bottle of unscented chlorine bleach, without other additives, is often advised as a purifying agent. The usual formula for cleansing water with bleach is one-fourth tablespoon to each gallon. The water should then be allowed to sit for at least sixty minutes before drinking.

Chlorine tablets for water purification can also be purchased and are much easier to use, transport, and store than chlorine liquid. Of course, hard-boiling is also a way to purify most water supplies, especially if there are any doubts at all about its cleanliness. Cloudy water should be filtered (using coffee filters, paper towels, cheesecloth, clean clothing, or a cotton plug in a funnel) before boiling.

If the water is suspected to be unsafe because of chemicals, oils, poisonous substances, sewage, or other contaminants, we should never drink it. Nor should we drink water that is dark in color, has an odor, or contains solid materials.

2. Shelter

Exposure to extreme elements such as heat, cold, rain, and snow, can be a killer, or at least a danger to our health and ability to survive. Emergency shelter preparation is as varied as the terrain, the environment, and our emergency situation.

Sometimes, something as simple as an automobile or a family camping tent will suffice as a shelter until other arrangements can be made. In worst-case situations, a rudimentary hut or canopy may need to be constructed. The main idea, of course, is to quickly secure protection from nature's extremes. There are many ways to accomplish rapid sheltering.

A quickly constructed wooden structure using 2' x 4' framing lumber, just big enough for one or two people, can be covered with a plastic tarp, sheets of tin, or other building materials. A lean-to shelter constructed from tree limbs and rope or twine can be assembled with a minimum of supplies for an immediate-need shelter. Again, a multitude of materials such as videos, books, and pictures are available to assist you in the construction of such shelter.

Why are we even talking about survival shelters and huts? It might be hard to imagine a scenario in which we would be forced to live outside without assistance *from anyone* for days on end. I understand how far-fetched it must sound to even have to consider such a scenario.

But please remember that starting in 2010, during Arab Spring, eventually hundreds of thousands of Iraq's Christians, living in the oldest

Christian communities in the world, were suddenly blasted from their homes, schools, and businesses and driven into the deserts and wilderness areas; they were fleeing for their lives.

At the time, many of these people were professionals with careers, homes, cars, businesses, and families. The next day, they were refugees, fending for themselves and seeking emergency shelter, food, and water—and most would never return to their homes or businesses, or have access to their bank accounts. If they survived at all, they had to start from scratch. Their first priority was basic survival.

I pray we are never faced with such horror, but why should we think that, as the world continues to turn, we are exempt from a similar possibility?

We are not.

When Disaster Strikes

I, as a former law enforcement officer, can assure you, when disaster strikes, those who have not prepared often panic.

We're embarking upon this journey of preparedness because we've also pretty well settled the fact that we are living in some precarious days. We don't know what tomorrow holds, but recent years have taught us that everything about our world and our personal lives can change, and in a moment's notice.

And here is the most important biblical principle of all: People who are prepared are also able to minister and attend to the needs of others more freely. This is a huge reason for the true child of God to faithfully prepare. We're not here to see how rich and comfortable we can become, only to leave everything behind to others when we depart. Rather, we are placed here by the Lord's design as ambassadors for Jesus Christ. We are the Noahs of our day. We are the ones who can bring light and hope in a world that continues to grow increasingly dark.

With that in mind, let's take a quick look at the remaining basic needs.

3. Food

Food supply is usually the first thing to get folks' attention when preparing for an emergency. However, as stated, a healthy person can survive without food for several weeks if necessary. It's not comfortable, nor is it advisable, but it can be done.

Of course, for those with life-and-death dietary needs (such as diabetes, high blood pressure, heart problems, and so forth), extra preparation and food storage plans will have to be made. It's also important to remember that local grocery stores only carry enough fresh food to supply their customer base for about three to four days before they need new shipments. Canned and bottled goods can disappear from the shelves within hours, even from the largest grocery stores, especially as the surrounding population perceives that danger is about to strike.

Massive runs on grocery stores and gas stations, for example, are a common affair in the region where I live—Hurricane Alley. Within hours, and certainly not more than a few days, many businesses close because of buyer panic, unprepared people stocking up at the last minute. We've recently seen that even the most basic supplies, like toilet paper, can disappear within hours—*from everywhere.*

We should also give thought to the shelf life of stored foods. Pest control is another consideration. If we aren't careful, we may wind up simply feeding the rats and bugs in the area, creating additional problems. The safety and relative ease in getting to our food supply in an emergency is also important.

On a simpler basis, as in hurricane supply preparation, canned goods, dried foods, bottled water, and jarred goods are plentiful and easy to store. They can be purchased in bulk, stored for weeks or months, and then used and rotated as we replenish our stock. Many of these goods can be eaten without cooking. Some canned goods, if stored properly and left unopened, can last for longer than a decade.

Needless to say, we can't plan on trying to eat a gourmet meal each day. We're talking about survival food! In the case of raw survival, calories are what's the most important. We'll need, normally speaking, a lot of them. Many nutrition sites recommend we intake several thousand calories per day. Believe it or not, we can now purchase survival bars that have as much as two to three thousand calories in a single bar of food.

Don't forget we'll also need to plan for the basic food prep items such as matches, grills, fuel, pots, utensils, plates, cups, and bowls. During a prolonged power outage, a closed, full, and properly sealed freezer will keep food safe for several days. After that, we can remove the food and cook it on a grill, smoker, or open fire. The cooked food will then last a little longer, plus we can use the extra food to share with and minister to those around us.

Food in a refrigerator should be fine as long as power is out no more than four hours. It's important to keep the door closed as much as possible, and discard any perishable food (such as meat, poultry, fish, eggs, and leftovers) that have been above 40 degrees Fahrenheit for more than two hours. We should be able to eat out of the refrigerator and freezer for several days, if we are careful about opening and closing the doors.

This is where having a well-stocked refrigerator and freezer comes into play. The refrigerator keeps things cool for two to three days, depending on location and the temperatures outside. The freezer then becomes the fridge in three to four days as things thaw out but stay cool.

4. Emergency Clothing

In emergency survival scenarios, it's also important to have ample and adequate clothing. Again, we probably want to avoid excess in the personal storage of clothing. However, few people think first of clothing as an emergency supply. Most of us are blessed to have plenty—but imagine if you had no shoes or heavy jacket in extremely cold weather.

What if you didn't have enough underclothing? Hmmm. I bet you're thinking about it now! I advise people, in preparing for their own or family emergency needs, to set aside a couple of pairs of shoes, used but in good repair—as well as a supply of T-shirts, pants, underclothing, and socks. In addition, we should throw in some clothing appropriate for our locale, taking weather extremes into consideration. These items can be stored in a box, plastic container, or a dedicated closet. We should always remember to think of others we're responsible for as we make these basic and minimum preparations concerning clothing.

5. Medical and Hygiene Supplies

We should give serious consideration to medical and hygiene needs when planning ahead for potential emergency situations. It is surprising how often a disaster strikes and many people are simply not prepared with emergency medical supplies. In some cases, what was once a simple daily, routine medication requirement can quickly become a matter of life and death. We should give thought to our particular medical needs and to those of the people around us, and prepare accordingly. Additionally, we can purchase adequate first-aid kits that have long shelf lives.

It's also wise to construct a list of contact information for those within our church family and circle of close acquaintances who are medical professionals (EMTs, nurses, doctors, surgeons, physician assistants, and pharmacists). These folks may well prove to be a lifesaver for us or a family member in an emergency scenario.

6. Protecting Your Stuff

It doesn't take long to learn that, no matter how many emergency supplies you have, if you can't protect them, you probably won't have them long. We've already spent much time considering the philosophy and biblical nature of armed protection. Sadly, in the case of an extreme disaster or emergency situation, this may be one of your most important preparations.

I, as a former law enforcement officer, can assure you that when disaster strikes, those who did not prepare often panic. Some who go into panic mode turn into something akin to crazed animals. They will kill, steal, and destroy anything and anyone to get to our supplies.

And they will often do it without thought or regret. This is an extreme scenario, to be certain, but it is realistic and happens almost every day somewhere in the world. If that unthinkable scenario ever presents itself in your life, please be prepared.

7. Tools and Equipment

The seventh need often proves to be an extremely important factor in emergency situations. Consider the following list of supplies:

- Air mattresses
- Axe
- Baby supplies
- Basic tool kit
- Cell phone and charger
- Chain saw, with gas and oil
- Charcoal
- Compass and map of the area
- Duct tape and electric tape
- Emergency flare gun and flares
- Zip ties
- Entertainment items (books, cards, games)
- Generator or power inverter
- Hammer
- Hand-crank emergency radio
- Hatchet
- Heavy-duty pry bar
- Knives (sheath, hunting, pocket, Swiss Army)
- Large plastic tarps
- Lighter fluid
- Lighting sources (flashlights, glow sticks, etc.)
- Limb saw
- Manual can opener
- Nails and other fasteners

- Notepad and pencils/pens
- Roll of strong twine or cord
- Pet supplies
- Portable propane container
- Propane cookstove
- Rain gear
- Scissors
- Shovel
- Strike-anywhere matches
- Whistle
- Work gloves

Depending upon your own personal needs, you may think of other items.

You may already have most of these items, but if you don't, consider purchasing them now. Or, partner with neighbors to share access to tools and supplies with each other in the case of a disaster situation. Remember, it may be days before we can get to a store. The idea in all of this, of course, is common sense planning and thoughtful preparation.

These seven basics are the beginning of a rational guide to planning. Thinking about these matters is the intelligent and godly thing to do. Talking about and formulating a plan is even better. However, nothing substitutes for actual preparation as well as hands-on, logistical gathering and stocking up on at least the basic survival needs.

Of course, we all pray that we'll never have to live in a genuine survival situation. The sad truth, though, is that tens of thousands of Americans every year are put in these types of circumstances: fires, floods, earthquakes, tornadoes, hurricanes, snowstorms, and more.

But now we are beginning to understand that disasters may prove to be the least of our concerns in the long run. More is on the way. Much more. We're in the days of Noah.

Are you and your family prepared? Noah and his family were. They were prepared physically, to be sure. But more importantly, when the final day came, they were also spiritually prepared.

And because they were prepared, they survived by God's grace in order to be used to accomplish His ongoing will.

The rest perished.

Spiritual Preparation and Daily Nourishment

In this section, I have provided more than two dozen Scripture promises for power, strength, and protection for the Lord's faithful, modern-day "Noahs."

Many more verses could be included, but I wanted to give you a quick reference of short passages that are packed with spiritual power. And, they're easy to memorize if you're so inclined.

At the end, I've left blank pages so you can add other passages—those that minister directly to your heart and soul.

Old Testament Promises

You are my hiding place; you will protect me from trouble and surround me with songs of deliverance.
—PSALM 32:7

God is our refuge and strength, an ever-present help in trouble.
—PSALM 46:1

Be strong and courageous. Do not be afraid or terrified because of them, for the Lord your God goes with you; he will never leave you nor forsake you.
—DEUTERONOMY 31:6

You make your saving help my shield, and your right hand sustains me; your help has made me great. You provide a broad path for my feet, so that my ankles do not give way.

—Psalm 18:35–36

"No weapon forged against you will prevail, and you will refute every tongue that accuses you. This is the heritage of the servants of the Lord, and this is their vindication from me," declares the Lord.

—Isaiah 54:17

Keep me safe, my God, for in you I take refuge.

—Psalm 16:1

The Lord is with me; I will not be afraid. What can mere mortals do to me?

—Psalm 118:6

You are my refuge and my shield; I have put my hope in your word.

—Psalm 119:114

Above all else, guard your heart, for everything you do flows from it.

—Proverbs 4:23

Even to your old age and gray hairs I am he, I am he who will sustain you. I have made you and I will carry you; I will sustain you and I will rescue you.

—Isaiah 46:4

I keep my eyes always on the Lord. With him at my right hand, I will not be shaken.

—Psalm 16:8

As for God, his way is perfect: The Lord's word is flawless; he shields all who take refuge in him.
—PSALM 18:30

But I will sing of your strength, in the morning I will sing of your love; for you are my fortress, my refuge in times of trouble.
—PSALM 59:16

Even though I walk through the valley of the shadow of death, I will fear no evil, for you are with me; your rod and your staff, they comfort me.
—PSALM 23:4

But you, Lord, are a shield around me, my glory, the One who lifts my head high.
—PSALM 3:3

Every word of God is flawless; he is a shield to those who take refuge in him.
—PROVERBS 30:5

It is better to take refuge in the Lord than to trust in humans.
—PSALMS 118:8

The name of the Lord is a fortified tower; the righteous run to it and are safe.
—PROVERBS 18:10

The Lord will rescue his servants; no one who takes refuge in him will be condemned.
—PSALMS 34:22

For who is God besides the Lord? And who is the Rock except our God?

—2 Samuel 22:32

The Lord is good, a refuge in times of trouble. He cares for those who trust in him.

—Nahum 1:7

The prudent see danger and take refuge, but the simple keep going and pay the penalty.

—Proverbs 27:12

New Testament Promises

Put on the full armor of God, so that you can take your stand against the devil's schemes.

—Ephesians 6:11

So we say with confidence, "The Lord is my helper; I will not be afraid. What can mere mortals do to me?"

—Hebrews 13:6

I can do all this through him who gives me strength.

—Philippians 4:13

What, then, shall we say in response to these things? If God is for us, who can be against us?

—Romans 8:31

And lead us not into temptation, but deliver us from the evil one.

—Matthew 6:13

Do you think I cannot call on my Father, and he will at once put at my disposal more than twelve legions of angels?
—Matthew 26:53

The Lord will rescue me from every evil attack and will bring me safely to his heavenly kingdom. To him be glory for ever and ever. Amen.
—2 Timothy 4:18

Never again will they hunger; never again will they thirst. The sun will not beat down on them, nor any scorching heat. For the Lamb at the center of the throne will be their shepherd; he will lead them to springs of living water. And God will wipe away every tear from their eyes.
—Revelation 7:16–17

Add Your Own Personal Favorites

About the Author

Carl Gallups has been the senior pastor of Hickory Hammock Baptist Church in Milton, Florida, since 1987. He is a graduate of the Florida Law Enforcement Officer Academy, Florida State University (BSC Criminology), and New Orleans Baptist Theological Seminary (MDiv Theology), and has served on the Board of Regents at the University of Mobile in Mobile, Alabama, since 2000.

Carl is a former decorated Florida law enforcement officer, having served under three sheriffs with two different offices, as well as working in an administrative capacity in the Central Office of the Florida Department of Corrections. He was also appointed as a special deputy, in January 2016, under former Sheriff Joe Arpaio, Maricopa County, Arizona.

Pastor Gallups is a critically acclaimed, Amazon Top 60 bestselling author, an internationally known talk-radio host since 2002, and a regular guest pundit on numerous television and radio programs. He is also a frequent guest preacher at national prophecy and Bible conferences. He has preached the gospel of Jesus Christ on three continents, in four nations, including Peru and Israel, and all over the United States—including Hawaii and Alaska. He has also preached in the Canadian provinces of British Colombia, Alberta, and Ontario.

Carl was featured on Fox News Business Report in 2016 as an "influential evangelical leader" publicly endorsing candidate Donald

Trump for the office of president. Carl was asked by the Trump campaign to open the internationally broadcast *Trump for President Rally* in Pensacola, Florida, in January 2016. More than twelve thousand people attended that rally.

Carl lives in Milton, Florida, with his wife, Pam. You can find more information about him at www.carlgallups.com.

Notes

1. There is an insurmountable difference between the "visible" and the "invisible" church. Largely, the visible church is represented by the institutional, denominational megaliths supposedly representing "Christianity" as a whole. That visible church is fractured, often at war within its own bodies and offices, and even against its own elements of denominational membership. The "invisible" church, however, is made up of truly born-again individuals who are sold out to the gospel of Jesus Christ alone, regardless of any particular institutional affiliation. Jesus is not returning for an institution, a denomination, or an ecclesiastical man-made structure. He is returning for the church "invisible."

   Jamieson-Fausset-Brown Bible Commentary expresses the matter like this:

   Satan's first effort was to root out the Christian Church, so that there should be no visible profession of Christianity. Foiled in this, he wars against *the invisible Church*, namely, "those who keep the commandments of God, and have the testimony of Jesus." These are "the remnant," or rest of her seed, as distinguished from her seed, "the man-child." Unable to destroy Christianity and the Church as a whole, Satan directs his enmity against true Christians, the elect remnant: the others he leaves unmolested. (Emphasis added)

   Revelation 12, "Jamieson-Fausset-Brown Bible Commentary," Biblehub.com, https://biblehub.com/commentaries/jfb/revelation/12.htm.

2. Collins, Charles. "UK Government Imposes Sanctions on Those Involved in Religious Persecution," *The Crux*, 7-10-20, https://cruxnow.com/church-in-uk-and-ireland/2020/07/uk-government-imposes-sanctions-on-those-involved-in-religious-persecution.

3. *Barnes' Notes on the Bible*:

Gather my saints together unto me—This is an address to the messengers employed for assembling those who are to be judged. Similar language is used by the Saviour Matthew 24:31: "And he (the Son of Man) shall send his angels with a great sound of a trumpet, and they shall gather together his elect from the four winds, from one end of heaven to the other." The idea is, that God will bring them, or assemble them together. All this is language derived froth the notion of a universal judgment, "as if" the scattered people of God were thus gathered together by special messengers sent out for this purpose. The word "saints" here refers to those who are truly his people. The object—the purpose—of the judgment is to assemble in heaven those who are sincerely his friends; or, as the Saviour expresses it Matthew 24:31, his "elect." Yet in order to this, or in order to determine who "are" his true people, there will be a larger gathering - an assembling of all the dwellers on the earth.

See: https://biblehub.com/commentaries/psalms/50-5.htm.

4. Richardson, Lindsay. "'Hundreds' of Inmates Quietly Released from Federal Prisons over Covid-19 Fears: Blair," OPTN National News, 4-20-20, https://www.aptnnews.ca/national-news/hundreds-of-inmates-quietly-released-from-federal-prisons-over-covid-19-fears-blair/?fbclid=IwAR36Oaz qBOAlqctUxaMIn0G-uwx8dTPv4FVFg8yrhnGEHuKca0lboT9ERoo.

5. Curtis, Mark. "Covid-19 Hits Five West Virginia Churches," WOWK, 6-15-20, https://www.wowktv.com/news/west-virginia/covid-19-hits-five-west-virginia-churches.

6. Ibid.

7. Author's Note: At the time of this writing, Pastor MacArthur is still embroiled in this political and spiritual battle over the government's authority to indefinitely "control" the church during a supposed pandemic.

Anugrah Kumar. "Pastor John MacArthur May Face Fine, Arrest for Holding Indoor Services: 'We will obey God rather than men'," Christian Post, 8-3-20, https://www.christianpost.com/news/pastor-john-macarthur-may-face-fine-arrest-for-holding-indoor-services-we-will-obey-god-rather-than-men.html?fbclid=IwAR3ETIOhU1NkrqYaN P5g-iO1fdkAyygmZ5U-ueQOjpe0p84ZgdN9UhiTSEM.

By August 15, 2020, a California judge finally ruled in favor of Dr. MacArthur and his church. The judge ruled they could meet as a congregation and could sing in their services. The full hearing was set for September 4, 2020.

Starnes, Todd. "VICTORY! California Judge Says John MacArthur Can Hold Indoor Church," Todd Starnes, 8-14-20, https://www.toddstarnes.

com/faith/victory-california-judge-says-john-macarthur-can-hold-indoor-church/?utm_source=izooto&fbclid=IwAR3EZ6ZhwwtdYqok
QSICOVzoFYMBLhv93SynVUoznenbaM_QyZcdioEFBCs.

8. Blankley, Bethany. "Pastor, Church Sue Newsom, Los Angeles County Officials over Orders," Center Square, 8-14-20, https://www.thecentersquare.com/california/pastor-church-sue-newsom-los-angeles-county-officials-over-orders/article_77e0d6ee-de26-11ea-ad3d-5fa535a592d5.html.

9. The Summit Church: Gathering Plans for 2020. Accessed 8- 21-20, https://summitchurch.com/coronavirus.

   "For the remainder of the year, we will not gather in person at our campuses on the weekend. Our plan is to equip you to be the church in your homes, in your communities, and online…"

10. From the Fox News article:

    The SBC president made the comments **in the wake of George Floyd's May 25 death** while in police custody, something that he said shed light on the injustices "that our black brothers and sisters have been telling us for years."

    The leader of the **largest Protestant Christian denomination** in the country **shocked many** when he urged his members to declare "black lives matter" and denounced using "all lives matter…. And, oh by the way, let's not respond by saying 'all lives matter,'" Greear said.

    See: Parke, Caleb. "Southern Baptist President Calls for Members to Declare: 'Black lives matter'," Fox News, 6-11-20, https://www.foxnews.com/us/black-lives-matter-southern-baptist.

11. Goldman, Russell. "Chinese Police Dynamite Christian Megachurch," *New York Times*, 1-12-18, https://www.nytimes.com/2018/01/12/world/asia/china-church-dynamite.html.

12. Foust, Michael. "'Whatever Means Are Necessary': Chicago Threatens to Close Church That Defied Order," Christian Headlines, 5-26-20, https://www.christianheadlines.com/contributors/michael-foust/whatever-means-are-necessary-chicago-threatens-to-close-church-that-defied-order.html.

13. Horowitz, Daniel. "Horowitz: SCOTUS Rules Nevada Churches Can Be Restricted More Than Casinos," Conservative Review, 7-27-20, https://www.conservativereview.com/news/horowitz-scotus-rules-nevada-churches-can-restricted-casinos.

14. Huston, Warner Todd. "Chicago Mayor Launches Police Raid to Shut Down Black Church's Sunday Services," Breitbart.com, 5-24-20, https://www.breitbart.com/politics/2020/05/24/chicago-mayor-launches-police-

raid-shut-down-black-church/?fbclid=IwAR0AYx311PXv5Q4_JN0b6eOB
V2K4I2f7TvRYMfqXSHQXdMRFSTf-aDV_LnM.

15. Durden, Tyler. "One Nation Under House Arrest: How Do COVID-19
Mandates Impact Our Freedoms?" Zero Hedge, 7-30-20, https://www.
zerohedge.com/political/one-nation-under-house-arrest-how-do-covid-19-
mandates-impact-our-freedoms.

16. Aaro, David. "Utah School Students, Staff Defying Mask Mandate Could
Face Charges: Reports," FOX News, 8-21-20, https://www.foxnews.
com/politics/utah-school-students-staff-defying-mask-mandate-could-
face-charges-reports?fbclid=IwAR2SNBx28Il9MwNX0ybRBD1sctuDFq
O1v-i1gU9NqzN4cz68RLJyRCCxgrw.

17. Golden, C. Douglas. "Expert Warns America: Here's What States May
Do If You Refuse a COVID Vaccine," *Western Journal*, 8-22-20, https://
www.westernjournal.com/expert-warns-america-states-may-refuse-
covid-vaccine/?utm_source=Email&utm_medium=aa-breaking&utm_
campaign=can&utm_content=firefly&ats_es=2064cabe67f590ed52b3bee4
705e4c01.

18. Deadliest Pandemics in History

The deadliest pandemic recorded in human history was the Black
Death, or the Bubonic Plague (mid-1300s), resulting in 75–200 million
deaths worldwide. (See: ABC Science, "Black Death 'Discriminated'
between Victims," 1-29-08, http://www.abc.net.au/science/
articles/2008/01/29/2149185.htm).

The 1918 flu, also known as the Spanish Flu, lasted until 1920 and
is considered the deadliest pandemic in modern history. There were an
estimated fifty million deaths worldwide. (See: National Geographic, "How
Some Cities 'flattened the curve' During the 1918 Flu Pandemic," 3-27-20,
https://www.nationalgeographic.com/history/2020/03/how-cities-flattened-
curve-1918-spanish-flu-pandemic-coronavirus/#close). In the United States,
various cities and states ordered the closing of schools, theaters, public
gathering places, and even churches. However, some areas of the country
did not order the closing of churches. Even among the ones that ordered
church closings, they were closed on average no longer than a few weeks to a
couple of months. The US military was hit particularly hard near the end of
its engagement in World War 1. There was no vaccine or treatment for this
particular strain of H1N1.

While the COVID-19 global pandemic of 2020 was billed as a similar
situation to the Spanish Flu, there really is little spiritual and societal

comparison between the two. Church shutdowns during the Spanish Flu were by and large not a global, government-ordered phenomenon, in nearly the same way as was COVID. Nor were casinos, bars, and restaurants deemed by the US Supreme Court to have more of a right to be open during a pandemic than did a church (See: Conservative Review, "SCOTUS Rules Nevada Churches Can Be Restricted More Than Casinos," 7-27-20, https://www.conservativereview.com/news/horowitz-scotus-rules-nevada-churches-can-restricted-casinos).

During the Spanish Flu, National Guard troops were not called to churches. Pastors and congregants were not threatened with fines, jails, or the bulldozing of their churches for not complying with closure orders. I can find no records of global major media sources constantly accusing the churches of being the major culprit in the spreading of the disease, as was the case with the COVID outbreak. And in 1918 in America, there was very little "anti-church" sentiment running through our culture. In fact, the exact opposite was true. The microscope that could actually see viruses was not invented until the 1930s. In 1918, there was little that medical science could offer in the way of alleviation. Today's technology and medications are much more advanced. So is global communication technology. So is global *fake news* and purposed disinformation designed to affect national elections and the continued disruption of people's personal lives and privacy. The ability to "force" people to take a new vaccine and even to put human tracking technology inside of those formulations would have been considered pure science fiction in 1918. Not so today. We live in a completely different age than the world of 1918. What happened in America and around the world in the COVID pandemic was not even within the same prophetic ball park as the Spanish Flu.

19. Dr. Lee, Lionel. "Big Tech Silencing Physicians: A Very Dangerous Road for American Medicine," Association of American Physicians and Surgeons (AAPS), 8-5-20, https://aapsonline.org/big-tech-silencing-physicians-a-very-dangerous-road-for-american-medicine.

"It would appear now that we are allowing social media tech giants to practice medicine, instead of keeping this sacred relationship between the doctor and patient."

20. Pinkerton, James P. "If the Viruses Keep Coming, Here's How We Should Respond," Breitbart, 7-11-20, https://www.breitbart.com/health/2020/07/11/pinkerton-if-the-viruses-keep-coming-heres-how-we-should-respond.

21. *Benson Commentary*:

So far **mercy prevailed**, that **a reprieve was obtained** for six-score years [120 years]; and **during this time Noah was preaching righteousness** to them, and, to assure them of the truth of his doctrine, was preparing the ark. (Emphasis added)

Genesis 6:13. "Benson Commentary on the Bible," Biblehub.com, https://biblehub.com/commentaries/genesis/6-3.htm.

Keil and Delitzsch Biblical Commentary on the Old Testament:

"Therefore his days shall be 120 years:" this means, not that human life should in future never attain a greater age than 120 years, but that *a respite of 120 years should still be granted to the human race* [during Noah's day]. This sentence, as we may gather from the context, was made known to Noah in his 480th year, to be *published by him as "preacher of righteousness"* (2 Peter 2:5) to the degenerate race. (Emphasis added)

Genesis 6:13. "Keil and Delitzsch Biblical Commentary on the Old Testament," Biblehub.com, https://biblehub.com/commentaries/genesis/6-3.htm.

Jamieson-Fausset-Brown Bible Commentary:

Yet his days shall be an hundred and twenty years—It is probable that the corruption of [Noah's] world, which had now reached its height, had been long and gradually increasing, and *this idea receives support from the long respite granted.* (Emphasis added)

Genesis 6:13. "Jamieson-Fausset-Brown Bible Commentary," Biblehub. com, https://biblehub.com/commentaries/genesis/6-3.htm.

22. "A thousand years in your sight…"

Cambridge Bible for Schools and Colleges:

A whole millennium to God, as He reviews it, is but as the past day when it draws towards its close,—a brief space with all its events still present and familiar to the mind.

Barnes' Notes on the Bible:

The idea here is, that the longest human life, even if it should be lengthened out to a thousand years, would be in the sight of God, or in comparison with his years, but as a single day.

23. This topic is thoroughly explored beginning with the chapter titled "A Certain Tree."

24. See Matthew 24 and Luke 17.

25. Schmidt, Charles, "Genetic Engineering Could Make a COVID-19 Vaccine in Months Rather Than Years," *Scientific American*, 6-1-20, https://www.

scientificamerican.com/article/genetic-engineering-could-make-a-covid-19-vaccine-in-months-rather-than-years1.

Also see note 18 above titled "Deadliest Pandemics in History."

26. Bowman, Amanda. "New Epidemic Model Indicates COVID-19 Here to Stay, Likely to Cause 235,000 U.S. Deaths by October," MedicalXpress. com, 6-24-20, https://medicalxpress.com/news/2020-06-epidemic-covid-deaths-october.html.

27. Of course, the Genesis narrative does not say that Noah had such a vision. But such visions were indeed recorded by King David and the prophet Isaiah (Psalm 22, Isaiah 53). I am merely suggesting that Noah, who was foreshadowing the entire ministry of Jesus and the offering of the "only" means of escape from God's coming wrath and judgment, might also have been given some prophetic insight concerning the eternal purpose for which he was currently being used. Certainly, the apostle Peter understood that Noah' life and mission foreshadowed the entire gospel event. See 1 Peter 3 and 2 Peter 2.

28. Genesis 6:7–16:

[7] And Noah and his sons and his wife and his sons' wives entered the ark to escape the waters of the flood. [8] **Pairs of clean and unclean animals**, of birds and of all creatures that move along the ground, [9] male and female, *came to* **Noah** and *entered the ark*, as God had commanded Noah. [10] And after the seven days the floodwaters came on the earth.

[11] In the six hundredth year of Noah's life, **on the seventeenth day of the second month**—on **that day** all the springs of the great deep burst forth, and the floodgates of the heavens were opened. [12] And rain fell on the earth forty days and forty nights.

[13] *On that very day* Noah and his sons, Shem, Ham and Japheth, together with his wife and the wives of his three sons, entered the ark. [14] They had with them every wild animal according to its kind, all livestock according to their kinds, every creature that moves along the ground according to its kind and every bird according to its kind, everything with wings. [15] **Pairs of all creatures that have the breath of life in them** *came to Noah and entered the ark.* [16] The *animals going in* were male and female of every living thing, as God had commanded Noah. **Then the Lord shut him in.** (Emphasis added)

29. The next narrative chapters are a fictionalized account of Jesus' journey from the region of Galilee on down toward Jericho, by way of the Jordan Valley. From there, Jesus and the disciples made their way up to Jerusalem, on the way to the cross. Based upon Matthew 22–24 and Luke 17.

30. **Baruch.** A Hebrew name for a male meaning "blessing." This is a fictional name inserted here to make the narrative more personal. Baruch was the name of Jeremiah's scribe, mentioned numerous times in that book.

31. *Hashem* is a Hebrew title used in Judaism to refer to God, and literally means "the Name."

32. Zechariah 12:10:

    And I will pour out on the house of David and the inhabitants of Jerusalem a spirit of grace and supplication. They will look on me, the one they have pierced, and they will mourn for him as one mourns for an only child, and grieve bitterly for him as one grieves for a firstborn son.

    Isaiah 53:5:

    But he was pierced for our transgressions, he was crushed for our iniquities; the punishment that brought us peace was on him, and by his wounds we are healed.

    Psalm 22:1, 16–8 (A Psalm of David):

    My God, my God, why have you forsaken me? Dogs surround me, a pack of villains encircles me; they pierce my hands and my feet. All my bones are on display; people stare and gloat over me. They divide my clothes among them and cast lots for my garment.

33. *Bengel's Gnomen*:

    You ought not to look to times that are future, or places that are remote: for the kingdom of God is **within** you; **even as the King Messiah is in the midst of you: John 1:26** ["There standeth one among you whom ye know not"]. (Emphasis added; brackets in the original)

    Pulpit Commentary:

    The kingdom of God **could not be said to be in the hearts of those Pharisees** to whom the Master was especially directing his words of reply here. It should be *rather understood in the midst of your ranks.* [In the person of Jesus]. (Emphasis added)

    Matthew Poole's Commentary:

    The kingdom of God is **now in the midst among you,** though you **observe it not.** (Emphasis added)

    All three commentary entries are found at: https://biblehub.com/commentaries/luke/17-21.htm.

34. Luke 19:11.

35. John 12:1.

36. Matthew 21:18–22.

37. Matthew 24:32–35. This book devotes a later chapter entitled "A Certain Tree" to what Jesus most likely meant by using this specific parable.

38. See John 10:18 and Matthew 26:5–7.

39. Psalm 22:1, 7–8, 15–18.

40. After the crucifixion and resurrection (and even before), there were believers among the Pharisees, priests, and teachers of the law, as well as among rabbis, leaders in the synagogues, and even Roman centurions.

    See: Acts 6:7, Acts 15:5, Acts 18:8, John 19:38–39, and Acts 10.

41. Copeland, Terry. "It Might Be That God Is Just Trying to Get Our Attention," *Cumberland Times-News*, 3-23-20, https://www.times-news.com/opinion/it-might-be-that-god-is-just-trying-to-get-our-attention/article_4a5caf74-6ad4-11ea-bc8f-d31651b7bb4b.html.

42. Hobbs, Billy. "Pastor Believes God Has Clear Message Amid Pandemic," *Union-Recorder*, 4-14-20, https://www.unionrecorder.com/news/pastor-believes-god-has-clear-message-amid-pandemic/article_5b7d40b2-7e88-11ea-b8d2-47da178fff86.html.

43. Mattia Ferraresi. "God vs Coronavirus," *New York Times*, 3-10-20, https://www.nytimes.com/2020/03/10/opinion/coronavirus-church-religion.html.

44. Market Insights. "Global Antidepressant Market: Increased Stress Levels over the Covid-19 Outbreak," accessed July 23, 2002, https://www.globenewswire.com/news-release/2020/06/30/2055610/0/en/Global-Antidepressant-Market-Increased-Stress-Levels-over-the-Covid-19-Outbreak-PMI.html.

45. Kahzan, Olga. "The Millennial Mental-Health Crisis: Suicides and overdoses among young adults were already skyrocketing before the pandemic started. Now experts fear that the situation is going to get even worse." *Atlantic*, 6-11-20, https://www.theatlantic.com/health/archive/2020/06/why-suicide-rates-among-millennials-are-rising/612943.

    See also: Mora, Edwin. "CDC Confirms: 'Adverse' Mental Health Problems 'Increased Considerably' During Lockdowns," Breitbart, 8-13-20, https://www.breitbart.com/politics/2020/08/13/cdc-confirms-adverse-mental-health-problems-increased-considerably-during-lockdowns.

46. US National Library of Medicine. "The COVID-19 Pandemic Brings a Second Wave of Social Isolation and Disrupted Services," National Institutes of Health, Accessed August 23, 2020, https://www.ncbi.nlm.nih.gov/pmc/articles/PMC7227800.

47. Luke 21:26. *Jamieson-Fausset-Brown Bible Commentary*, Biblehub.com, https://biblehub.com/commentaries/luke/21-26.htm.

48. William Wan, Joel Achenbach, Carolyn Y. Johnson and Ben Guarino. "Coronavirus Will Radically Alter the U.S." *Washington Post*, March

19, 2020. https://www.washingtonpost.com/health/2020/03/19/
coronavirus-projections-us.

49. NBC News, "Americans Warned That as Many as 240,000
    May Die," 4-1-20, https://www.nbcnews.com/health/health-
    news/live-blog/2020-03-31-coronavirus-news-n1172706/
    ncrd1173016#blogHeader.

50. Bowman, Amanda. "New Epidemic Model Indicates COVID-19 Here to
    Stay, Likely to Cause 235,000 U.S. Deaths by October," MedicalXpress.
    com, 6-24-20, https://medicalxpress.com/news/2020-06-epidemic-covid-
    deaths-october.html.

51. Bleau, Hannah. "Controversial IHME Forecast over 410k Coronavirus
    Deaths by January 1: 'The Worst Is Yet to Come'," Breitbart, 9-4-20,
    https://www.breitbart.com/politics/2020/09/04/controversial-ihme-forecast-
    over-410k-coronavirus-deaths-by-january-1-the-worst-is-yet-to-come.

52. Stewart, Katherine. "Is Crippling Our Coronavirus Response: Trump's
    response to the pandemic has been haunted by the science denialism of his
    ultraconservative religious allies," March 27, 2020, https://www.nytimes.
    com/2020/03/27/opinion/coronavirus-trump-evangelicals.html.

53. Wilson, Jason. "The Rightwing Christian Preachers in Deep Denial over
    Covid-19's Danger," *Guardian*, 4-4-20, https://www.theguardian.com/
    us-news/2020/apr/04/america-rightwing-christian-preachers-virus-hoax.

54. Merritt, Jonathan. "Some of the Most Visible Christians in America Are
    Failing the Coronavirus Test," *Atlantic*, 4-24-20, https://www.theatlantic.
    com/ideas/archive/2020/04/christian-cruelty-face-covid-19/610477.

55. Cohen, Ben. "Covid-19 Conspiracy Theories Putting Christian Minorities at
    Risk," Evangelical Alliance, 4-22-20, https://www.eauk.org/news-and-views/
    covid-19-conspiracy-theories-putting-christian-minorities-at-risk.

56. *Christian Today*, staff writer. "More Suffering for Persecuted Christians as
    They're Blamed for Coronavirus," April 20, 2020, https://christiantoday.
    com/article/more-suffering-for-persecuted-christians-as-theyre-blamed-for-
    coronavirus/134722.htm.

57. Vision Christian Radio. "Coronavirus Sparks New Persecution
    Threat for Christians," 5-5-2020, https://vision.org.au/radio/news/
    coronavirus-sparks-new-persecution-threat-for-christians.

58. EWTN News Nightly. "Virginia Governor Makes Attending Church a
    Criminal Offense," YouTube video, March 26, 2020, https://www.youtube.
    com/watch?v=ItexA8bH79Q.

59. Curtis, Mark. "Covid-19 Hits Five West Virginia Churches,"

WOWK, 6-15-20, https://www.wowktv.com/news/west-virginia/covid-19-hits-five-west-virginia-churches/.

60. Kate Conger, Jack Healy, and Lucy Tompkins. "Churches Emerge as Major Source of Coronavirus Cases: Churches Were Eager to Reopen. Now They Are Confronting Coronavirus Cases." *New York Times*, 7-8-20, https://www.nytimes.com/2020/07/08/us/coronavirus-churches-outbreaks.html.

61. As of 8-20-20, the following was the HTML <HEAD> coding of that NYT article. It was designed to display one headline on Google, and a different one at the article itself.

    <head><meta content=images/branding/googleg/1x/googleg_standard_color_128dp.png" itemprop="image"><meta content="origin" name="referrer"><title>Churches Emerge as Major Source of Coronavirus Cases. NYT - Google Search</title>.

    The headline at the actual article reads: "Churches Were Eager to Reopen. Now They Are Confronting Coronavirus Cases," https://www.nytimes.com/2020/07/08/us/coronavirus-churches-outbreaks.html.

62. *Los Angeles Times*. "Despite Coronavirus, These Experts Support the Protests for Health Reasons,"6-9-20, https://www.latimes.com/california/story/2020-06-09/coronavirus-protests-health-experts.

    Also see: Jones, Jonathan. "Sen. McConnell Exposes Democrats for 'Double Standard' in Banning Gatherings," *Western Journal*, 6-9-20, https://www.westernjournal.com/sen-mcconnell-exposes-democrats-double-standard-banning-gatherings/?utm_source=Email&utm_medium=aa-breaking&utm_campaign=can&utm_content=firefly.

63. Daniela Hernandez, Sarah Krouse, Brianna Abbott, and Charity L. Scott, "Early Data Show No Uptick in Covid-19 Transmission From Protests," *Wall Street Journal*, 6-21-20, https://www.wsj.com/articles/recent-protests-may-not-be-covid-19-transmission-hotspots-11592498020.

64. Fiore, Kristina. "So Far, So Good: No Covid-19 Spread from Protests… Yet." Med Page Today, 6-18-20, https://www.medpagetoday.com/infectiousdisease/covid19/87148.

65. Magan, Christopher. "Early Test Results Show Few Protesters Caught Covid-19," *Twin Cities*, 6-12-20, https://www.twincities.com/2020/06/12/mn-coronavirus-george-floyd-early-test-results-show-few-protesters/.

66. Carney, John. "Increased Social Distancing to Avoid Protests May Have Held Down Coronavirus Infections: Study," Breitbart.com, 6-22-20, https://www.breitbart.com/economy/2020/06/22/increased-social-distancing-to-avoid-protests-may-have-held-down-coronavirus-infections-study.

67. PBS. "The Great Fire of Rome – Background," May 29, 2014, https://www.pbs.org/wnet/secrets/great-fire-rome-background/1446.

68. Turley, Jonathan. "Why the Government Can Shut Down Church Gatherings During Pandemic," *The Hill*, 4-11-20, https://thehill.com/opinion/judiciary/492332-why-the-government-can-shut-down-church-gatherings-during-pandemic.

69. Parke, Caleb. "California County's Order Criticized for Limiting Online Worship: 'No singing'," Fox News, 4-15-20, https://www.foxnews.com/us/coronavirus-california-church-online-order-county-worship-limit.

70. Pollack, Joel. "California Bans Singing in Church," Breitbart, 7-2-20, https://www.breitbart.com/politics/2020/07/02/california-bans-singing-in-church.

71. Ibid.

72. Associated Press. "Experts See Little Evidence That Protests Spread the Coronavirus in U.S." 7-1-20, https://www.latimes.com/science/story/2020-07-01/experts-see-little-evidence-that-protests-spread-coronavirus.

73. DW.com, "Coronavirus: Germans Go Back to Church—But No Singing Allowed," 3-5-20, https://www.dw.com/en/coronavirus-germans-go-back-to-church-but-no-singing-allowed/a-53316113.

74. Horowitz, Daniel. "Horowitz: SCOTUS Rules Nevada Churches Can Be Restricted More Than Casinos," *Conservative Review*, 7-27-20, https://www.conservativereview.com/news/horowitz-scotus-rules-nevada-churches-can-restricted-casinos.

    Also see the following article, wherein after the SCOTUS ruling, a church decided to meet in a casino. The governor fined the casino for allowing it, proving that the governor's edict against churches was blatantly and supremely prejudicial against churches alone.

    Nolte, John. "Nevada's Democrat Governor Punishes Casino for Holding Worship Service," Breitbart, 8-11-20, https://www.breitbart.com/politics/2020/08/11/nolte-nevadas-democrat-governor-punishes-casino-for-holding-worship-service.

75. Quintanilla, Milton. "Trump's Personal Attorney to Represent John MacArthur amid Threats of Fines, Arrest for Holding Indoor Services," Christian Headlines, 8-6-20, https://www.christianheadlines.com/contributors/milton-quintanilla/trumps-personal-attorney-to-represent-john-macarthur-amid-threats-of-fines-arrest-for-holding-services.html?utm_source=wnd&utm_medium=wnd&utm_campaign=syndicated&fbclid=Iw

AR3z36dZnYUfJn2nFCgpi6nCdb1sRLClPD
JAEmSwRUVixWEJ0vbpvVGgkXY.

76. Dr. Rodney Stark is an American sociologist of religion. He served as a long-time professor of sociology and of comparative religion at the University of Washington. He is now the Distinguished Professor of the Social Sciences at Baylor University. Dr. Stark also serves as the co-director of the university's Institute for Studies of Religion, and he is the founding editor of the *Interdisciplinary Journal of Research on Religion*. Stark has written more than thirty books, including *The Rise of Christianity* (1996), and more than 140 scholarly articles. See: https://en.wikipedia.org/wiki/Rodney_Stark.

77. Stark, Rodney. *The Triumph of Christianity: How the Jesus Movement Became the World's Largest Religion*, (New York: Harper One, 2011), 114–119.

See also this excellent article wherein Rodney Stark's work is quoted:

Dr. Berding, Kenneth. "How Did Early Christians Respond to Plagues? Historical Reflections as the Coronavirus Spreads," Biola. edu, 3-16-20, https://www.biola.edu/blogs/good-book-blog/2020/ how-did-early-christians-respond-to-plagues.

78. Haskins, Justin. "Al Gore, UN Secretary-General, Others Now Demanding 'Great Reset' of Global Capitalism," Fox News, 6-25-20, https://www.foxbusiness.com/markets/ al-gore-un-secretary-general-great-reset-global-capitalism.

79. "A temporary form." Yet one would be hard pressed to provide examples of instances when major global power brokers were given the reigns to literally control the economic and social engines of nations across the globe, only to wield that great authority "temporarily" and then freely hand back the reins to the nations over which the newly constructed governing body had been "temporarily" ruling.

80. Elliott, Larry. "Gordon Brown Calls for Global Government to Tackle Coronavirus," *Guardian*, March 26, 2020. https://www.theguardian.com/politics/2020/mar/26/ gordon-brown-calls-for-global-government-to-tackle-coronavirus.

81. Brinded, Lianna (head of Yahoo Finance UK). "Coronavirus Marks the Real Beginning of the End of Cash," Yahoo News, 4-26-20, https://news. yahoo.com/coronavirus-covid-19-marks-the-real-beginning-of-the-end-of-cash-104855087.html.

82. Haskins, Justin. "Al Gore, UN Secretary-General, Others Now Demanding 'Great Reset' of Global Capitalism."

83. WeForum. "The Great Reset," Accessed July 1, 2020, https://www. weforum.org/great-reset.

Also see this article at *The Hill*: Haskins, Justin. "Introducing the 'Great Reset,' World Leaders' Radical Plan to Transform the Economy," The Hill, 6-25-20, https://thehill.com/opinion/energy-environment/504499-introducing-the-great-reset-world-leaders-radical-plan-to.

84. Simon, Kent. "U.N. Chief Guterres Renews Call for More Global Governance, Bureaucratic Regulation," Breitbart, 7-2-20, https://www.breitbart.com/politics/2020/07/02/u-n-chief-guterres-renews-call-for-more-global-governance-bureaucratic-regulation.

85. Lopez, German. "What Diseases Have Vaccines Eradicated?" Vox. com, 8-25-16, https://www.vox.com/2018/8/21/17588074/vaccines-diseases-wiped-out.

86. World Economic Forum. "The Great Reset," Accessed July 23, 2020, https://www.weforum.org/great-reset.

There is an urgent need for global stakeholders to cooperate in simultaneously managing the direct consequences of the COVID-19 crisis. To improve the state of the world, the World Economic Forum is starting The Great Reset initiative.

87. One of the most famous cases was the forty-year "experiment" upon a portion of Alabama's black population called the **Tuskegee Study of Untreated Syphilis in the African American Male.** This was a clinical study conducted between 1932 and 1972 by the United States Public Health Service.[1][2] The purpose of this study was to observe the natural history of untreated syphilis; the African-American men in the study were only told they were receiving free health care from the Federal government of the United States.

See:

Brandt, Allan M. (December 1978). "Racism and Research: The Case of the Tuskegee Syphilis Study." Hastings Center Report. 8 (6): 21–29. doi:10.2307/3561468. JSTOR 3561468. https://www.jstor.org/stable/3561468?seq=1.

"Tuskegee Study - Timeline - CDC - NCHHSTP". www.cdc.gov. March 2, 2020. Retrieved May 14, 2020. https://www.cdc.gov/tuskegee/timeline.htm.

Reverby, Susan (2009). Examining Tuskegee: The Infamous Syphilis Study and its Legacy. Chapel Hill: The University of North Carolina Press.

Tuskegee syphilis experiment: https://en.wikipedia.org/wiki/Tuskegee_syphilis_experiment#cite_note-:0-1.

88. Mark, Michelle. "Dr. Deborah Birx said 'there is nothing from the

CDC that I can trust' in a White House coronavirus task force meeting," *Business Insider*, 5-9-20, https://www.businessinsider.com/deborah-birx-cdc-comments-coronavirus-task-force-meeting-2020-5.

89. Guaderrama, Robert. "Fox 35 Investigates: Florida DOH, Several Labs in Dispute over COVID-19 Data," Fox News 35, 7-23-20, https://www.fox35orlando.com/news/fox-35-investigates-florida-doh-several-labs-in-dispute-over-covid-19-data.

90. Gates, Bill. "31 Questions and Answers about Covid-19: My thoughts on what to do now and other topics," GatesNotes.com, March 19, 2020, https://www.gatesnotes.com/Health/A-coronavirus-AMA.

91. Crespo, Gisela. "Fauci: There Might Be 'merit' to the Idea of Coronavirus Immunity Certificates," CNN, 4-10-2020, https://www.cnn.com/world/live-news/coronavirus-pandemic-04-10-20/h_22356f654296c004330e2149b8afd5eb.

92. Scudelarrie, Megan. "Quantum Dots Encode Vaccine History in the Skin," Spectrum.ieee.org, 12-18-2019, https://spectrum.ieee.org/the-human-os/biomedical/imaging/quantum-dots-encode-vaccine-history-in-skin.

93. Gates, Bill. "What You Need to Know about the Covid-19 Vaccine," GatesNotes.com, 4-30-20, https://www.gatesnotes.com/Health/What-you-need-to-know-about-the-Covid-19-vaccine.

94. Lovelace, Berkeley. "Bill Gates Denies Conspiracy Theories That Say He Wants to Use Coronavirus Vaccines to Implant Tracking Devices," CNBC, 7-22-20, https://www.cnbc.com/2020/07/22/bill-gates-denies-conspiracy-theories-that-say-he-wants-to-use-coronavirus-vaccines-to-implant-tracking-devices.html.

95. Schmidt, Charles. "Genetic Engineering Could Make a COVID-19 Vaccine in Months Rather Than Years," *Scientific American*, 6-1-20, https://www.scientificamerican.com/article/genetic-engineering-could-make-a-covid-19-vaccine-in-months-rather-than-years1.

96. Wadman, Meredith. "Abortion Opponents Protest COVID-19 Vaccines' Use of Fetal Cells," *Science Magazine*, 6-5-20, https://www.sciencemag.org/news/2020/06/abortion-opponents-protest-covid-19-vaccines-use-fetal-cells.

97. Sowders, Jeffrey. "Alan Dershowitz: "You Have No Right to Refuse to Be Vaccinated," May 17, 2020, https://www.youtube.com/watch?v=Hjk1-a98xag.

98. Diego, Raul. "Africa to Become Testing Ground for 'Trust Stamp' Vaccine Record and Payment System," Mint

Press, July 10, 2020, https://www.mintpressnews.com/
africa-trust-stamp-covid-19-vaccine-record-payment-system/269346.

99. Dr. Michael Lederman, Maxwell J. Mehlman and Dr. Stuart Youngner.
     "Defeat COVID-19 by requiring vaccination for all. It'ss Not
     Un-American, It's Patriotic," *USA Today*, 8-6-20, https://www.usatoday.
     com/story/opinion/2020/08/06/stop-coronavirus-compulsory-universal-
     vaccination-column/3289948001/?fbclid=IwAR2gWxMyO458JSZMM
     mdaCCntxLN3-Ol7TIRM5AXUnzJYyaNE6pM_cBDd_vU.

100. Reuters Fact Check, "False Claim: Bill Gates Wants to Microchip People;
     Anthony Fauci Wants people to Carry Vaccination Certificates," Reuters.
     com, 5-5-20, https://www.reuters.com/article/uk-factcheck-gates-fauci/
     false-claim-bill-gates-wants-to-microchip-people-anthony-fauci-wants-
     people-to-carry-vaccination-certificates-idUSKBN22H2JD.

101. Actually, Mr. Dershowitz is "legally" correct. There have been several
     Supreme Court decisions to this effect.
         See: https://www.latimes.com/opinion/opinion-la/la-ol-vaccines-
     supreme-court-parents-20150203-story.html.
         See: https://reason.com/2020/04/30/
     when-the-supreme-court-upheld-a-compulsory-vaccination-law.

102. Rogers, Michelle. "Fact Check: Hospitals Get Paid More if Patients Listed
     as COVID-19, on Ventilators," USA Today, 4-24-20, https://www.
     usatoday.com/story/news/factcheck/2020/04/24/fact-check-medicare-
     hospitals-paid-more-covid-19-patients-coronavirus/3000638001.

103. Ibid.

104. Made possible by the unprecedented pervasiveness of global information
     and communications technologies.

105. See the note 18 titled "Deadliest Pandemics in History."

106. Wikipedia. "Shavuot," Accessed 6-22-20, https://en.wikipedia.org/wiki/
     Shavuot.

107. Huckabee, Tyler. "The Problem with Saying 'All Lives Matter'"
     Relevant Magazine, 6-5-20, https://relevantmagazine.com/current16/
     problem-saying-all-lives-matter.

108. This common but contextually unbiblical argument is often leveled
     against Christians who are attempting to walk in faithfulness to the
     Word of God in spite of godless edicts handed down by governmental
     authorities. The biblical truth is addressed in the first chapter of the
     Addendum in the subsection titled "Must We Obey the Government?"

109. Rainer, Thom S. "Five Types of Church Members
     Who Will Not Return after the Quarantine," Church

Answers, 8-9-20, https://churchanswers.com/blog/
five-types-of-church-members-who-will-not-return-after-the-quarantine.

110. Noah's Flood encompasses three full chapters in Genesis and involves
the lives of eight people. It also involves eighty-eight verses, nine specific
measurements, sixteen dates and/or times, and a multitude of specific
instructions. SEE: "God's Grand Design" at https://www.godsgranddesign.
com/noahs-flood.

111. Tom Krattenmaker. "Creationism Support Is at a New Low. The Reason
Should Give Us Hope," *USA Today*, 7-13-17, https://www.usatoday.com/
story/opinion/2017/07/13/creationism-evolution-template-for-easing-
divisions-tom-krattenmaker-column/467800001/.

112. White, Monty. "Flood Legends," AIG, 3-29-07, https://answersingenesis.
org/the-flood/flood-legends/flood-legends.

113. Keep, Lennlee. "A Flood of Myths and Stories," PBS, 2-14-20, https://
www.pbs.org/independentlens/blog/a-flood-of-myths-and-stories.

114. The fact that stories of the Flood existed long before Moses gave us
Genesis is only further proof that it happened. The Bible, however, is the
one place where the information surrounding the Flood can be trusted
completely. It was given by the mouth of God Himself to Moses, on Sinai.
Of course, Jesus also affirmed the biblical account of Noah's Flood. The
secularists would have us believe that since these stories existed before the
Bible, then, somehow Moses merely copied the story into his writings.

115. Tharoor, Ishaan. "Before Noah: Myths of the Flood Are Far
Older than the Bible," *Time*, 4-1-14, https://time.com/44631/
noah-christians-flood-aronofsky.

116. Eric Cline is professor of anthropology, classics and history and director
of the Capitol Archaeological Institute at George Washington University.
A former Fulbright Scholar, he is an award-winning author and teacher
with degrees in classical archaeology, Near Eastern archaeology, and
ancient istory. Author and editor of sixteen books and almost one hundred
articles, Dr. Cline has three times won the Biblical Archaeology Society's
Publication Award for "Best Popular Book on Archaeology." See more
here: https://www.biblicalarchaeology.org/scholar/eric-cline.

117. Jenna Millman, Bryan Taylor and Lauren Effron. "Evidence
Noah's Biblical Flood Happened, Says Robert Ballard,"
ABC News, 12-5-12, https://abcnews.go.com/Technology/
evidence-suggests-biblical-great-flood-noahs-time-happened/
story?id=17884533.

118. Cotterell, Arthur. *'Nu'u' A Dictionary of World Mythology*. (Oxford University Press, 1997). Oxford Reference Online. Oxford University Press. 30 September 2010, http://www.oxfordreference.com/views/ENTRY.html?subview=Main&entry=t73.e525.

119. White, Monty. "Flood Legends: The Significance of a World of Stories Based on Truth," Answers in Genesis, 8-11-08, https://answersingenesis.org/the-flood/flood-legends/flood-legends.

120. Ibid. See also: Greshko, Michael. "Geologic Evidence May Support Chinese Flood Legend," National Geographic, 8-4-16, https://www.nationalgeographic.com/news/2016/08/china-yellow-river-great-flood-xia-dynasty-yu/#close.

121. Tharoor, Ishaan. "Before Noah: Myths of the Flood Are Far Older than the Bible."

122. Ibid.

123. Consider this example. If a person dies a normal death and is buried, will we ever come back to that burial site and find a fossilized human being? Of course not—not in a million years. Eventually, the body will turn back to dust, and then it will vanish completely. However, if that same person were to die in a catastrophic burial (volcano, earthquake, or flood for example), we very well could find the fossilized remains of that person. This is the only way fossils are formed.

124. Dr. Horner, John R. (paleontologist). *Digging Dinosaurs: The Search That Unraveled the Mystery of Baby Dinosaurs* (Cataclysmic Burial), (Workman, November 1, 1988),131.

125. Robert Duane Ballard (born June 30, 1942) is a retired United States Navy officer and a professor of oceanography at the University of Rhode Island who is noted for his work in underwater archaeology: maritime archaeology and archaeology of shipwrecks. He is most known for the discoveries of the wrecks of the *RMS Titanic* in 1985, the battleship *Bismarck* in 1989, and the aircraft carrier *USS Yorktown* in 1998. He discovered the wreck of John F. Kennedy's PT-109 in 2002 and visited Biuku Gasa and Eroni Kumana, who saved its crew. He leads ocean explorations on E/V Nautilus. See: https://en.wikipedia.org/wiki/Robert_Ballard.

126. Jenna Millman, Bryan Taylor and Lauren Effron. "Evidence Noah's Biblical Flood Happened, Says Robert Ballard," ABC News, 12-5-12, https://abcnews.go.com/Technology/evidence-suggests-biblical-great-flood-noahs-time-happened/story?id=17884533.

127. Ridley, M. "Who Doubts Evolution?" *New Scientist*, Vol. 90, June 1981, p.832.

128. Andrew Snelling, PhD, geologist, accessed May 1, 2020, https://isgenesishistory.com/andrew-snelling.

   From the referenced site:

   He worked for six years in the exploration and mining industries across the nation of Australia. For over ten years, Dr. Snelling was a research consultant to the Australian Nuclear Science and Technology Organization for an international collaborative research project funded by the US Department of Energy. That work also involved university and government research scientists from the USA, UK, Australia, Japan, Korea, Sweden, Austria and Belgium.

129. Dr. Andrew A. Snelling. "The World's Graveyard," Answers in Genesis, 2-12-2008, https://answersingenesis.org/fossils/fossil-record/the-worlds-a-graveyard.

130. Trefil, James. "Evidence for a Flood: Sediment Layers Suggest That 7,500 Years Ago Mediterranean Water Roared into the Black Sea," SmithsonianMag.com, 4-1-2000, https://www.smithsonianmag.com/science-nature/evidence-for-a-flood-102813115.

131. Ibid.

132. Dimmick, Pamela, "Seashells in the Desert, Fossilized Shells," Desert USA, accessed 4-24-20, https://www.desertusa.com/desert-california/seashells-in-desert.html.

133. Ibid.

134. Ibid.

135 Ibid.

136. Father Font was the chaplain of Juan Bautista de Anza's expedition that explored Alta California from 1775 to 1776. See: Zephyrin Engelhardt (1912). *The Missions and Missionaries of California*, Volume II: Upper California. pp. xxix, 173–190.

137. Dimmick, Pamela, "Seashells in the Desert Fossilized Shells."

138. Charles Q. Choi. "Vast Bed of Ancient Bones and Shark Teeth Explained," *Live Science*, June 09, 2009, https://www.livescience.com/3656-vast-bed-ancient-bones-shark-teeth-explained.html.

139. Ibid.

140. Ibid.

141. NASA. "Minturn Formation, Colorado," accessed 4-22-20, https://earthobservatory.nasa.gov/images/6255/minturn-formation-colorado.

142. Psalm 104:8. "Jamieson-Fausset-Brown Bible Commentary," Biblehub.
     com, https://biblehub.com/commentaries/psalms/104-8.htm.

143. Psalm 104:8. "Adam Clarke Commentary," Studylight.org, https://www.
     studylight.org/commentary/psalms/104-8.html.

144. Genesis 7:11–12
        In the six hundredth year of Noah's life, on the seventeenth day of the
     second month—on that day all **the springs of the great deep burst forth**,
     and the floodgates of the heavens were opened. And rain fell on the earth
     forty days and forty nights. (Emphasis added)

145. Psalm 104:8. "Cambridge Bible for Schools and Colleges," Biblehub.com,
     https://biblehub.com/commentaries/psalms/104-8.htm.

146. Dr. Andrew A. Snelling. "High and Dry Sea Creatures," Answers in
     Genesis, 12-7-2007, https://answersingenesis.org/fossils/fossil-record/
     high-dry-sea-creatures.

147. Mishana Khot. "Why Are There Fish Fossils High Up in the Himalayas?"
     Weather.com, 6-29-18, https://weather.com/en-IN/india/news/
     news/2018-06-29-fish-fossil-himalayas.

148. The Flood and the New Testament: 1 Peter 3:20, 2 Peter 2:5, Hebrews
     11:7.

149. My inspiration for this portion came from Eric Hovind's teachings.
     However, the actual message you are reading in this book is in my own
     words.
        Hovind, Eric. "Fossils Are Gospel Tracts from Noah's Flood,"
     Creation Today, accessed March 21, 2020, https://creationtoday.org/
     fossils-are-gospel-tracts-from-noahs-flood.

150. Romans 1:18. "Gill's Exposition of the Scriptures," Biblehub.com, https://
     biblehub.com/commentaries/romans/1-18.htm.

151. Dr. Stephen J. Cole. "Lesson 6: Is God's Wrath Justified? (Romans
     1:18-23)" Bible.org, accessed April 4, 2002. https://bible.org/seriespage/
     lesson-6-god-s-wrath-justified-romans-118-23.

152. Daniel 9:26: "The end will come like a flood: War will continue until the
     end, and desolations have been decreed."

153. Heb. #127, Adamah. "Hebrew Dictionary," Biblehub.com, https://
     biblehub.com/hebrew/127.htm.

154. Those translations include the King James Version, the New King James
     Version, the Berean's Study Bible, the Christian Standard Bible, the
     English Revised Version, and others of the same caliber.
        Genesis 1:25. "Parallel Translations," Biblehub.com, https://biblehub.
     com/genesis/1-25.htm.

155. Heb. #776, Erets. "Hebrew Dictionary," Biblehub.com, https://biblehub.com/hebrew/776.htm.

156. For example, see these passages: Genesis 6:7, 7:3, 7:4, and 8:9.

157. Genesis 6:7. "Barnes' Commentary," Biblehub.com, https://biblehub.com/commentaries/genesis/6-7.htm.

158. Genesis 6:7. "Ellicott's Commentary for English Readers," Biblehub.com, https://biblehub.com/commentaries/genesis/6-7.htm.

159. Genesis 7:19. Such as *Keil and Delitzsch Biblical Commentary on the Old Testament*, *Matthew Poole's Commentary*,– and *Gill's Exposition of the Entire Bible*. https://biblehub.com/commentaries/cambridge/genesis/7.htm.

160. Genesis 7:19. "Cambridge Bible for Schools and Colleges," Biblehub.com, https://biblehub.com/commentaries/cambridge/genesis/7.htm.

161. Genesis 7:19. "Benson Commentary," Biblehub.com, https://biblehub.com/commentaries/cambridge/genesis/7.htm.

162. See: Hill, Carol. "A Worldview Approach to Science and Scripture," Kregel Academic (November 19, 2019) https://www.amazon.com/Worldview-Approach-Science-Scripture/dp/0825446147.

163. Carol A. Hill, Consulting Geologist. "The Noachian Flood: Universal or Local?" Perspectives on Science and Christian Faith—California State University, Northridge (Volume 54, Number 3, September 2002), http://www.csun.edu/~vcgeo005/Carol%201.pdf.

164. See my book, *Gods of the Final Kingdom* (Crane, MO: Defender Publishing, 2016), in which I lay out the biblical and scientific truth of these matters in great and reliably referenced detail.

165. See Ephesians 1:9.

166. Dr. Lehman Strauss, professor of Old Testament. "The Importance of Bible Prophecy" (The First Prophecy – Compound Prophecy), Bible.org, https://bible.org/article/bible-prophecy.

167. Dr. Thomas Constable graduated from Moody Bible Institute in 1960 and later graduated from Dallas Theological Seminary. He is the founder of Dallas Seminary's Field Education department (1970) and the Center for Biblical Studies (1973), both of which he directed for many years before assuming other responsibilities. https://www.studylight.org/commentaries/dcc.html.

168. Matthew 24:32. "Expository Notes of Dr. Thomas Constable," https://www.studylight.org/commentaries/dcc/matthew-24.html.

169. Matthew 24. "Arno Gaebelein's Annotated Bible," Studylight.org, https://www.studylight.org/commentaries/gab/matthew-24.html.

170. See: Ezekiel 31. The entire chapter is a parabolic metaphor of the "nations" being represented as "all the trees of Eden." It is a well-known passage among the Jews.

171. Matthew 24. "Arno Gaebelein's Annotated Bible," Studylight.org, https://www.studylight.org/commentaries/gab/matthew-24.html.

172. Matthew 24. "Lange's Commentary on the Holy Scriptures: Critical, Doctrinal, and Homiletical," Studylight.org, https://www.studylight.org/commentaries/lcc/matthew-24.html.

173. Matthew 24. "Expository Notes of Dr. Thomas Constable," Studylight.org, https://www.studylight.org/commentaries/lcc/matthew-24.html.

174. Matthew 24. "John Trapp Complete Commentary," Studylight.com, https://www.studylight.org/commentaries/lcc/matthew-24.html.

175. International Bible Encyclopedia. "Eschatology of the New Testament, I-IV (Signs Preceding the Parousia)," Accessed August 3, 2020, https://www.internationalstandardbible.com/E/eschatology-of-the-new-testament-i-v.html.

176. "This is what the Sovereign Lord says: I will take the Israelites out of the nations where they have gone. I will gather them from all around and bring them back into their own land. I will make them one nation in the land, on the mountains of Israel. There will be one king over all of them and they will never again be two nations or be divided into two kingdoms" (Ezekiel 37:21–22; emphasis added)

When I have brought them back from the nations and have gathered them from the countries of their enemies, I will be proved holy through them in the sight of many nations. Then they will know that I am the Lord their God, for though I sent them into exile among the nations, I will gather them to their own land, not leaving any behind. (Ezekiel 39:27–28; emphasis added)

177. Matthew 24:32. "Pulpit Commentary," Biblehub.com, https://biblehub.com/commentaries/matthew/24-32.htm.

178. F. W. Grant. "Volume 5 of the Numerical Bible: The Fifth Pentateuch of the Bible," (Division 6: Matthew 24, 25), STEM Publishing, accessed July 12, 2020, https://www.stempublishing.com/authors/FW_Grant/Numerical_Bible/FWG_Numerical_Bible21f.html.

179. Regarding "the hope of Israel," see the following two entries:

1. "Hatikvah" (pronounced [hatik′va], lit. English: "The Hope") is a 19th-century Jewish poem and **the national anthem of Israel.** The theme of the romantic composition reflects the Jews' 2,000-year-old hope of

returning to the Land of Israel, restoring it, and reclaiming it as a free and sovereign nation. (Emphasis added); https://en.wikipedia.org/wiki/Hatikvah.

2. Stallard, Mike. "Prophetic Hope in the Writings of Arno C. Gaebelein: A Possible Demonstration of the Doxological Purpose of Biblical History," Accessed July 12, 2020, pp.105–106; https://www.clarkssummitu.edu/wp-content/uploads/2018/06/6_Stallard_FINAL_Prophetic-Hope_3-12-18.pdf.

From that paper, a quote from Arno C. Gaebelien:

And the people Israel have been thus preserved because the other **great promise of Hope** and Glory, **the promise of the land, their national restoration**, spiritual regeneration, and the promise of future blessing to "all the families of the earth" will have to be fulfilled. **Such is Israel's Hope,** and, when it is reached, it **will mean the Hope** and blessing for all the world.

And **this has been going on generation after generation**, century after century, during the darkest ages, during the times when satanic powers attempted their complete extermination. "This year here—next year in Jerusalem." **The Jewish Hope is a never dying Hope. Israel is the nation of Hope. In addition, this hope was not known by other nations.** (Emphasis added)

180. Matthew 24. "Arno Gaebelein's Annotated Bible," Studylight.org, https://www.studylight.org/commentaries/gab/matthew-24.html.

181. Matthew 24:32. "Expository Notes of Dr. Thomas Constable," https://www.studylight.org/commentaries/dcc/matthew-24.html.

182. David Guzik is the pastor of Calvary Chapel Santa Barbara, California. Before that, he was director and teacher at Calvary Chapel Bible College, Germany, following more than twenty years of pastoral ministry. He currently serves as senior pastor of Calvary Chapel Santa Barbara. He has been a premier commentator for the Blue Letter Bible online Bible study program for more than a decade. He is the author of the eleven thousand-page Guzik Bible Commentary—Enduring Word, https://www.blueletterbible.org/commentaries/guzik_david.

183. Matthew 24. "David Guzik—Enduring Word Commentary," Enduringword.com, https://enduringword.com/bible-commentary/matthew-24.

184. Ed Rickard (full name: Stanley Edgar Rickard, Jr.) received a BS with highest honors from Wheaton College in 1963, graduating in three years with a major in chemistry, then a PhD from Northwestern University

in 1967. His field was social psychology with emphasis on statistics and research methodology, and his dissertation and two subsequent publications (one of which is viewable online) dealt with the causal analysis of correlations. In college, he was a National Merit Scholar, and in graduate school he was a National Science Foundation Fellow.

He began his career teaching at the undergraduate and graduate levels in the field of his doctorate. Later he taught Bible courses at a Christian college. His subjects included the book of Daniel, Christian evidences, and graduate apologetics. More recently, he has served as principal of a Christian academy. For a leading publisher of Christian school curricula, he wrote a high school physics text that has been widely used. See https://www.themoorings.org/information.html.

185. Dr. Rickard, Stanley Edgar, Ph.D., "The Place of Israel in Christian Hope," The Moorings, accessed July 12, 2020, https://www.themoorings.org/Bible_prophecy/Israel/fig_tree.html.

186. Ibid.

187. International Standard Bible Encyclopedia. "Fig Trees," Internationalstandardbible.com, accessed July 23, 2020, https://www.internationalstandardbible.com/F/fig-fig-tree.html.

188. A breba is a fig that develops on a common fig tree in the spring on the previous year's shoot growth.

189. Facts about Israel—Truths about our Future: The Mystery of Israel the Fig Tree, Accessed July 12, 2020, https://www.factsaboutisrael.uk/israel-fig-tree.

190. April–May of 1948.

The "Fig Tree" of a newly birthing Israel was beginning to put forth its shoots. It happened in April–May of 1948.

April 22, 1948 (Thursday)

The Battle of Haifa ended in Haganah victory.

The Palmach launched Operation Yevusi to assert Jewish control over Jerusalem. (https://en.wikipedia.org/wiki/April_1948).

April 23, 1948 (Friday)

The UN Security Council voted 8-0 to set up a three-power commission consisting of Belgium, France and the United States to supervise the implementation of a truce in Palestine. (https://en.wikipedia.org/wiki/April_1948).

Just two weeks after these events in late April, on May 14, 1948 - in Tel Aviv, Jewish Agency Chairman David Ben-Gurion proclaims the State

of Israel, establishing the first Jewish state in 2,000 years. Ben-Gurion
became Israel's first premier.... At midnight, the State of Israel officially
came into being upon termination of the British mandate in Palestine.

    History.com. "State of Israel Declared," https://www.history.com/
this-day-in-history/state-of-israel-proclaimed#:~:text=On%20May%20
14%2C%201948%2C%20in,Gurion%20became%20Israel's%20
first%20premier.&text=At%20midnight%2C%20the%20State%20
of,the%20British%20mandate%20in%20Palestine.

191. See: Deuteronomy 30:1–5 and Deuteronomy 31:14–29.
192. Ezekiel 37:20. For examples of those scholars who thought this meant a
symbolic return of Israel "through the presence of the Church," or after
the return of Jesus, see:

    Benson Commentary:

    The expressions here made use of, seem to…refer, in their full sense,
to the final restoration of the Jews, **after their conversion to Christianity,
when Christ, in a peculiar sense, shall be their king.**

    Barnes' Notes on the Bible:

    The gathering together of the children of Israel was to take effect in
the first place in the return from Babylon, when the distinction of Israel
and Judah should cease. **The full completion concerns times still future,
when all Israel shall come in to acknowledge the rule of Christ.**

    The Pulpit Commentary:

    Viewed in this light, their own land was first Canaan, in so far as after
the exile it was cleansed from idolatry; **now it is those portions of the
earth in which the Christian Church has been planted.**

    Elliott's Commentary for English Readers:

    A fulfilment on a larger scale was perpetually prevented by the sins
of the people; God did for them all that their obdurate disobedience
would allow Him to do. Yet He did not wholly reject them, but **allowed
a remnant to keep alive His Church, and become the channel of those
richer blessings of the new covenant,** in which all who will accept His
salvation are united in a holier bond, and led to a land of higher promise
than Israel after the flesh could ever know.**A Literal Return of Israel—**
Other scholars saw this to mean a literal return of Israel in the very last
days before the return of the Lord:

    Gill's Exposition of the Scriptures:

    "For what follows is a prophecy **of what shall be in the latter day.**"

    As does *Jamieson-Fausset-Brown Bible Commentary*:

"A future complete fulfilment must therefore be looked for."

Each of the above commentary entries is found at: https://biblehub. com/commentaries/ezekiel/37-21.htm.

193. Jewish Virtual Library, "Vital Statistics: Latest Population Statistics for Israel," 4-28-2020, https://www.jewishvirtuallibrary.org/ latest-population-statistics-for-israel.

194. Wikipedia. "List of Israeli Nobel Laureates," accessed April 12, 2020, https://en.wikipedia.org/wiki/List_of_Israeli_Nobel_laureates.

195. For more info on this topic, please see my book (written with Messianic Rabbi Zev Porat of Tel Aviv, Israel— www.messiahofisraelministries.com) titled *The Rabbi, The Secret Message, and the Identity of Messiah.* (Crane, MO: Defender Publishers, 2019), 221–226.

196. Isaiah 49:22. "The Cambridge Bible for Schools and Colleges," Biblehub. com, https://biblehub.com/commentaries/isaiah/49-22.htm.

197. Isaiah 49:22. "The Pulpit Commentary," Biblehub.com, https://biblehub. com/commentaries/isaiah/49-22.htm.

198. Isaiah 49:22. "Jamieson-Fausset-Brown Bible Commentary," Biblehub. com, https://biblehub.com/commentaries/isaiah/49-22.htm.

199. Tova Cohen, Steven Scheer. "Israel's Soaring Population: Promised Land Running Out of Room?" Reuter's News, 9-25-15, https://www.reuters. com/article/us-israel-demographics/israels-soaring-population-promised-land-running-out-of-room-idUSKCN0RP0Z820150925.

200. Surkes, Sue. "With Its Population Set to Double in 30 Years, How Will Israel Cope?" *Times of Israel,* 6-26-19, https://www.timesofisrael.com/ with-its-population-set-to-double-in-30-years-how-will-israel-cope.

201. Tol, Alon. "Racing Toward Disaster: Israel's Unsustainable Population Bomb," *Jerusalem Post,* 9-23-17, https://www.jpost.com/jerusalem-report/ racing-toward-disaster-israels-unsustainable-population-bomb-504249.

202. The Six-Day War was a brief but high-casualty war that was fought in June 1967. The war commences between Israel and the Arab states of Egypt, Syria, and Jordan, when those states attacked what they thought to be an "unsuspecting" Israel. During that Six-Day War of 1967, Israel captured the West Bank from Jordan, Gaza Strip and Sinai Peninsula from Egypt, and Golan Heights from Syria. On September 22, 1948, during a truce in the war, the Provisional State Council of Israel passed a law to annex all land that Israel had captured in the war, and declaring that from then on, any part of Palestine taken by the Israeli army would automatically be annexed to Israel. Since that time, Israel has already given

up the Sinai Peninsula and the Golan Heights in various "peace deals."
For Netanyahu to have ceded their further territories to a currently non-
existing "State of Palestine" would have indeed left Israel in a veritable
indefensible state of affairs, with its nation being "too narrow."

Editors, History.com. "Six-Day War," History.com, 8-21-18, https://
www.history.com/topics/middle-east/six-day-war.

203. Jeffrey Heller, Matt Spetalnick. "Israeli Rebuke of Obama Exposes
Divide on Mideast," Reuters, 5-20-11, https://www.reuters.com/article/
us-obama-mideast-netanyahu/israeli-rebuke-of-obama-exposes-divide-on-
mideast-idUSTRE74I7L720110520.

204. See the following two references:

1. Hebrew/English Interlinear of Isaiah 49:8: https://biblehub.com/
interlinear/isaiah/49-8.htm.

2. O.T. 3444. Yeshuah [salvation], https://biblehub.com/
hebrew/3444.htm.

205. The name "Yeshua" is a shortened version of the name "Yehoshua" or
"Joshua" and is the literal Hebrew word for "salvation." Note that around
AD 1600, Protestant Bible translators started to transcribe ישׁוע in the
Old Testament into English as "Jeshua," but kept transcribing Ιησους in
the New Testament into English as "Jesus," obscuring the connection
between the equivalent Greek and Hebrew versions of the same name.
The name "Jesus" is a transliteration of the Greek name "Iesous," which is
a transliteration of the name "Yeshua."

See: Price, R. (28 September 2013). "Jesus or Yeshua?" Yeshua.org.
https://yeshua.org/who/yeshua-or-jesus.

206. Isaiah 49:8. "Pulpit Commentary," Biblehub.com, https://biblehub.com/
commentaries/isaiah/49-8.htm.

207. Isaiah 49:8. "Keil and Delitzsch Biblical Commentary on the Old
Testament," Biblehub.com, https://biblehub.com/commentaries/
isaiah/49-8.htm.

208. Isaiah 49:8. "Keil and Delitzsch Biblical Commentary on the Old
Testament," Biblehub.com, https://biblehub.com/commentaries/
isaiah/49-8.htm.

209. Isaiah 49:8. "Barnes' Notes on the Bible," Biblehub.com, https://biblehub.
com/commentaries/isaiah/49-8.htm.

210. Isaiah 49:9. "Keil and Delitzsch Biblical Commentary on the Old
Testament," Biblehub.com, https://biblehub.com/commentaries/
isaiah/49-8.htm.

211. International Bible Encyclopedia. "Eschatology of the New Testament, I-IV (Signs Preceding the Parousia)," accessed August 3, 2020, https://www.internationalstandardbible.com/E/eschatology-of-the-new-testament-i-v.html.

212. For examples, see:

"Major Rabbis Agree: 'Gog and Magog Can Come in the Form of a Virus'," Breaking Israel News, 3-22-20, https://www.breakingisraelnews.com/147354/major-rabbis-agree-gog-and-magog-can-come-in-the-form-of-a-virus.

Adam Eliyahu Berkowitz. "400-Year-Old Prophecy Connects Recent Events in Iran to the War of Gog and Magog," Breaking Israel News, 6-23-19, https://www.breakingisraelnews.com/131964/iran-prophesized-flashpoint-gog-umagog.

CBN broadcast posted on YouTube. "Middle East Expert to CBN News: 'Russia, Iran and Turkey May Be the Gog and Magog of Ezekiel 38-39'", Youtube.com, https://www.youtube.com/watch?v=btT42KJkrL0.

213. Chismar, Janet. "'This Could Be America's Last Call…'" Billy Graham.org, 10-16-12, https://billygraham.org/story/this-could-be-americas-last-call.

214. Gryboski, Michael, "Franklin Graham: 'US on Path of Destruction,'" *Christian Post*, Nov. 7, 2012, https://www.christianpost.com/news/franklin-graham-u-s-on-path-of-destruction-84559/.

215. Stunningly, this date corresponds with the Hebrew calendar date of the 9th of Tammuz, the day that Babylon's Nebuchadnezzar **breached the walls** of old Jerusalem and entered the city. Four weeks later, the Holy Temple was destroyed, and the Jews were exiled to Babylon. It became a national day of mourning and fasting. It represented a day of God's judgment upon a disobedient Israel. The 9th of Tammuz represented the day when the "walls of security" for the nation of Israel had been breached by the most godless world power of its day. Similarly, the US Supreme Court, on the 9th of Tammuz, breached the walls, or borders, of security for the foundations of civilization itself. I take this to be a clear warning sign for America, direct from Heaven's throne.

See: https://www.chabad.org/calendar/converter.asp?tdate=6/26/2015 (Hebrew Calendar Conversion Chart)

And: https://www.aish.com/dijh/Tammuz_9.html (Understanding Tammuz 9).

216. Gallups, Carl. "Irrefutable Proof—The 2015 SCOTUS Ruling on

Homosexual Marriage Was Illegal and Unconstitutional," CarlGallups. com, accessed June 2, 2020, http://carlgallups.com/scotusgaymarriage.

Excerpts from the SCOTUS rulings:

In *U.S. v. Windsor* (the 2013 SCOTUS decision that overturned the Defense of Marriage Act), the five majority justices explicitly and correctly ruled that the federal government and Supreme Court had no jurisdiction over marriage laws—whatsoever. They ruled that those decisions rested only with the individual states. Two years later they violated their own ruling, irrefutably proving that their 2015 ruling was illegal. Below are a few excerpts from that opinion. They are "positions" that SCOTUS took in order to overturn the Defense of Marriage Act. Get ready to be shocked. HERE is the Windsor 2013 ruling:

(https://www.supremecourt.gov/opinions/12pdf/12-307_6j37.pdf)

STATES UNITED v. WINDSOR

Excerpts from WINDSOR:

"Regulation of domestic relations is an area that has long been regarded as a virtually exclusive province of the States."

"Each state as a sovereign has a rightful and legitimate concern in the marital status of persons domiciled within its borders."

"The definition of marriage is the foundation of the State's broader authority to regulate the subject of domestic relations with respect to the protection of offspring, property interests, and the enforcement of marital responsibilities."

"The states, at the time of the adoption of the Constitution, possessed full power over the subject of marriage and divorce…[and] the Constitution delegated no authority to the Government of the United States on the subject of marriage and divorce."

"The whole subject of the domestic relations of husband and wife, parent and child, belongs to the laws of the States and not to the laws of the United States."

"Consistent with this allocation of authority, the Federal Government, through our history, has deferred to state law policy decisions with respect to domestic relations."

"The significance of state responsibilities for the definition and regulation of marriage dates to the Nation's beginning; for when the Constitution was adopted the common understanding was that the domestic relations of husband and wife and parent and child were matters reserved to the States."

"Marriage laws vary in some respects from State to State."

"Federal intrusion on state power is a violation of the Constitution because it disrupts the federal balance."

217. Miller J., Zeke. "Axelrod: Obama Misled Nation When He Opposed Gay Marriage In 2008," *Time*, Feb. 10, 2015, https://time.com/3702584/gay-marriage-axelrod-obama.

218. Flax, Billy. "Hobby Lobby Fights the Good Fight Against Obamacare Tyranny," *Forbes*, 1-8-13, https://www.forbes.com/sites/billflax/2013/01/08/hobby-lobby-fights-the-good-fight-against-obamacare-tyranny/#3be804f7648e.

219. Julie Hirschfeld Davis and Matt Apuzzo. "U.S. Directs Public Schools to Allow Transgender Access to Restrooms," *New York Times*, 5-12-16, https://www.nytimes.com/2016/05/13/us/politics/obama-administration-to-issue-decree-on-transgender-access-to-school-restrooms.html.

Even the leftist fact-checking site Snopes had to admit the veracity of what Obama's administration had accomplished in this regard:

Snopes, quoting from the order:

Restrooms and Locker Rooms. A school may provide separate facilities on the basis of sex, but must allow transgender students access to such facilities consistent with their gender identity. A school may not require transgender students to use facilities inconsistent with their gender identity or to use individual-user facilities when other students are not required to do so. A school may, however, make individual-user options available to all students who voluntarily seek additional privacy.

https://www.snopes.com/fact-check/obama-transgender-bathrooms.

220. Helene Cooper and Robert F. Worth. "In Arab Spring Obama Finds a Sharp Test," *New York Times*, 9-24-12, https://www.nytimes.com/2012/09/25/us/politics/arab-spring-proves-a-harsh-test-for-obamas-diplomatic-skill.html.

221. Sherwood, Harriet. "Binyamin Netanyahu Attacks Arab Spring Uprisings," *Guardian*, 11-24-11, https://www.theguardian.com/world/2011/nov/24/israel-netanyahu-attacks-arab-spring.

222. Cohen, Tom. "Obama Calls for Israel's Return to Pre-1967 Borders," CNN Politics, 5-19-11, http://www.cnn.com/2011/POLITICS/05/19/obama.israel.palestinians/index.html.

223. Federation for American Immigration Reform. "President Obama's Record of Dismantling Immigration Enforcement," FAIR, February 2016, https://www.fairus.org/issue/publications-resources/president-obamas-record-dismantling-immigration-enforcement.

224. Genesis 3:15.

225. *Decision Magazine*. "Abortion Leading Cause of Death
     Worldwide in 2019," 2-2-20, https://decisionmagazine.com/
     abortion-leading-cause-death-worldwide-2019.

     Abortion was the leading cause of death worldwide in 2019,
     according to figures released from Worldometers.info, a website that uses
     reporting from the world's governments to track demographics and vital
     statistics.

     LifeNews.com, a pro-life website, was among the few outlets to
     report on the 2019 abortion numbers, which show 42.3 million preborn
     babies killed worldwide. Worldometers recorded 58.6 million deaths
     last year from violence, illness and natural causes. Abortion statistics are
     recorded separately from mortality numbers. "The abortion number is
     incomprehensible, but each of those 42 million abortions represents a
     living human being whose life was violently destroyed in their mother's
     womb," wrote Steven Ertelt and Micaiah Bilger for LifeNews. "Each
     unborn baby already had their own unique DNA, making them distinct
     from their mother."

226. Andrew, Arthur R. "The Border Crisis Goes Global," Center
     for Immigration Studies, 6-1919, https://cis.org/Arthur/
     Border-Crisis-Goes-Global.

227. Mintz, Stephen, Ph.D. "Is Marriage in Decline?" *Psychology Today*, 3-7-
     15, https://www.psychologytoday.com/us/blog/the-prime-life/201503/
     is-marriage-in-decline.

228. Fight the New Drug. "By The Numbers: Is The Porn Industry Connected
     to Sex Trafficking?" July 29, 2019, https://fightthenewdrug.org/
     by-the-numbers-porn-sex-trafficking-connected.

     See also:

     Blanchard, R. Varieties of Autogynephilia and Their Relationship
     to Gender Dysphoria. Arch Sex Behav 22, 241–251 (1993). https://doi.
     org/10.1007/BF01541769.

     See also: Stoller, R. J. (1970). "Pornography and Perversion." Archives
     General Psychiatry. 22: 490–499. https://jamanetwork.com/journals/
     jamapsychiatry/article-abstract/490252.

     See also: Dr. Donald L. Hilton, Jr and Dr. Clark Watts. "Pornography
     Addiction: A Neuroscience Perspective," *Surgical Neurology International*,
     2-21-11, https://www.ncbi.nlm.nih.gov/pmc/articles/PMC3050060.

229. Editorial Board. "The U.N. Hates Israel," *Wall Street Journal*, 3-25-
     18,https://www.wsj.com/articles/the-u-n-hates-israel-1522014994.

230. "On December 6, 2017, US President Donald Trump announced the United States recognition of Jerusalem as the capital of Israel and ordered the planning of the relocation of the U.S. Embassy in Israel from Tel Aviv to Jerusalem. Benjamin Netanyahu, the Prime Minister of Israel, welcomed the decision and praised the announcement. Trump's decision to recognize Jerusalem as Israel's capital was rejected by a majority of world leaders. The United Nations Security Council held an emergency meeting on December 7 where 14 out of 15 members condemned Trump's decision, but the motion was vetoed by the United States."

    See:https://en.wikipedia.org/wiki/United_States_recognition_of_Jerusalem_as_capital_of_Israel#:~:text=During%20the%202016%20US%20Presidential,of%20the%20US%20embassy%20to.

231. Greene, Emma. "What the Supreme Court's Abortion Decision Means: Trump promised to appoint justices who would "automatically" overturn *Roe v. Wade*. The chief justice just made sure that won't happen before the 2020 election." *The Atlantic*, 6-29-2020,

    https://www.theatlantic.com/politics/archive/2020/06/supreme-court-abortion-trump/613642.

232. Mangan, Dan. "Trump: I'll appoint Supreme Court justices to overturn *Roe v. Wade* abortion case," CNBC, 10-19-16, https://www.cnbc.com/2016/10/19/trump-ill-appoint-supreme-court-justices-to-overturn-roe-v-wade-abortion-case.html.

233. Human Rights Campaign. "Donald Trump: Opposes Nationwide Marriage Equality," accessed June 2, 2020, https://www.hrc.org/2016RepublicanFacts/donald-trump-opposes-nationwide-marriage-equality.

234. Rebecca Hersher and Carrie Johnson. "Trump Administration Rescinds Obama Rule On Transgender Students' Bathroom Use," NPR, 2-22-17, https://www.npr.org/sections/thetwo-way/2017/02/22/516664633/trump-administration-rescinds-obama-rule-on-transgender-students-bathroom-use.

235. Tyrrell, Emmett. "Waiting for Shoe to Drop on Obama's Use of Spying," *Boston Herald*, 12-2-19, https://www.bostonherald.com/2019/12/02/waiting-for-shoe-to-drop-on-obamas-use-of-spying.

    Also see: Forgey, Quint. "Barr Taps U.S. Attorney to Investigate 'Unmasking' as Part of Russia Probe Review," *Politico*, 5-28-20, https://www.politico.com/news/2020/05/28/barr-russia-probe-attorney-286920.

236. Graves, Chris. "The Killing of George Floyd: What We Know:

The in-custody killing of George Floyd by a Minneapolis police officer ignited uprisings in Minnesota and across the nation." MPR News, 6-1-20, https://www.mprnews.org/story/2020/06/01/the-killing-of-george-floyd-what-we-know.

237. Jack Evans and Romy Ellenbogen. "How 'Defund the Police' Went Mainstream, and What That Means," *Tampa Bay Times*, 6-19-20, https://www.tampabay.com/news/2020/06/19/how-defund-the-police-went-mainstream-and-what-that-means.

238. Blue, Hannah. "Hypocrisy: NBC Highlights Danger of Trump's Rallies, Paints BLM and LGBT Protests in Positive Light," Breitbart, 6-15-20, https://www.breitbart.com/politics/2020/06/15/hypocrisy-nbc-highlights-danger-of-trumps-rallies-paints-blm-and-lgbt-protests-in-positive-light.

239. 15 Bible Verses about God's Activity in the Nations, accessed July 12, 2020, https://bible.knowing-jesus.com/topics/God-s-Activity-In-The-Nations.

240. Gryboski, Michael, "Franklin Graham: 'US on Path of Destruction,'" *Christian Post*, Nov. 7, 2012, https://www.christianpost.com/news/franklin-graham-u-s-on-path-of-destruction-84559/.

241. Horowitz, Daniel. "Horowitz: Trump-appointed Judge: Idaho can't block men from competing in women's sports," *Conservative Review*, 8-18-20, https://www.conservativereview.com/news/horowitz-trump-appointed-judge-idaho-cant-block-men-competing-womens-sports.

242. Yes. The play on words was intended by the author.

243. I have documented many of the more detailed matters of this phenomenon in several of my previous books, quoting the latest Barna Group polling statistics, and other academically reliable sources and studies. The drastic decline in global biblical literacy is shocking. And it shows.

    Showalter, Brandon. "Only 1 in 10 Americans Have Biblical Worldview, Just 4 Percent of Millennials: Barna," *Christian Post*, 2-28-17, https://www.christianpost.com/news/1-in-10-americans-have-biblical-worldview-just-4-percent-of-millennials-barna.html.

244. Cohen, Debra Nussbaum. "Protestant Churches Split Over anti-Israel Divestment Resolutions," *Haaretz*, 5-7-15, https://www.haaretz.com/jewish/.premium-protestant-churches-split-over-bds-1.5375228.

245. Herding mentality.Before 2001 there was no such thing as TSA at airports, for example. No scanning, screening, body and cavity searches before you took a trip to grandma's. Now, it's routine, and simply tolerated as normal. This also applies to the new normal of universal mandates to "wear

masks," "shelter at home," and "don't go to church" lest you become one of the "dangerous ones" to society at large.

246. Miller, Caroline. "Does Social Media Cause Depression?" Child Mind Institute, accessed July 2, 2020, https://childmind.org/article/is-social-media-use-causing-depression/.

247. US National Library of Medicine. "Gender Dysphoria in Adolescence: Current Perspectives," National Institutes of Health, accessed June 3, 2020, https://www.ncbi.nlm.nih.gov/pmc/articles/PMC5841333.From the article:

    Increasing numbers of adolescents are seeking treatment at gender identity services in Western countries. An increasingly accepted treatment model that includes puberty suppression with gonadotropin-releasing hormone analogs starting during the early stages of puberty, cross-sex hormonal treatment starting at ~16 years of age and possibly surgical treatments in legal adulthood, is often indicated for adolescents with childhood gender dysphoria (GD) that intensifies during puberty.

    However, virtually nothing is known regarding adolescent-onset GD, its progression and factors that influence the completion of the developmental tasks of adolescence among young people with GD and/or transgender identity. Consolidation of identity development is a central developmental goal of adolescence, but we still do not know enough about how gender identity and gender variance actually evolve. Treatment-seeking adolescents with GD present with considerable psychiatric comorbidity.

248. Suicide. "Key facts," World Health Organization, 9-2-2019, https://www.who.int/news-room/fact-sheets/detail/suicide.

    From the article:

    Every year close to 800 000 people take their own life and there are many more people who attempt suicide. Every suicide is a tragedy that affects families, communities and entire countries and has long-lasting effects on the people left behind. Suicide occurs throughout the lifespan and was the second leading cause of death among 15–29 year-olds globally in 2016. Suicide does not just occur in high-income countries, but is a global phenomenon in all regions of the world.

249. The Conquer Series. "Science Confirms Bible on Generational Curses," accessed July 12, 2020, https://conquerseries.com/science-confirms-bible-on-generational-curses.

250. Especially see my book, *Masquerade: Preparing for the Biggest Con Job in*

History. (Crane, MO: Defender Publishing, 2020), particularly chapters 35–38.

251. The word "**Nephilim**" is usually translated as "giants." And the word often carries with it the connotation of something out of the ordinary. See: Nephilim, OT# 5303. Biblehub.com, http://biblehub.com/hebrew/5303. htm.

   In Genesis 6:4, the word translated "heroes" comes from the Hebrew word #1368 (*gibbor*). The word means, "A powerful warrior, a tyrant, a mighty man—and a giant of a man." So, in both cases, Nephilim and *gibbor*, we find the connection to giants in the most literal sense of the word.

   See: Gibbor, OT #1368. (See Strong's Concordance), Biblehub.com, http://biblehub.com/hebrew/1368.htm.

   The word translated as "**renowned**" simply means "well-known." So, what we truly have here are notorious tyrant-warriors who were overwhelmingly powerful and huge—even gigantic in stature. On top of that, the next verse (5) tells us that these individuals were causing untold violence to flourish over the earth. To put it in modern vernacular, the Nephilim were brutal terrorists. These were terrifying beasts of men. And their existence was at least a part of the reason God destroyed every living thing on the earth.

252. **Septuagint**, abbreviation LXX, the earliest extant Greek translation of the Old Testament from the original Hebrew. The Septuagint was presumably made for the Jewish community in Egypt when Greek was the common language throughout the region. Analysis of the language has established that the Torah, or Pentateuch, the first five books of the Old Testament, was translated near the middle of the 3rd century BCE and that the rest of the Old Testament was translated in the 2nd century BCE. https://www.britannica.com/topic/Septuagint.

253. Genesis 6:2. "Ellicott's Commentary for English Readers," Biblehub.com, https://biblehub.com/commentaries/genesis/6-2.htm.

254. Ibid. "The word Nephilim is usually translated as 'giants.' And the word often carries with it the connotation of something out of the ordinary."

255. Dickason, C. Fred, Th.D., *Names of Angels*, (chapter: "Sons of God") (Chicago: Moody Press, August 1, 1997) copyright by C. Fred Dickason. All rights reserved.

256. Genesis 6:4, Cambridge Bible for Schools and Colleges, Biblehub.com, http://biblehub.com/commentaries/genesis/6-4.htm.

257. Genesis 6:4, Jamieson-Fausset-Brown Bible Commentary (from Jamieson,

Fausset, and Brown Commentary, Electronic Database. Copyright ©
1997, 2003, 2005, 2006 by Biblesoft, Inc. All rights reserved.).

Note: These commentators try hard to shy away from the "angel"
interpretation of "sons of God." Yet, in attempting to do so, they still had
to regrettably admit that "many of the fathers" (those closest to the original
interpretation of Jesus and His disciples who, by the way, were not in the
minority) "applied it to" the angels.

258. Genesis 6:1–2, Biblical Commentary on the Old Testament, by Carl
Friedrich Keil and Franz Delitzsch, accessed March 11, 2017, https://
www.studylight.org/commentaries/kdo/genesis-6.html9.

Note: These commentators try hard to shy away from the "angel"
interpretation of "sons of God." Yet, in attempting to do so, they still
had to regrettably admit that the sons of God *most naturally* should be
interpreted as "angels."

259. Guzik, David. "Genesis 6, Guzik Bible Commentary," Biblehub.com,
http://biblehub.com/commentaries/guzik/genesis/6.htm.

260. Job 38:7, "Barnes' Notes on the Bible," Biblehub.com, http://biblehub.
com/commentaries/job/38-7.htm.

261. Job 38:7. "Matthew Poole's Commentary," Biblehub.com, https://
biblehub.com/commentaries/job/38-7.htm.

262. Heiser, Michael S., *The Unseen Realm: Recovering the Supernatural World
View of the Bible*," Lexham Press, September 1, 2015, p. 101.

263. Genesis 6:2. "International Standard Version," Biblehub.com, https://
biblehub.com/genesis/6-2.htm.

264. Genesis 6:2. "The Good News Translation," Biblehub.com, https://
biblehub.com/genesis/6-2.htm.

265. Genesis 6:2. "The New International Version," Biblehub.com, https://
biblehub.com/genesis/6-2.htm.

266. Hebrew 120. Adam. "Hebrew Dictionaries," Biblehub.com, https://
biblehub.com/hebrew/120.htm.

The Hebrew word *adam* means "man" or "humans." As a proper
name for the first "man" is how we most readily recognize it. However, it is
often used in the Bible to represent humanity at large.

The Christian Standard Bible, the Holman Christian Standard Bible,
the New English Translation (NET) Bible, Heart English Bible, and God's
Word Translation all use the word "humans" or some derivative thereof to
translate the context of what the reader should take away from this verse.
See: https://biblehub.com/genesis/6-2.htm.

267. Hebrew 1320, Basar. "Hebrew," Biblehub.com, (See particularly Brown-Driver-Briggs Hebrew Dictionary) https://biblehub.com/hebrew/1320.htm.

268. Genesis 6:13. "Parallel Translations," Biblehub.com, https://biblehub.com/genesis/6-13.htm.

269. Hebrew 187. Derek. "Hebrew Dictionaries," Biblehub.com, https://biblehub.com/hebrew/1870.htm.

270. Hebrew 7843, Shachath. "Hebrew Dictionaries," https://biblehub.com/hebrew/7843.htm.

271. Vocabulary.com. "Corrupt," accessed June 23, 2020, https://www.vocabulary.com/dictionary/corrupt.

272. For a detailed study of this topic, please see my book, *Gods and Thrones* (Crane, MO: Defender Publishing, 2017), chapter 27: "Like the Angels in Heaven."

   Some Bible students will argue, "I thought Jesus said angels don't marry, therefore they can't have sex either."

   A number of the scholars will make this argument as their rock-solid proof that Genesis 6 simply cannot be referring to angelic beings. The dispute comes from Jesus' pointed statement in Matthew 22:30 (also Mark 12:25, Luke 20:35-36): "At the resurrection people will neither marry nor be given in marriage; they will be like the angels in heaven."

   First, Jesus says absolutely nothing about angels being sexless. He speaks only of the *human institution of marriage*, which indeed appears to be of no concern in the divine realm.

   Secondly, regarding marriage between angels, Jesus was referring to angels who were in heaven. These are *the obedient angels* living in divine bliss. Jesus was not referring to the fallen angels who apparently came to earth in lustful temptation and played house with the daughters of men in pre-Flood days, as the Genesis 6 narrative recounts. So the "Jesus said angels don't have sex" argument simply does not stand up to biblical scrutiny—despite arguments to the contrary.

   Expositor's Greek New Testament:

   [We will be] as angels, so far as marriage is concerned, not necessarily implying sexlessness.

   Matthew 22:28, *Expositor's Greek New Testament*, http://biblehub.com/commentaries/matthew/22-30.htm.

273. The "doctrine" of which *Meyer's* speaks is the Book of Enoch's postulation that the divine beings (sons of God) of Genesis 6 descended to the earthly

regions and had actual physical relations with earthly women—producing the Nephilim giants of the pre-Flood age.

274. The Book of Enoch—While the book of Enoch (Noah's great-grandson) is non-canonical, it is an influential ancient Jewish work, with parts of it dating to around 300 BC. Eleven fragments of the book were found among the Dead Sea Scrolls, proving its impact upon at least some within the earliest Jewish community. There is a particular passage in the book of Enoch that is very similar to the reference in Jude 1:6–7:

Enoch is mentioned by name in the New Testament in three different places (Luke 3:37, Hebrews 11:5, Jude 1:14). It is also alleged that there are a number of allusions (paraphrased quotes, etc.) to the Book of Enoch throughout the New Testament as well. The identification of those particular passages as having Enochian influence is disputed, and hold varying degrees of interpretation among Bible students. However, the greater point is the indisputable fact that a good portion of early Jewish thought was that the sons of God were fallen elohim. This understanding apparently came from biblical, as well as non-biblical, sources and was prevalent among early orthodox Jews as well as the early church.

Wayne, Jackson, "Did Jude Quote from the Book of Enoch?" *Christian Courier*, accessed March 11, 2017, https://www.christiancourier.com/articles/562-did-jude-quote-from-the-book-of-enoch.

275. Jude 1:6. "Meyer's New Testament Commentary," Biblehub.com, https://biblehub.com/commentaries/jude/1-6.htm.

276. Ibid. **The Book of Enoch,** "While the book of Enoch (Noah's great-grandson) is non-canonical, it is an influential ancient Jewish work…".

277. Jude 1:6. "Gill's Exposition of the Entire Bible," Biblehub.com, https://biblehub.com/commentaries/gill/jude/1.htm.

278. Jude 1:6. "Pulpit Commentary," Biblehub.com, https://biblehub.com/commentaries/jude/1-6.htm.

279. Jude 1:6. "Lange's Commentary on the Holy Scriptures: Critical, Doctrinal, and Homiletical," Studylight.org, https://www.studylight.org/commentaries/lcc/jude-1.html.

280. 2 Peter 2:4. "Cambridge Bible for Schools and Colleges," Biblehub.com, https://biblehub.com/commentaries/2_peter/2-4.htm.

281. International Standard Bible Encyclopedia. "Sons of God," Edited by James Orr, published in 1939 by Wm. B. Eerdmans Publishing Co. Accessed July 2, 2020, https://www.internationalstandardbible.com/S/sons-of-god.html.

282. 2 Peter 2:4ff. "Peter Pett's Commentary on the Bible," Studylight.org, https://www.studylight.org/commentary/2-peter/2-4.html.

283. ANF07. Fathers of the Third and Fourth Century. "Lacantius." Accessed June 23, 2020, https://ccel.org/ccel/schaff/anf07.iii.ii.ii.xv.html.

284. 2 Peter 2:4. "Myers New Testament Commentary," Biblehub.com, https://biblehub.com/commentaries/2_peter/2-4.htm.

285. Jude 1:7. "Expositor's Bible Commentary," Biblehub.com, https://biblehub.com/commentaries/jude/1-7.htm.

286. Jude 1:7. "Cambridge Bible for Schools and Colleges," Biblehub.com, https://biblehub.com/commentaries/jude/1-7.htm.

287. International Standard Bible Encyclopedia. "Sons of God," Edited by James Orr, published in 1939 by Wm. B. Eerdmans Publishing Co. Accessed July 2, 2020, https://www.internationalstandardbible.com/S/sons-of-god.html.

288. Jude 1:7. "Pulpit Commentary," Biblehub.com, https://biblehub.com/commentaries/jude/1-7.htm.

289. Jude 1:7. "Gill's Exposition of the Entire Bible," Biblehub.com, https://biblehub.com/commentaries/jude/1-7.htm.

290. Jude 1:7. "Meyer's New Testament Commentary," Biblehub.com, https://biblehub.com/commentaries/jude/1-7.htm.

291. See my book, *Gods and Thrones* (Crane, MO: Defender Publishing, 2017), for a detailed understanding of the "gods" of which Satan spoke of as being the angelic realm itself. These were the true "sons of God," the *bene elohim* in Hebrew.

292. Aparna Vidyasagar. "Human-Animal Chimeras: Biological Research & Ethical Issues," *Live Science*, 9-29-16, https://www.livescience.com/56309-human-animal-chimeras.html.

293. "CRISPR-Cas9 is a unique technology that enables geneticists and medical researchers to edit parts of the genome by removing, adding or altering sections of the DNA sequence."
See: What is CRISPR-Cas9, Accessed June 30, 2020, https://www.yourgenome.org/facts/what-is-crispr-cas9.

294. Mark Shwartz. "Target, Delete, Repair: CRISPR Is a Revolutionary Gene-editing Tool, But It's Not without Risk," *Stanford Medicine*, Winter 2018, https://stanmed.stanford.edu/2018winter/CRISPR-for-gene-editing-is-revolutionary-but-it-comes-with-risks.html.
"When it comes to experiments on animals, plants and microbes, two things worry me," says Stanford bioethicist Hank Greely, JD, a professor

of law. "One is the intentional misuse of CRISPR. The other is that people with good intentions will inadvertently cause harm."

295. Guzik. "Genesis 6, Guzik Bible Commentary," Biblehub.com, http://biblehub.com/commentaries/guzik/genesis/6.htm.

296. "The Latter Times"

Pulpit Commentary:

This "falling away" is to take place in…"the latter times." [the very last days] The adjective ὕστερος is only found here in the New Testament. But in the LXX [Septuagint—the Grk translation of the Old Testament]. (e.g., 1 Chronicles 29:29; Jeremiah 1:19; Jeremiah 27:17, LXX.), ὕστερος means "the last," as opposed to "the first." (Brackets added for clarification) See: https://biblehub.com/commentaries/1_timothy/4-1.htm.

297. Please see by book *Masquerade: Preparing for the Greatest Con Job in History* (Crane, MO: Defender Publishing, March 2020), Part II, "The Holy Place," chapters 9–20.

Following are only a few revelations from that book regarding Paul's statement concerning the "temple of God," as those words appear in the context of every one of its usages throughout *all of his writings*. I have added the emphasized bold-type to each of these commentaries, to make it easier for you to quickly get the gist of each one.

Pulpit Commentary:

It appears *more correct* to refer the expression *metaphorically to the Christian Church*. It is a *favorite metaphor of Paul* to compare believers in particular, or *the Church in general, to the temple of God* (comp. 1 Corinthians 3:17; 1 Corinthians 6:19; Ephesians 2:20–22)

See: "Pulpit Commentary," Biblehub.com, https://biblehub.com/commentaries/2_thessalonians/2-4.htm.

Whedon's Commentary on the Bible:

Temple of God—*Not the Jewish temple*, which is never called so in the New Testament, but *unquestionably the Christian Church*. See 2 Corinthians 6:16; Ephesians 2:21.

See: "Whedon's Commentary on the Bible, 2 Thessalonians 2," studylight.org, https://www.studylight.org/commentaries/whe/2-thessalonians-2.html.

Benson's Commentary:

After the death of Christ *the temple at Jerusalem is never called by the apostles the temple of God*; and that when they mention the house or temple of God, *they mean the Christian Church in general*, or every particular

believer; which indeed is *evident from many passages* in their epistles: see 1
Timothy 3:15; 1 Corinthians 6:19; 2 Corinthians 6:16; Ephesians 2:19-
22; 1 Peter 2:5.

See: "Joseph Benson's Commentary of the Old and New Testaments,"
https://www.studylight.org/commentaries/rbc/2-thessalonians-2.html.

International Standard Bible Encyclopedia:

Here we would only indicate what seems to us *the most plausible view
of the Pauline doctrine.* It had been revealed to the apostle by the Spirit that
the church was to be exposed to a more tremendous assault than any it had
yet witnessed.

See: International Standard Bible Encyclopedia. "Antichrist,"
(Published 1915), accessed July 18, 2019, https://www.
internationalstandardbible.com/A/antichrist.html.

International Critical Commentary:

The difficulty with the reference to the temple in Jerusalem is that
the evidence adduced for this interpretation is not convincing.… **The
[temple] elsewhere used in the writings of Paul is used metaphorically.**
The ***Christians are the temple of God***, or the body is the temple of the
Spirit.

See: "The International Critical Commentary," Accessed July 12,
2019, https://archive.org/details/criticalexegetic00framuoft/page/256.

Commentary on 2 Thessalonians 2: Views of the Early Church
Fathers

Only the Church (or Antichrist "becomes" the counterfeit
"temple"-church.

(St. Andrew of Caesarea) *[This passage] referred to the churches*, in
which he will arrogate to himself pride of place, ***striving to declare himself
God***. Theodore of Mopsuestia, Theodoret of Cyrus and Oecumenius
include only the Christian Churches and not the Temple of Jerusalem. St.
Augustine, Thietland and Lyra propose that the text may mean that the
Antichrist becomes the counterfeit temple in comparison to Christ as the
Temple.

See: 2 Thessalonians 2. "Commentary on 2 Thessalonians 2," (Views
of the early church fathers), accessed August 21, 2019, https://sites.google.
com/site/aquinasstudybible/home/2-thessalonians/2-thess-q/2-thess-2.

Additional Commentary Analysis of 2 Thessalonians 2:4:

At this site: https://www.studylight.org/commentaries/, there are
over 60 classical commentaries (some of them already referenced in this

chapter) indexed on a single page that address 2 Thessalonians 2:4. *The overwhelming majority indicated that the "temple of God" is the church* – based upon the context of all of Paul's other writings that use that phrase.

298. *Meyer's New Testament Commentary:*

[When the writer of Hebrews wrote this] The signs of this were already in the air, and that approaching Day of the Lord was destined to be "the bloody and fiery dawn" of the Last Great Day—"the Day of days, the Ending-day of all days, the Settling-day of all days, the Day of the promotion of Time into Eternity, the Day which for the Church breaks through and breaks off the night of this present world."

Hebrews 10:25. "Meyer's New Testament Commentary," Biblehub. com, https://biblehub.com/commentaries/hebrews/10-25.htm.

299. Phillips, Tom. "China on Course to Become 'World's Most Christian Nation' Within 15 Years," *The Telegraph* 6-23-2020, https://www. telegraph.co.uk/news/worldnews/asia/china/10776023/China-on-course-to-become-worlds-most-Christian-nation-within-15-years.html.

300. Saavedra, Ryan. "China Forces Christians to Renounce Faith, Destroy Christian Symbols or Be Cut Off from Welfare, Reports Say," *Daily Wire*, July 21,2020, https://www.dailywire.com/news/china-forces-christians-to-renounce-faith-destroy-christian-symbols-or-be-cut-off-from-welfare-reports-say?utm_source=facebook&utm_medium=social&utm_campaign=benshapiro&fbclid=IwAR0f50_qxU4gyUgpkoFhdGDz9JLf6h4wO06c1F3RzWGVHpQe_irO8EWnfuw.

301. Ibid.

302. Ephesians 6:13, "Meyer's New Testament Commentary," Biblehub.com, https://biblehub.com/commentaries/ephesians/6-13.htm.

303. Ephesians 6:13, "Expositor's Greek Testament," Biblehub.com, https://biblehub.com/commentaries/ephesians/6-13.htm.

304. Ephesians 6:13, "Cambridge Bible for Schools and Colleges," Biblehub. com, https://biblehub.com/commentaries/ephesians/6-13.htm.

305. Ephesians 6:13, "McLaren's Exposition," Biblehub.com, https://biblehub. com/commentaries/ephesians/6-13.htm.

306. Revelation 12:9. "Barnes's Notes on the Bible," Biblehub.com, https://biblehub.com/commentaries/revelation/12-9.htm.

307 Arno C. Gaebelein

With a ministry that bridged two centuries and endured two world wars, Gaebelein never doubted the relevance of the study of prophecy for spiritual growth and for interaction with the chaos of culture.... Gaebelein was a devout student and fervently studied and mastered Hebrew, Aramaic, Syriac, and Arabic. https://www.studylight.org/commentaries/gab.html.

308. Ephesians 6: 10–20. "Arno C. Gaebelein's Annotated Bible," (Verses 10–20 - 6. The Warfare and the Panoply of God), Studylight.org, https://www.studylight.org/commentaries/gab/ephesians-6.html.

309. Haggai 2:6. "Barnes' Notes on the Bible," Biblehub.com, https://biblehub.com/commentaries/haggai/2-7.htm.

310. Dr. Lehman Strauss, professor of Old Testament. "The Importance of Bible Prophecy" (The First Prophecy—Compound Prophecy), Bible.org, https://bible.org/article/bible-prophecy.

311. Haggai 2:6. "Barnes' Notes on the Bible," Biblehub.com, https://biblehub.com/commentaries/haggai/2-7.htm.

312. Ibid.

313. Matthew 24:29. "Bengel's Gnomen," Biblehub.com, https://biblehub.com/commentaries/matthew/24-29.htm.

314. Matthew 24:29. "Meyer's New Testament Commentary," Biblehub.com, https://biblehub.com/commentaries/matthew/24-29.htm.

315. Matthew 24:29. "Pulpit Commentary," Biblehub.com, https://biblehub.com/commentaries/matthew/24-29.htm.

316. Greek 3772. Ouranos (Heavens). "Thayer's Greek Lexicon," Biblehub.com, https://biblehub.com/greek/3772.htm.

317. Luke 21:26. "Cambridge Bible for Schools and Colleges," Biblehub.com, https://biblehub.com/commentaries/luke/21-26.htm.

318. Greek 1411. Dunamis. "Thayer's Greek Lexicon," Biblehub.com, https://biblehub.com/greek/1411.htm.

319. Revelation 9:3. "Expositor's Greek Testament," Biblehub.com, https://biblehub.com/commentaries/revelation/9-3.htm.

320. Revelation 9:3. "Ellicott's Commentary on the Bible," Biblehub.com, https://biblehub.com/commentaries/revelation/9-3.htm.

321. Revelation 9:3. "Matthew Henry's Concise Commentary," Biblehub.com, https://biblehub.com/commentaries/revelation/9-3.htm.

322. Revelation 9:3. "Geneva Study Bible," Biblehub.com, https://biblehub.com/commentaries/revelation/9-3.htm.

323. Revelation 9:11. "Ellicott's Commentary for English Readers," Biblehub.com, https://biblehub.com/commentaries/revelation/9-11.htm.

324. Revelation 9:11. "Meyer's New Testament Commentary," Biblehub.com, https://biblehub.com/commentaries/revelation/9-11.htm.

325. Revelation 9: "Commentary Critical and Explanatory on the Whole Bible," Bible Study Tools, https://www.biblestudytools.com/commentaries/jamieson-fausset-brown/revelation/revelation-9.html.

326. Revelation 9:1–6. "The IVP New Testament Commentary Series," https://www.biblegateway.com/resources/ivp-nt/Opening-Abyss.

327. Revelation 9: "Expository Notes of Dr. Thomas Constable," https://www.studylight.org/commentaries/dcc/revelation-9.html.

328. Revelation 9:11. "Pulpit Commentary," Biblehub.com, https://biblehub.com/commentaries/revelation/9-11.htm.

329. Greek #12, Abussos. "Thayer's Greek Lexicon," Biblehub.com, https://biblehub.com/greek/12.htm.

330. Ephesians 6:11. "Meyer's New Testament Commentary," Biblehub.com, https://biblehub.com/commentaries/ephesians/6-11.htm.

331. Ephesians 6:11. "Expositor's Greek New Testament," Biblehub.com, https://biblehub.com/commentaries/ephesians/6-11.htm.

332. Isaiah 59:20. "Benson Commentary," Biblehub.com, https://biblehub.com/commentaries/isaiah/59-20.htm.

333. I urge you to read the passage of Isaiah 11:1–5 as well. Similar imagery of the coming Redeemer and certain other elements of the Ephesians 6 armor are also employed there.
    "Righteousness will be his belt, and faithfulness the sash around his waist" (Isaiah 11:5).

334. Isaiah 59:17. "Lange's Commentary on the Holy Scriptures: Critical, Doctrinal, and Homiletical," Studylight.org, https://www.studylight.org/commentaries/lcc/isaiah-59.html.

335. Isaiah 59:17. "Ellicott's Commentary for English Readers," Biblehub.com, https://biblehub.com/commentaries/isaiah/59-17.htm.

336. Isaiah 59:17. "Cambridge Bible for Schools and Colleges," Biblehub.com, https://biblehub.com/commentaries/isaiah/59-17.htm.

337. Isaiah 59:17. "Barnes' Notes on the Bible," Biblehub.com, https://biblehub.com/commentaries/isaiah/59-17.htm.

338. Isaiah 59:17. "Gill's Exposition of the Scriptures," Biblehub.com, https://biblehub.com/commentaries/isaiah/59-17.htm.

339. Isaiah 59:17. "Biblical Illustrator," Studylight.org, https://www.studylight.org/commentary/isaiah/59-17.html.

340. Isaiah 59:17. "John Trapp Complete Commentary," Studylight.org, https://www.studylight.org/commentary/isaiah/59-17.html.

341. Luke 17:26. "Coffman's Commentary on the Bible," Studylight.org, https://www.studylight.org/commentary/luke/17-26.html.

342. Dr. Reagan, David. *Wrath and Glory: The Meaning of the Book of Revelation,* 2nd Edition (Lamb and Lion Ministries; May 1, 2016), 112–113.

> **The oldest viewpoint** [about the doctrine of the Rapture] is called **historic premillennialism** [the Rapture occurs at the end of the Tribulation, and just before God pours out His wrath—as in Noah's day].
>
> It is termed "historic" for two reasons: to differentiate it from modern premillennialism and to indicate that it was the historic position of the early church…. This view is **based on a literal interpretation of what the Bible says** will happen in the end times. One of its distinctive features is that it places the Rapture of the Church at the end of the Tribulation, combining it with the Second Coming as one event…. This is the only systematic view of end-time events that existed during the first 300 years of the Church." (Emphasis added).

343. Reznick, Leibel. "Biblical Archeology: Sodom and Gomorrah" (Does archeological data support the biblical story?) Aish.com, accessed July 7, 2020, https://www.aish.com/ci/sam/48931527.html.

> From the article:
>
> Sodom and Gomorrah were part of a metropolis assumed to have been located on the eastern bank of the Dead Sea consisting of five cities, each with its own king. There was (1) Bera, king of Sodom, (2) Birsha, king of Gomorrah, (3) Shinab, king of Admad, (4) Shember, king of Zeboiim, and (5) the king of Bela, which is also called Zoar (Genesis 14:8). This thriving group of city-states is referred to in the Bible (Genesis 13:12) as the Cities of the Plain. The five kings were under the dominion of a coalition of eastern Mesopotamian overlords. According to the Torah, with the help of the patriarch Abraham, the cities gained their independence, though their independence was only short-lived. A few years later, God destroyed the cities in a hail of fire and brimstone.

344. Some who hold to the pre-Tribulation Rapture framework of eschatology will insist that since Noah was instructed by the Lord to enter the ark exactly *seven days* before the Flood was loosed upon the planet that this "escape" into the ark stood as a symbol of the Rapture—seven "years" *before* God's final wrath will fall. However, there are several problems with this exegetical scheme:

> A. Upon closer examination of the context of that passage we discover that Noah was indeed ordered to enter the ark. But he was told to do this in order to "escape the waters of the flood." Those waters represent *God's wrath*. They were not the waters of "tribulation."

B. Noah and his family were already living in the midst of the tribulation of their days. They went into the ark primarily to make the final preparations before the actual Flood. This is when the animals would begin coming to him, on the first day of those seven days.

C. Noah and his family were not "hiding" in the ark. Neither were they "separated" from their world entirely. The next verses make it clear that they were merely instructed to make the last preparations of all that was necessary before the flood waters of God's wrath fell. At the outpouring of that wrath is when they were then "separated" from the world and finally "taken out."

D. Besides these facts, Jesus made it clear that the last days would also be "just like" Lot's days as well—*equally so*. There is no corresponding pre-departure, *seven-day scenario* in Lot's instance.

345. **Tribulation.** The Greek word that is often translated as "tribulation" in our English versions of the Bible is *thlipsis*. "Tribulation" means extreme pressure. Hopelessness. Helplessness. Tribulation is different than wrath. See the following two verses for examples:

These things I have spoken to you, that in Me you may have peace. In the world you will have tribulation; but be of good cheer, I have overcome the world (John 16:33, KJV).

HELPS Word-studies

2347 thlípsis—properly, pressure (what constricts or rubs together), used of a narrow place that "hems someone in"; tribulation, especially internal pressure that causes someone to feel confined (restricted, "without options").

2347 thlípsis ("compression, tribulation") carries the challenge of coping with the internal pressure of a tribulation, especially when feeling there is "no way of escape" ("hemmed in").

See: 2347. Thlipsis, "Greek," Biblehub.com, https://biblehub.com/greek/2347.htm.

346. *amieson-Fausset-Brown Bible Commentary*:

The **great tribulation.** Including retrospectively **all the tribulation** which the saints **of all ages** have had to pass through.... Their number was waiting to be completed, but here [Revelation 7:14] it is completed, and *they are seen taken out* of the earth *before the judgments* [wrath from God] on the *Antichristian apostasy*. (Emphasis added)

See: https://biblehub.com/commentaries/revelation/7-14.htm.

Wrath. The Greek word is Orgē. It is Greek word #3709.

HELPS Word-studies:

Orgē comes from the verb oragō meaning, "**to teem, to swell**"; and thus implies that it is not a sudden outburst, but rather *(referring to God's) fixed, controlled, passionate feeling against sin...* a settled indignation (so Hendriksen). (D. E. Hiebert, at 1 Thes 1:10).) (Emphasis added, parenthesis in original) See: https://biblehub.com/greek/3709.htm.

For God did not appoint us to suffer wrath but to receive salvation through our Lord Jesus Christ. (1 Thessalonians 5:9).

Bengel's Gnomen (1 Thessalonians 5:9)

347. *Helps Word Studies* (Greek):

2347 **thlípsis**—properly, pressure (what constricts or rubs together), used of a narrow place that "hems someone in"; tribulation, especially internal pressure that causes someone to feel confined (restricted, "without options"). https://biblehub.com/greek/2347.htm.

Following is a listing of every single one of the KJV passages that use the word "tribulation" as derived from the Greek *thlipsis*:

Matthew 13:21, Matthew 24:21, Matthew 24:29, Mark 13:24, John 16:33, Acts 14:22, Romans 2:9, Romans 5:3, Romans 8:35, Romans 12:12, 2 Corinthians 1:4, 2 Corinthians 7:4, 1 Thessalonians 3:4, 2 Thessalonians 1:6, Revelation 1:9, Revelation 2:9, Revelation 2:10, Revelation 2:22, and Revelation 7:14.

This list includes the only two verses that include the exact words "great tribulation" when used in the potential sense of a certain period of time (Matthew 24:21 and Revelation 7:14). However, as you will soon observe, in their proper grammatical context they each mean *the daily trials and pressures of living in a fallen world that is under the domain of Satan*, especially as time draws closer to the return of Jesus.

Interestingly, the term "great tribulation" is found only one other time in the KJV, besides the two just mentioned. It's in Revelation 2:22. But here, this specific term is not used to denote a "special dispensation" of time at all. In fact, the majority of the scholarly translations of that passage render the phrase "intense suffering," or something similar. The use of the phrase "great tribulation" in this manner serves as a clue that the two words are certainly not meant to be understood only as a very specific time in human history.

Behold, I will cast her into a bed, and them that commit adultery with her *into great tribulation*, except they repent of their deeds. (Revelation 2:22, KJV; emphasis added)

Barnes' Notes on the Bible:

Into great tribulation—*Great suffering,* **disease of body or tortures of the soul.** Except they repent of their deeds—It is only by repentance that we can avoid *the consequences of sin.* (Emphasis added) https://biblehub.com/commentaries/revelation/2-22.htm.

Out of the Great Tribulation

Some might argue that the wording of Revelation 7:14 makes the biblical case that God's people of the last days were *delivered "out" of the "great tribulation"* as though somehow they were able to "miss" it altogether. They would then refer to Matthew 24:21 as referring to the corresponding period.

They would further claim that in the last days God's people will "escape" or be *raptured out* of that period of time. Matthew 24 and Revelation 7 are the only two places where the words *great tribulation* are found in that potential context.

For then shall be *great tribulation*, such as was not since the beginning of the world to this time, no, nor ever shall be. (Matthew 24:21, KJV; emphasis added)

And I said unto him, Sir, thou knowest. And he said to me, **these are they which came *out of great tribulation*,** and have washed their robes, and made them white in the blood of the Lamb. (Revelations 7:14, KJV; emphasis added)

Following are what the scholars who understand the Greek language and its nuances say about the subject of "coming out" of "great tribulation," as stated in Revelation 7:14 (and related to Matthew 24:21).

International Bible Encyclopedia:

[Tribulation] The word *thlipsis* is used generally of *the hardships* **which Christ's followers *would* suffer** (Mt 13:21; 24:9,21,29; Mark 4:17; 13:19,24; Joh 16:33; 1Co 7:28); or **which they *are now passing through*** (Ro 5:3; 12:12; 2Co 4:17; Philippians 4:14); **or through which they *have already come*** (Ac 11:19; 2Co 2:4; Re 7:14). (Emphasis added)

See: Pollard, Edward. "Tribulation: In the New Testament," International Bible Encyclopedia, https://www.internationalstandardbible.com/T/tribulation.html.

Ellicott's Commentary for English Readers:

They are those who come, *not all at once, but gradually.* The saints of God are *continually passing into the unseen world,* and taking their place among the spirits of just men made perfect. [Thus] They come *out of the great tribulation.* Is not the great tribulation the tribulation which those must encounter who are on the side of Christ and righteousness, and refuse to receive the mark of worldliness and sin on their heart, conscience, and life?

In all ages it is true that we must through much tribulation enter the Kingdom of God; and **the vision here is surely not of those who will come safe out of some particular trials**, but of **the great multitude from every age** and every race who waged war against sin, and who, in the midst of that protracted conflict, endured **the great tribulation which is to continue until Christ's return.** (Emphasis added)

Expositor's Greek Testament:

But the situation of the Apocalypse is so acute, that **mission operations are at a standstill.** Instead of the gospel invading and pervading the pagan world, the latter has closed in *upon the churches* with threatening power, **and in the brief interval before the end** practically nothing can be looked for except the preservation of the faithful. (Emphasis added)

Pulpit Commentary:

The repeated article is especially emphatic. The question arises: What is "the **great tribulation**" referred to? Probably **all the tribulation** which has been passed through by the redeemed, **all that which pertained to the life** though which they have passed. This tribulation is now completed and past, and is therefore referred to as "the great tribulation." "These are they which have passed through **the great tribulation** of their life on earth." (Emphasis added)

Jamieson-Fausset-Brown Bible Commentary:

The **great tribulation.** Including retrospectively **all the tribulation** which the saints **of all ages** have had to pass through. … Their number was waiting to be completed, but here it is completed, and *they are seen taken out* of the earth *before the judgments* [wrath from God] on the *Antichristian apostasy.* (Emphasis added)

Gill's Exposition of the Entire Bible:

Out of *great tribulation*: seeing this company designs *all the elect* of God, that *ever were, are, or shall be in the world*; "the great tribulation," out of which they came, is *not to be restrained to any particular time* of trouble, but includes all that has been, is, or shall be. (Emphasis added)

The above commentary entries are all found on the same page, for ease of verification, at https://biblehub.com/commentaries/revelation/7-14.htm.

Barnes' Notes on the Whole Bible:

The word rendered "tribulation" - θλίψις thlipsis- is **a word of general character, meaning "affliction,"** though perhaps there is here an allusion to persecution. The sense, however, would **be better expressed by the phrase great trials.** The object seems to have been to set before the mind of the apostle **a view of those who had suffered much, and who by their sufferings had been sanctified and prepared for heaven, in order to encourage those who might be yet called to suffer.** (Emphasis added)

Coffman's Commentary on the Bible:

These are they that came out of the **great tribulation…** This verse is the principal proof-text for sponsors of the Great Tribulation theory; but the words *"they that came"* are translated *from the present middle participle, meaning they "continue to come."* Bruce translated this, "These are the comers. The whole history of the church is a time of tribulation." (Emphasis added)

Robertson's Word Pictures in the New Testament:

Present middle participle with the idea of continued repetition. "The martyrs *are still arriving from the scene of the great tribulation"* (Emphasis added)

Peter Pett's Commentary on the Bible:

All through the present tribulation and the greater tribulations to come Christians will be dying, but now they know that they need not fear. For it is to this that they will come. "Those who are coming," the present participle. We may be intended to read it as "the coming ones who have come."

Whedon's Commentary on the Bible:

Out of great tribulation—*the epithet great is emphatic*, by **being placed with its article after the noun,** which our English idiom does not permit. **Plainly, this company** robed in white is that of Revelation 7:9, which *embraces all the redeemed.* The *great tribulation is, therefore, the battle of probationary life under pressure of the world, the flesh, and the devil.* (Emphasis added)

The last five commentary entries are also found on a single page at: https://www.studylight.org/commentary/revelation/7-14.html.

The historical viewpoint from the time of Jesus through the next three hundred years:

Following are the historical observations from Dr. David Reagan's book, *Wrath and Glory*. Dr. Reagan is a well-known pre-Tribulation

Rapture teacher and conference speaker. Yet, in that book, Dr. Reagan candidly sets forth the following historically accurate admissions concerning our current topic:

"*The oldest viewpoint* [about the doctrine of the Rapture] is **called historic premillennialism** [the Rapture occurs at the end of the Tribulation, and just before God pours out His wrath—as in Noah' day].

It is termed "historic" for two reasons: to differentiate it from modern premillennialism and to indicate that *it was the historic position of the early church*.... This view is *based on a literal interpretation* of what the Bible says *will happen* in the end times. One of its distinctive features is that it places *the Rapture of the Church at the end of the Tribulation*, combining it with the Second Coming as *one event*....

This is the only systematic view of end-time events that existed *during the first 300 years* of the Church." (Emphasis added)

See: Reagan, David. *Wrath and Glory: The Meaning of the Book of Revelation*, Lamb and Lion Ministries; 2nd Edition (May 1, 2016), 112–113.

348. **Ecclesia** is defined as a political assembly of citizens in the definition of ancient Greece, or the church members. A group of ancient Greek politicians who came to Athens to debate is an example of an ecclesia. The collective congregation of a church is an example of an ecclesia. https://www.yourdictionary.com/ecclesia#:~:text=Ecclesia%20is%20defined%20as%20a,an%20example%20of%20an%20ecclesia.

349. Ibid. Regarding Matthew 24:31. Various commentary entries.

350. Luke 17:20–37. "The IVP New Testament Commentary Series – How Does the Consummation Come? (17:20-37)," Biblegateway.com, https://www.biblegateway.com/resources/ivp-nt/How-Does-Consummation-Come.

351. Luke 17:26. "Coffman's Commentary on the Bible," Studylight.org, https://www.studylight.org/commentary/luke/17-26.html.

352. Luke 17:26. "Matthew Poole's English Annotations on the Holy Bible," Studylight.org, https://www.studylight.org/commentary/luke/17-26.html.

353. Genesis 7:16, "Matthew Henry's Concise Commentary," Biblehub.com, https://biblehub.com/commentaries/genesis/7-16.htm.

354. Genesis 6:13. "Benson Commentary on the Bible," Biblehub.com, https://biblehub.com/commentaries/genesis/6-3.htm.

355. Genesis 6:13. "Keil and Delitzsch Biblical Commentary on the Old Testament," Biblehub.com, https://biblehub.com/commentaries/genesis/6-3.htm.

356. Genesis 6:13. "Jamieson-Fausset-Brown Bible Commentary," Biblehub. com, https://biblehub.com/commentaries/genesis/6-3.htm.

357. Gallups, Carl. *The Rabbi Who Found Messiah: The Story of Yitzhak Kaduri* (WND Books, Washington DC, 2014). (See: http://www.carlgallups. com/books).

358. Missler, Chuck. "The Gospel in Genesis: A Hidden Message," Koinonia House Ministries, 2-1-96, https://www.khouse.org/articles/1996/44.

359. As of the writing of this chapter, I could find no one else claiming to be the original discoverer of this amazing biblical revelation. I do not see, on Dr. Missler's website presentation, where he credited anyone else with the discovery either. As far as I know, Dr. Missler's claim to its discovery has not been seriously disputed.

360. Missler, Chuck. "The Gospel in Genesis: A Hidden Message."

361. Ibid.

362. Ibid.

363. Acts 17:26. "Robertson's Word Pictures in the New Testament," Studylight.org, https://www.studylight.org/commentary/acts/17-26.html.

364. Acts 17:26. "Matthew Poole's English Annotations on the Holy Bible," Studylight.org, https://www.studylight.org/commentary/acts/17-26.html.

365. Acts 17:26. "Gill's Exposition of the Entire Bible," Biblehub.com, https:// biblehub.com/commentaries/acts/17-26.htm.

366. "Fall from your secure position"….

    Barnes' Notes on the Bible:

    Fall from your own steadfastness—Your firm adherence to the truth. The particular danger here referred to is not that of falling from grace… but from the firm and settled principles of religious truth into error.

    Gill's Exposition:

    Though the saints can never finally and totally fall into sin, or from the truth, yet they may fall from their steadfastness, both as to the exercise of the grace of faith, and as to their profession of the doctrine of faith; and to be fluctuating, hesitating, and doubting in either respect, must be very uncomfortable and dishonorable.

    See: https://biblehub.com/commentaries/2_peter/3-17.htm.

367. From Barna's website:

    "In its 30-year history, Barna Group has conducted more than one million interviews over the course of hundreds of studies, and has become a go-to source for insights about faith and culture, leadership and vocation, and generations. Barna Group has carefully and strategically tracked the role of faith in America, developing one of the nation's most comprehensive databases of spiritual indicators." Barna.com, accessed 7-14-20, https://www.barna.com/about.

368. The quotations are from Chris Woodward, "Barna: Many Pastors Wary of Raising 'Controversy,'" OneNewsNow, August 1, 2014, accessed January 2015, http://www.onenewsnow.com/hurch/2014/08/01/barna-many-pastors-wary-of-raising-controversy#.U-ED1KO0uSr.

369. Gallups, Carl. *Be Thou Prepared: Equipping the Church for Persecution and Times of Trouble.* (Washington, DC: WND Books, 2015). You can purchase this book, individually or in bulk, or in combination with any other of my books, at www.carlgallups.com/books or by email at bookcarlgallups@gmail.com.

370. Matthew 5:39. "Ellicott's Commentary for English Readers," Biblehub.com, https://biblehub.com/commentaries/matthew/5-39.htm.

371. Matthew 5:39. "Barnes' Notes on the Bible," Biblehub.com, https://biblehub.com/commentaries/matthew/5-39.htm.

372. Luke 22:36. "Bengel's Gnomen," Biblehub.com, https://biblehub.com/commentaries/luke/22-36.htm.

373. Luke 22:36. "Barnes' Notes on the Bible," Biblehub.com, https://biblehub.com/commentaries/luke/22-36.htm.

374. Matthew 6:25. "Pulpit Commentary,"Biblehub.com, https://biblehub.com/commentaries/matthew/6-25.htm.

375. Matthew 6:25. "Matthew Henry's Commentary,"Biblehub.com, https://biblehub.com/commentaries/matthew/6-25.htm.

376. Matthew 6:25. "Benson Commentary,"Biblehub.com, https://biblehub.com/commentaries/matthew/6-25.htm.